MW01265624

1|6|17

Off Grid and Free

My Path to the Wilderness

Ron Melchiore

Publisher: Moon Willow Press http://www.moonwillowpress.com
Coquitlam, British Columbia, Canada

Dedication

Dedicated to my mom, who supplied my daily fix of sweets, and my dad, who was always available to throw the baseball or football and wondered why I had such boundless energy--I got to the chocolate chip cookies first, Dad.

And to off gridders, homesteaders, and other self-reliant people worldwide who dare to be different and free.

Preface

Humans are ideally supposed to be visitors who do not *remain* in the wilderness—at least if we go by the U.S. Wilderness Act and a variety of laws and regulations that have been enacted throughout the world to preserve wilderness. To preserve it, that is, by separating human nature from nature. The notion of the separation of people and wilderness, or society and nature, has lately been subject to a great deal of criticism because it ignores the traditional practices and land claims of both indigenous populations and settlers who have made wilderness their place of dwelling and because it has historically resulted in countless evictions and displacements of wilderness residents following the legal designation of a tract of land as park or reserve. So can any human being, nowadays, up and move into the wilderness? How can one manage to live full-time in the wilderness? And is a wilderness area still wild after a human has chosen to remain there?

I spent two years between 2011 and 2013 travelling across all of Canada's provinces and territories to find people who live off the grid (i.e. in homes disconnected from electricity and natural gas networks) and document their way of life. Many of the off gridders I found lived in exurban, rural, and peripheral areas. But in February of 2013 I met a couple who lived full-time far more remotely than anyone else and who indeed lived further away from human civilization than anyone I had ever heard of. Ron and Johanna lived in Northern Saskatchewan, 100kms away from the nearest road of any kind and 160kms away from the nearest town. They had lived there for about a decade.

Ron and Johanna's home could only be accessed by small planes equipped for landing on water or ice. Soon after I got off that floatplane in the middle of February I learned that they typically chartered it only twice a year to stock up on the few supplies they could not otherwise grow or build on their own. Their home was entirely self-sufficient for electricity and heat, thanks to a hybrid system that made use of solar and wind (with a small back-up diesel generator) to generate power, and locally harvested firewood for heating and cooking. Water was sourced from a well. Waste and sewage were sustainably disposed of locally. And, while they bought a good deal of meat and other provisions during their twice-yearly trips, they managed to grow much of their calorie intake right there in their garden and greenhouse. Old-fashion home-making and building skills allowed them to build, repair, and craft a good deal of the things and technologies they needed on a daily basis. Despite all this, Ron and Johanna were no hermits: they kept connected to the rest of the world via a satellite link that permitted them to watch television, access the internet, and make (emergency) phone calls.

What brought Ron and Johanna from their previous home in New England so far away from the rest of society? And how did they manage to not only survive but indeed thrive in a place so remote? In the wonderful tales this book contains, the answer will ring clear and true, and you will have to read to find out.

While their remoteness was unusually dramatic, their values are common to many people who call "the bush" home across much of Canada, the United States, and Australia. Getting away from it all is indeed an increasingly sought-after form of lifestyle migration driven—unlike much migratory patterns—not by economic reasons but rather by the existential need to live life on one's own terms, in a more basic and simple (though obviously at times very complicated!) manner. In this way, wilderness areas serve as prime testing grounds for such lifestyle experiments, allowing individuals to start fresh, to clean the slate—as it were—and re-invent modern living.

Did Ron and Johanna "undo" wilderness in virtue of choosing to *remain* there? In other words, did they—in light of choosing to stay, rather than simply visit and leave—turn their wilderness into a less pristine, less wild environment? One could very well argue that their cozy home—with its stocked pantry and warm rooms—wasn't wild. As a permanent structure meant to give them comfort and convenience, their off-grid home wasn't much different from your home or ours. But just a few steps away from their wind turbine, the bush was as wild as it would have been before, or without, their arrival. As Ron and I would walk the trail surrounding their land— as we did daily for the time I was their guest—we would quickly and punctually lose sight and sound of anything that wasn't wild. Meeting them taught me that choosing to remain in a wilderness area, and practising a low-impact lifestyle, does not spoil the experience of the wild. People belong in the wilderness. And they can do so without becoming wild themselves, but rather simply by accepting the value of wildness and welcoming some of that wildness—instead of simply confining it to a distant "park" or "reserve"—into their home.

-Phillip Vannini, Professor, Royal Roads University, July 10, 2015

Acknowledgments

To bring this book to fruition, I counted on a small circle of family and friends for their input. I am thankful to all for their support and feedback. I took everyone's recommendations to heart and carefully considered implementing the various suggestions to help clarify the story.

Foremost, I need to thank my wife Johanna for her effort in reading the chapters numerous times and for correcting my mistakes. I am the creative force behind the book, but Johanna refined and polished it. She is convinced that without the excellent instruction she received from her high school English teacher, Mr. Pusey, in the topics of grammar and composition, she would not have been as effective. Johanna and I make a good team, and she certainly had an eye towards improving grammar and the flow of the story by rearranging sentences or even entire paragraphs.

A sincere thank you to my publisher, Mary Woodbury at Moon Willow Press, an environmentally aware publishing firm. She believed I had a good story to share, and her editing skills and advice were key in the quality of the finished manuscript. She is a true pro, and I look forward to a long-term relationship with her.

I'd like to thank my friend Bob Vitullo, a penpal I've never met in person. Years after a few of our magazine articles had been published, Bob found them while perusing magazines in his local library. He was intrigued with our lifestyle and contacted the magazine publisher for permission to write directly to us. Imagine our surprise when a letter from Bob arrived in our semi-annual mail delivery. This was a letter that had traveled from the United States to Canada. Then it made its way onto a float plane and finally out to us. Bob and I have remained in contact over many years. He was kind enough to read the entire first manuscript and offer suggestions. That initial manuscript, as it turns out, was a bit too concise and to the point. At 41,000 words, I told the story and got to the conclusion in a hurry. Bob was one of several preliminary readers who advised a more gradual approach with more detail. By the time I finished the second version, I had more than doubled the size of the book. Then he re-read each chapter. He was one of many who encouraged me to write this book, and I am grateful for his honest feedback throughout this process.

I feel very privileged to have met Phillip Vannini, a university professor who sought us out and stayed with us for several days. He was in the process of writing his own book, *Off the grid: re-assembling domestic life*, and was simultaneously filming a documentary, *Life off Grid*, which is about Canadians who are self-reliant and live off grid. We have remained in touch with Phillip over the years as well. He was an additional sounding board, who took time to read my early manuscript and suggested slowing down the pace of the book and giving more detail. His encouragement was invaluable.

A special thank you is in order to my niece Michelle Crean, a graphics designer. I wrestled, fought, and pleaded with a graphics program on my computer for a solid day, trying to generate a respectable front book cover. When I asked her what she thought of it, she said it was okay and gave me a few suggestions. Then, thankfully, she offered to whip out a few sample covers for me. Inside of a few hours, I had five professionally done covers from which to choose and my designs went into the great computer scrap heap, otherwise known as the trash can.

Another special thank you goes to my old friend and work supervisor, William Chadwick. Without a doubt, Bill had the biggest influence on my life's direction when he mentioned the concept of homesteading to me so many years ago. I'm sure he never thought a mere casual suggestion would have had such life altering ramifications.

My long-time friends Chris and Kathy Carroll, who I have known since our days from living in Maine, were anxious to read and offer their feedback on my composition.

And, finally, my parents read each chapter and took time to critique and point out punctuation errors. My siblings were always there when I needed to take a quick survey. For anyone I have missed, I apologize. Without the contributions of the above, the book would likely not exist, other than as a tattered, partially completed file on my computer. I thank them all!

Chapter 1 –

Which Way Do
I Go?

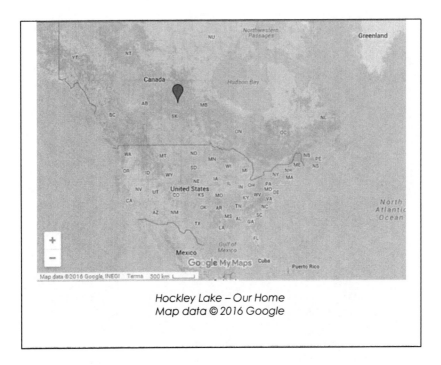

Hockley Lake – Our Home
Map data © 2016 Google

"There's a bear at the door!" shouted my wife Johanna.

She had gone downstairs to fetch a book and had heard a strange noise at the front door. Looking over, she was startled to see a pair of large paws groping at the door window pane, the claws making telltale click-click sounds on the glass.

I raced downstairs, grabbed the shotgun and was out the door in a flash, barely pausing long enough to put on my shoes. The bear, sensing my frantic activity, had not stuck around. By the time I managed to get outside, our intruder was making a beeline for the cover of the woods. Nevertheless, I fired a warning shot. A loud boom reverberated through the air and, for emphasis, I shouted a few choice words to discourage a return visit. Fortunately, I've never had to use our thunder stick as anything other than a noisy deterrent.

It's an alarming sight to see a bear at the door--the animal's bulky outline framed by the door window, as if it were a wildlife picture mounted on a wall. A couple of thin panes of window glass are all that separate you from the bear. There's only one reason it's there, and it's not to make a delivery. It wants in. Generally, building access doors swing to the inside, but our front door swings out, an inadvertent but lucky choice. An animal would need manual dexterity to turn the doorknob and pull the door outward before gaining entry to our home. Unless it's smarter than the average bear, it will likely try pushing inward, then give up when nothing happens.

Horror stories abound of marauding bears breaking into unoccupied cabins and wreaking havoc. Contents, including mattresses, can be dragged outside and are gnawed and shredded, while cabin interiors, rummaged in the search for food, don't fare any better. Bears, with their long claws and strength superior to a man's, can be terribly destructive. Our metal clad freezer has indentations on the lid that serve as a visual reminder of the power of those claws. Long canine teeth, used in conjunction with powerful jaw muscles, have left scars and puncture wounds on our snowmobile and boat motor.

Although we have little fear of bears when we are close to the homestead, we are alert and cautious when they're coming out of their dens after a long winter's hibernation, especially when a mother and her cubs are together. Hunger is the driving factor as they go about foraging for food. Black bear, the species in our area, are the least aggressive bears in North America, but on rare occasions, we hear a news report of someone being mauled or killed, so the bears need to be respected. Surprising a bear is a good way to get into trouble, so if I venture into the woods, an occasional warning shout gives any animal in the area a heads-up that I'm passing through.

My wife and I have lived in bear country for the last 36 years, first in the state of Maine, and now in the wilderness of northern

Saskatchewan. The above incident is just one of the many occasions we've encountered bears, with the majority of those encounters being short, fleeting glimpses. Most members of the ursine community will run as soon as they spot us, but a curious bear may stop to view us from a distance. When a bear is near and shows no fear, it's time to be concerned. In that event, they've become a little too accustomed to being around humans, or worse, their hunger has overcome any natural fear they normally have. Neither situation is good.

A fortuitous series of events brought us to this place, a remote lake, far out in the Canadian wilderness, 100 miles from the nearest supply point. And, by wilderness, I mean the real thing.

As far as your eye can see, from the vantage point of a float plane high above the ground, you can gaze upon an aerial tapestry of multi-hued green forest intermingled with jutting rock formations, lowland bogs, and glistening lakes. Exposed rocky hill tops, sparsely vegetated with stunted trees that have managed to gain a tenuous foothold, along with low shrubbery and lichen, are sure signs you are flying over Precambrian shield, a dominant surface feature in the north. Serpentine rivers and streams cut through the landscape, the rivers occasionally flashing a churning white, where rapids lie in wait for the unwary canoeist. All of this is the perfect habitat for wildlife and outdoor adventurer alike.

We are surrounded by pure virgin forest, where the only human tracks are our own and the only neighbors are animals. There are no roads or trails to get here. We are well beyond any population centers, and a flight on a float plane is the only way you will reach us. The electrical grid, which the majority of the world's population relies on to power industry and appliances, was left behind the moment we took off from the float plane base. We severed the electrical tether by vanquishing the utility company long ago.

We know we live here, at this particular location, and yet we have no street address. Our address is a set of coordinates, a latitude and longitude, given in degrees, minutes, and seconds. With the area so vast, any plane seeking to find us best be accurate down to the second, lest the plane fly by and miss us completely. There are no traffic signs, no mileage indicators, no flashing neon lights telling a guest they are closing in on our off-grid homestead. Our location is a mere pinprick on the Earth's surface, blending in with mile after mile of picturesque landscape. Generally, twice a year we fly out for resupply and appointments. These biannual trips out are the only times we pick up our mail, buy food, and interact with other humans.

At epochal turning points in our lives, each of us are faced with the question, "Which way do I go?" I've asked myself that key question many times throughout my life, and my answer has always been to take the least traditional road. Of course, each of us has our own "What should I do, which way do I go?" moment. We each have our own road to travel--a lengthy road if blessed with health, but where every step along the way is a potential encounter with a roadblock, twist, or fork. I've certainly opted to take a few forks. Who would have thought that living in the Canadian wilderness, at this point in our lives, would be the destination for my wife and me? Certainly not I.

Over the years, I have been urged by friends and countless strangers to write a narrative of some of the events that have occurred in my life. I resisted for a time, but I've compiled some true stories, interspersed with some humor, arranged in a loose chronological order. I hope you will find these stories entertaining and informative. I'll share accounts of survival and living in the

Canadian wilderness, of hiking the Appalachian Trail in winter, of cross country bicycling, and of the horror of watching my world catch on fire. I write and pass on these experiences to provide encouragement for others to pursue their dreams, regardless of how far-fetched those dreams may be. If you are as lucky as I have been, you will have the support of your family, spouse, or both.

"Which way do I go?" Let's start at the beginning by heading north to Maine!

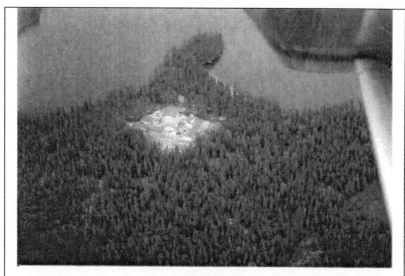

Aerial view

House facing south; note the solar panels and wind turbine

Chapter 2–

Northbound to Maine

Exhausted from an overnight drive, I was motoring up a desolate stretch of I-95 in northern Maine, well beyond civilization's background glow of lights. It was a perfectly clear, starlit night during the early dark morning hours, when I saw the Northern Lights beckoning to me for the first time. I was on a mission to search for a suitable site for an off-grid homestead, and this light display would be the first of many times I would enjoy watching it through the years. Since I've lived in northern latitudes for the last 36 years, viewing the lights is now a common occurrence, but at that time, it was quite the novelty.

Ironically, I began life in an urban setting. Born in the city of Philadelphia, I could never have envisioned the stepping stones of events that would lead to that long drive up a lonely stretch of I-95 so many years ago. I grew up in the nearby suburbs and led the life of a normal kid. I didn't do exceptionally well in school and averaged B to C grades. Not applying myself to my studies, I chose sports and music as the outlet for my high energy drive. As a young guy, I played drums in a rock and roll band.

Many cities have a large arena where concerts are played. Perhaps you've heard of the Spectrum in Philadelphia? Back in those days, it was the "go to" venue for lesser known bands as well as the famous, big name bands…

I never played there!

My claim to fame was playing music with friends in my basement and driving my parents nuts. Although I participated in a variety of neighborhood sports, track was the only sport I joined in high school. I considered making track my life's work, but realized I'd just be going in circles! The wilderness destination in which I ultimately arrived was never on the radar screen.

In fact, I had every reason to bail out on life and live every day as if it was my last. Our suburban neighborhood was like most, and we kids would put on local fun houses or carnivals. A basement would be decorated with what we thought at the time were really scary things, and local kids would be charged a pittance to come through the haunted house. Or someone would put on a carnival in their backyard with games and fun.

One summer day, during school vacation, I attended one of those neighborhood carnivals. A grade school friend had a table set up to do palm reading. I paid the prerequisite fee, and after analyzing the lines on my palm, my friend told me I was going to die young. This was quite the revelation since I was perhaps 11 years old.

I should have asked her, "Since I won't be around much longer, can I have my money back?!"

As I'm in my late fifties and haven't hit the checkout counter yet, it appears there was a technical glitch of some kind with the palm reading. For now, I've cheated death.

While attending high school, I concurrently took three years of courses in Industrial Electronics, which prepared me for a career in logging and tree farming, which then prepared me for a life in the bush. As odd as that last sentence may sound, and as unrelated as those careers are, that's how the twists and turns of this city boy's life led to living 100 miles out in the wilderness.

After graduating high school, I entered the workforce and worked several jobs in the electronics industry. Although I found electronics an interesting and challenging career, I'm a free spirit and I couldn't imagine continuing this daily routine for the duration of my life. I found the monotony of dragging myself out of bed in the mornings and making the drive to work a real chore. And all so I could make the owner of the company prosperous?

While working in one of those jobs, I was talking to a supervisor one day about life in general and the fact there had to be more to it than just working a nine-to-five job. He was a young man himself, likely 10 years older than me, in his early 30s, but he had been in the military, had traveled the world, and had done many things in his young life. He suggested homesteading. I had no idea what the term meant, but after some more discussion and research, I realized the term basically meant relying on yourself to live off the land and become as self-sufficient as possible.

This was one of those "oh wow" epiphany moments when everything gelled into an enormous fantasy. I was young, and visions of a simple life far in the woods with a small off-grid cabin and garden would be just the ticket. At the time, it never dawned on me that this was far beyond anything I'd ever contemplated before.

Self-reliant... it has such a nice ring to it!

The premise of taking my existence down to a bare-bones level, being carefree, leaving the rat race behind for others to savor, was an intoxicating allure. I would provide my own sustenance, generate my own power from sun, wind, or water; use fuel from my land in the form of firewood for heating and cooking; and rely on myself to take care of the daily chores with time left over to enjoy life as it was meant to be. Along with that self-reliance came independence, something we all strive for to a degree.

Because this sounded like such a noble cause, I immediately latched on to the concept. I bought books on the subject and researched land in several states, including West Virginia and Maine. Driving through both states, I made many trips seeking the right piece of land. I would take off after work on Friday, drive all night, look at properties, and make the return drive a couple of days later just in time for another work week. Ugh! My dad accompanied me on one trip to West Virginia, and I still remember the fun we had together while checking out the state. No question West Virginia is a beautiful, mountainous place, but ultimately, I decided to buy a 120 acre woodlot in northern Maine. That's how I ended up in a northern agricultural/forestry area, which was a major stepping stone toward living in the Canadian bush. I accepted the challenge at this early crossroad, and diverted to an unknown pathway.

Although the bank loan for this new property was in my name, it was secured by my parents' signature and help, and I am forever in their debt. They believed in me right from the start. This was a significant turning point in my young life, and without my parents support and encouragement, I am confident my life would have been far more blasé.

The back-to-the-land movement was in full swing in the 1970s, and I became part of that group by the end of the decade. My new property was at the dead end of a public road. At that time, it was a one-lane affair, and was so overgrown in places that the alder scraped the side of the vehicle as I drove down the road. That was part of the appeal of this land. It was isolated, and the paper company land surrounding me on three sides made me feel I was really living out in the wilderness. And to a degree I was if I compared it to the urban setting from which I had just come.

My property was essentially a large rectangle, completely forested except for a centrally located field perhaps 4 acres in size. A small stream meandered its way across the width of the woodlot, and in the ensuing years, I saw that little stream dry to a trickle as well as swell out of its banks.

Back in the early days, when the area was first being populated, my piece of real estate was part of a larger parcel that was home to several families. While exploring an area adjacent to my driveway, I found the remnants of a house foundation and a hand-dug well. How I wished I could have traveled back in time and seen what the old homestead looked like during that period. For a young guy from an urban setting, this was adventurous territory, all new and exciting.

After my land purchase, I didn't make the big move immediately but rather continued to work to accumulate money for building materials, equipment, and loan payments. During vacations, I made the long drive to Maine where I camped out on the property and prepared it to become home sweet home. On one of those early occasions, when I was camped out on site and was doing preliminary work, my dad made the drive to Maine for the first time in order to view my new prized possession. We explored not only my property but also the local communities, and after a few days he returned home.

Sometime the following day, I was alone, cutting brush, when I noticed some people walking down the driveway towards me. Familiar people! Imagine my surprise and joy at seeing my dad, mom, and sister. My dad had been so impressed with what he had seen, he drove all the way home, grabbed my mother and sister, and immediately ran the roads north again so they could see the place too. That would be the first of countless announced and unannounced surprise visits my family would make through the years. This was my first foray living away from family and friends, and the 13-hour driving commitment they made in order to come visit me was greatly appreciated. It was always a huge lift to see them.

Prior to my Maine adventure, I had never gone camping. It was an easy adaptation for me though, and I pitched my new tent at the terminus of the dead end road, which also happened to be one of the corners of my property, and used that as my base of operations. Campfires at night kept away all the ghosts and goblins. My family wasn't accustomed to sleeping in a tent or on the ground, yet when they came up to help, they accepted both as part of the overall experience. The locals could and did drive down the road and then turned around at my campsite, so in order to get a little more seclusion, I eventually moved the camping area a short distance down my driveway, setting up my gear there.

One night I slept out under the stars, right in the middle of my driveway. Away from any light sources, and with the fresh, clean air, the array of stars visible in the sky was spectacular. Snug in my sleeping bag, slumber came easy that night. I must have worked hard that day.

The next morning when I woke up, I saw large moose prints, which had come right up to where I had slept. They skirted around me and then continued on. A moose is a huge, imposing animal, and to this day, I can't imagine waking up in the middle of the night and seeing that bulky frame towering over me in the dark. Or in the light for that matter!

Another animal I liked having around was the coyote. It has a poor reputation, but it never bothered me, and I enjoyed hearing it howling, yipping, and barking at night. Their calls made the night-time forest come alive. It's an animal I miss hearing, as there are no coyotes where I now live.

Imagine sitting around the campfire, the silence of the night broken only by the crackling and sizzling of the fire, its glow reflecting off anyone fortunate enough to be there, sparks from the fire lazily drifting upward to disappear in the inky dark, and then a loud, mournful wail from nearby woods pierces the night. An answering howl follows from another coyote in the distance. For me, a nice memory. All in all, this was primitive camping at its best--cooking and heating water over an open fire, working by lantern light, star gazing in a sky free of light pollution, communing with the wildlife--and I reveled in it.

During one work trip, my parents and I were camped out and were visited by a beautiful, friendly Samoyed dog. We had no idea who it belonged to, and we couldn't persuade it to leave. Night time came, and the hamburgers were cooking on the grill; our stomachs were growling, and after a hard day's work, we were looking forward to dinner. The burger flipper who was responsible for cooking the meat to perfection, turned his back for just a split second, and the dog grabbed a burger off the grill and devoured it. It never even waited for a bun!

Bad dog! *I hate when that happens.*

Initially, my first priorities were to purchase the necessary gear and tools, design my castle, and pay off the land. Next on the agenda was to reclaim the old, overgrown access road that wound its way through the forest to an old potato field, the centrally located 4-acre field I mentioned earlier. Northern Maine is known for its potatoes, and the small town I lived in had a lot of potato farms. My little field, which would eventually be reclaimed, was just a fraction of the vast territory in northern Maine devoted to the crop. Additionally, a local farmer had used the property for cattle grazing. My property certainly had a diverse history.

To reclaim the old access road, I hired a local contractor with a bulldozer to clean up things so the field could be accessed by vehicle. This old road had become so overgrown, that in places the alder was so thick all I had was an animal path to follow. This 4/10ths of a mile-long access trail would eventually become my driveway, but first the road needed some serious gravel work. Countless loads of gravel were dumped in the road over the years, and I remember one time the dump truck even got stuck in the mud. The construction company charged me extra for the extrication of their truck. I've often wondered about that.

Why did they get it stuck in the first place?

The field the road led to was completely overgrown with alder and young saplings. The outline of the field was easily defined by the taller trees along the edges. I had the bulldozer clear the field up to the edge of the forest, and then piled all the debris into one humongous mound in the center of the field. In theory, it was to be burned. In reality, the pile contained so much embedded soil it would never burn completely. Over the course of many years, I picked away at cleaning up the pile by cutting the small trees into firewood. This was easy firewood to access, but because it was dirty from being pushed by the dozer, it had a tendency to quickly dull the chain on my saw. When cutting up the pile, if I noticed sparks flying, I knew I was hitting dirt or a hidden stone. But once I had the firewood salvaged, I burned the pile as best as I could and bulldozed the remainder into the surrounding woods.

In hindsight, it was an obvious mistake to bulldoze the field because a lot of the topsoil was removed in the process. My cleared field was destined to have a garden, orchard, grain, and hay fields, and I had shot myself in the foot by shaving the best soil off the top. It took years to improve the soil quality through the use of cover crops and manure. Cover crops are planted specifically for the purpose of being plowed back into the ground. They add lots of nutrients and organic matter back into the soil.

I had the notion of a quaint pond, so while the bulldozer was out, I had it do the excavation work in a corner of the field. Unfortunately, because of ledge rock, the dozer was unable to dig very deep. So instead of the pond being a summer swimming hole for me, it became a shallow puddle for the local frogs that set up residence there. It was a harbinger of summer when the first croaks filled the air. Who would have thought the cacophony of frogs on a warm summer's night could be so loud. Once the dozer was finished, I was left with a cleared field that would be my home for the next 20 years.

While searching for property in West Virginia and Maine, I owned a Dodge extended van. Since I was now going to live a more remote lifestyle, a van would never do. I needed a more appropriate vehicle that I could throw stuff in and not worry about ruining the van interior. A local dealer took my van as a trade for a small, sleek pickup truck. The first time I drove down my driveway and bogged down in the mud, I realized I had made a boo-boo. My new, snazzy truck looked good on the road, and it still looked good mired in mud, but it had a flaw when it came to off-road conditions, this flaw being rear-wheel-drive and low ground clearance. So at some point thereafter, I bought a proper 4-wheel-drive Dodge pickup. Now I could get somewhere.

I hired a local logger to harvest some trees from my property and had a portable sawmill saw those trees into lumber for my new home. The sawmill was set up in the new clearing, and although I wasn't there when the lumber was sawn, I was giddy when I first saw the stack of freshly cut lumber, 2x4s, 2x6s, 2x8s, and piles of boards that I'd use for my new abode. It wasn't until many years later I was able to finally clean the area of all the sawdust and slabs the sawmill had generated. Slabs were cut up for firewood, and the sawdust would eventually end up being used for animal bedding.

I also shopped in the local area for a used tractor. Tractors were a new concept to me as up until that point the only tractors I had ever seen were off in a field somewhere. I found an old Massey Harris 101 Jr. with a narrow front end, a dinosaur of 1940s vintage. Weathered and faded over the years, the dingy red painted exterior covered a well-used but mechanically sound machine. It was the perfect tractor for me to use to pull out my snazzy truck when I got it stuck in the mud. The tractor came with a small cart, which came in handy to lug around various items, as well as to haul the large quantities of firewood I would need to get me through a northern Maine winter. The tractor had a battery and starter, but if that failed, I could always pull out the crank handle and spin the motor by hand. This trick worked every time. Sort of like a windup toy. I just had to make darn sure the tractor wasn't in gear though when I did that, since I was standing directly in front of the machine when I cranked the handle.

Although I had no real world knowledge of carpentry, house wiring or plumbing, that didn't stop me from erecting a solid, toasty little house. Before I began construction, I read multiple books on the topic, and with a solid understanding of the hows and whys, I was able to design the house. My finances were limited, so cost was a paramount consideration in my selection of building materials. I drew my plans out on paper and knew where every piece of lumber was going to go. With a house plan and materials list, I was ready to tackle this project.

Spring of 1980 was the start of the construction and, at times, I had the good fortune of having family and friends lend a helping hand. My dad and I made the drive to Maine to pour the concrete posts, which would be the house foundation. When we arrived, the driveway was too wet to drive down, so bag after bag of redi-mix concrete was wheel-barrowed all the way down my driveway, through muddy sections, to the house site. With my driveway being 4/10ths of a mile long (one way) and each bag of redi-mix weighing in at 80 pounds, this was nothing short of a Herculean effort.

We laboriously hand-dug 12 holes down to bedrock. We placed wooden forms in the holes and then filled them with concrete. Once the concrete was set, we removed the forms and backfilled the empty space with dirt. We took water from the stream two hundred feet away from the house site and lugged it back to the work site, two buckets at a time. Then we mixed the concrete in the wheelbarrow by hand as two neophytes did their best to honor their Italian heritage.

Evidently, Italians are known for their excellent stone and concrete work, and I think we did our ancestors proud. I found out there was a right way and wrong way to mix concrete. I poured a bag of concrete into the wheelbarrow, and then Dad created a pocket in the middle where I was instructed to pour some water. Then, with a hoe, Dad methodically mixed in a little concrete until the batter slowly became the proper consistency. I added more water as needed. We then poured the concrete into one of the waiting wooden forms. That was the right way.

Then I took a turn at being the concrete foreman and did it the wrong way. I dumped a new bag of concrete into the wheelbarrow. I sloshed in a bucket of water and vigorously heaved the concrete around, to and fro, with the hoe. If I added too much water and it became soup… no problem, open another bag and throw in more dry concrete. We each had our own "technique," and in the end, it all worked out fine. Not only were the concrete piers solid, but the diagonals when measured were equal, signifying a square building.

Later that summer, I came back with some friends I worked with and we framed up the building. By the time we left, we had framed the building and tarpapered both roof and sides. Over the next couple of years, I built the chimneys, did the interior finish work, shingled the roof, and finished the exterior. On any visit, my parents were always willing to pick up a hammer and lend a helping hand. In fact, I have a picture of them up on the scaffolding, baking in the hot sun, pounding nails in board siding, sweat dripping off their brows as I offered encouragement while resting in the nearby shade. I write that with tongue in cheek since anybody who is familiar with me knows I'm a nonstop workaholic. But it is true; my parents were a real help in the building of the house.

When it came time to move my possessions and furniture up to Maine, I enlisted the help of my brother and one of my sisters. Renting a medium-sized U-Haul, I drove the van followed by my siblings in their car. We communicated between the two vehicles by citizens band (CB) radio. A funny thing happened along the way. All was going so well until I, as the lead vehicle, much to my consternation, missed a sign and took a wrong turn. Instead of taking us to the promised land of forest and quiet, I led us straight into the heart of the concrete jungle. We were now in the Bronx, and I was clueless as to where we were going. I did what any normal city driver would do; I made a big sweeping U-turn at a light, with my siblings tucked in behind me. The radio transmission went something like this.

My brother: "We got here quickly. So, which row house is the one you're moving into?"

Me: "Very funny!" while at the same time thinking, "Please, God, get me out of this maze."

This unintentional detour to the Bronx ended with a big sigh of relief when we came upon the I-95 North exit sign, accelerated on to the ramp, and mashed the gas to merge into northbound traffic. Pedal to the metal with the city in the rearview mirror. Maine or bust!

My new lifestyle was physically demanding, and I relished it. But I don't want to create the illusion I was living in utopia because there certainly were poor days and times too. Life is full of obstacles and frustrations, and in thinking back on that period of my life, one frustration that comes to mind is flies. Mosquitoes, black flies, no-see-ums, and the like were pests that were a part of summer life, but I could deal with them easily enough. Repellent, a bug net, or, as a last resort, going inside to get some relief were all methods I employed to cope with the biting insects.

But flies in fall and winter--that was too much!

Cluster flies, thousands of them, made my house their home. When cooler weather showed up, there was no escaping the hordes of flies as the sunny sides of the house would be covered with them. No matter how I tried, I was never able to find the openings they used to get into the house. On the inside, all the windows would be covered with flies, especially the large, west facing picture window.

Day after day, I used a portable vacuum cleaner to suck them up and still they came. The heat from the stove and the light from any sunny window kept them active long after cold winter temperatures had settled in for the season. Eventually, I always got the upper hand; the dwindling numbers on the windows offering encouragement I was winning the battle. My experience with cluster flies wasn't an isolated case. They are a part of life in northern Maine everyone has to deal with to some degree, and part of their life cycle is being a parasite of earthworms. Healthy soil meant healthy populations of earthworms, and by extension, meant lots of cluster flies. While I miss the coyotes, I do not miss cluster flies!

The house was a bare bones, basic shelter. No frills, with a hand pump outside for water, a greywater septic system, and an outhouse. The local well driller bored my well and then installed an old style hand pump, the type often seen at old farm houses. They still make them; hand pumps are a reliable way to draw water up from the ground. The suction pipe that went from the pump down into the well had a small hole located below the ground, which allowed water to drain back into the well after pumping, so no residual water remained in the pump to freeze during the cold months. In winter, if I pumped too vigorously and water slopped out the top of the pump, the mechanism would freeze. Fortunately, this was a rare occurrence, but when it happened, it was easily remedied by pouring enough hot water over the pump head to thaw it.

I bucketed in my water as needed. Regardless of the weather, if I needed water, I had to go outside to fetch it. Many times I had to pump water in bitter cold temperatures while being buffeted by wind. Or I had to don rain gear so I could pump water in the pouring rain. An insulated jug held my fresh drinking water, and buckets stored inside the house held water for hand washing, bathing, and dish washing.

Eventually, my quality of life was much improved when I installed a hand pitcher pump next to the kitchen sink. It was a chore to install since I had to dig a trench for a new pipe from the existing well, extend it under the house, and then run the pipe up into the kitchen. There was very little clearance for me to work under the house, so before I could start digging the pipe trench, I had to dig a depression for me to lay in just so I could fit under the house. I was so confined, my shoulders were in contact with the floor joists causing me to strain as I chipped rock out of the pipe trench with hammer and chisel. When I built the house, I never anticipated ever having to go under it, otherwise I would have made the concrete foundation piers a little taller. But it was all worthwhile, and it made life much easier to have "running" water at the sink, even though I still had to pump it by hand. No more going out in freezing temperatures or driving rain to secure the day's water supply.

I installed two wood stoves in the house. One was an old antique cook stove I bought at a consignment shop, and the other was a basic box heater stove. The cook stove had a decorative warming oven mounted over the cooking surface, and many a meal was prepared with that appliance. In the winter, the box stove did double duty as it both warmed the house and cooked meals. Since it had a large flat top, it was perfect for throwing on a pot of soup or a skillet of potatoes for dinner. A Dutch oven set on top filled with cubed beef, chunks of carrot and potato, and a few spices made a delicious one pot stew. To this day, I can't imagine living in a home without a wood stove.

I purchased and installed an old cast iron bathtub, complete with the claw feet, which still functioned well for getting myself clean. In those days, I was doing a lot of dirty, physical work and occasionally I'd get around to lounging in the tub for a good cleaning. In preparation for taking a bath, I pumped buckets of water, and poured their contents into a large pot, which was then set on one of the stoves to heat. Once it was good and hot, I dumped the steaming water into the cast iron tub, added a couple of buckets of cold water so the water temperature was something less than *scald*, and I had the luxury of soaking for a few minutes before it cooled off.

Once I was done with my bath, in order to be efficient with the still warm bath water, I sometimes took the latest and greatest mechanical device for clothes washing, the wash board, and did a load of laundry. I also had two washtubs on a stand specifically for clothes washing. In nice weather I used the washboard and the tubs outdoors, and during the winter, indoors.

I really didn't mind being out on a nice summer day, with one of the washtubs filled with hot sudsy water and the other filled with cold rinse water, taking each individual piece of clothing for a journey up and down the washboard. It was a little hard on the knuckles if I wasn't careful, but otherwise, the washboard did a fine job. Wringing out wet clothes by hand was also hard on hands and forearms, and by the time I was finished with my wash, I knew I'd had a workout.

No question--that was a hard way to do a load of laundry. I graduated to using a plumber's plunger (the kind used to free a clogged toilet--and no, it was never used for that purpose) which made a good agitator and saved the washboard for anything which needed extra persuasion, and eventually, I ramped up the modernization when I bought an old wringer/washer.

You may think living without a hot water heater was a hardship. But it really wasn't. In winter, the heating stove always had a fire going, so all I had to do was keep a full kettle of water on the stove, and I had hot water available when I needed it. Plus it provided a little moisture in the air to offset the drying effects of a wood stove. In summer, I always had a fire in the kitchen wood stove to cook the evening meal, so it was no chore to put a few more pieces of wood in the stove, set the pots of water on the stove to heat, and by the time the meal was over, there was hot water for dishes and bath.

I dealt with the wastewater from the sinks and tub by installing a greywater leach field. At first, all I had was a single drain pipe that emptied into a buried container behind the house. Eventually, I upgraded to the more traditional perforated pipe in a trench. The pipe terminated in a large, rock-lined hole, so even if the perforations plugged up, water could still flow out of the house and be filtered by the ground.

Utilizing a handy mound of dirt behind the house, I dug a deep hole from the top down and then built an outhouse over the hole.

From my high throne, with the door wide open to all my loyal subjects, I was able to gaze out over my empire--long, leisurely gazes in warmer months, quick glances at 0 degrees, and at minus 30, no gazing at all, in and out... no fooling around.

At cold temperatures, a visit to the outhouse really wasn't too bad since I had a piece of foam rubber cut in the shape of the seat. That toasty foam was placed between me and the toilet seat, and it eliminated the shock and awe of parking my tender flesh on a frozen seat when the daily need arose in the winter to use the outhouse. A sheet of Styrofoam cut out in the shape of a toilet seat would have worked well too. Years later, I incorporated a commercial composting toilet situated next to the tub, inside the house, but it never worked satisfactorily. It was a non-electric model, and by rights, it needed a fan and heating element to function properly.

My intention from the start was to be energy-independent. I had no desire to ever be connected to the conventional power grid. There was a learning curve to all this though, and one thing I learned immediately, was how much energy all our gadgets consume. I started out with one woefully inadequate solar panel and a car battery. Those two components bordered on the absurd and fell far short of an ideal system. There just wasn't enough power capacity in the battery, nor was there enough solar panel to recharge it. Plus a car battery isn't designed for this purpose.

Given my lack of financial resources at the time, I wasn't able to afford a more elaborate system. Many people have the misconception that alternative energy is free, as in "free energy from the sun." Not true. All costs are paid up front. Photovoltaic panels, wind turbines, batteries, electronic controllers, and inverters are all expenses that need to be factored in. Depending on the size of the system, it can be quite costly.

Eventually, my electrical situation improved when I added a couple more solar panels and two deep cycle marine batteries, but that didn't happen until years later. And even then, my system was still incapable of running more than a small TV, radio, and a few lights. My TV was small, maybe nine inches measured diagonally.

You know the kind: in order to watch it from across the room, one needed binoculars.

I lived with a chronic power shortage. During extended cloudy periods, I used a battery charger powered by a clunker of a gas generator to charge my battery bank. The generator was cheap, always in need of adjustment, and the adage 'you get what you pay for' certainly applied in this case.

To save on battery power, I reverted to the old-time kerosene lanterns. Those kerosene lanterns didn't throw off much light, but they shed enough light that I could easily maneuver around the house. In order to read, however, I needed to set the book right next to the lantern. Soot accumulation on the inside of the glass chimneys required cleaning every few days, and the wicks needed occasional trimming. To sum it all up, we're talking about a back–to-basics, lean, Spartan lifestyle.

My mailbox was located at the head of the driveway (.4 mile from the house), and it was my daily ritual to wander up the driveway just before lunch and fetch the mail. This was something I looked forward to every day, no matter the season. It was a wonderful walk through the woods, one that was always a source of enjoyment. I knew every inch of my driveway. With every day's hike, there was always something new to see, whether along the road or deep in the forest. Images were stashed away, deep in my mind, images that I can recall vividly to this day. Bear or moose tracks embedded in the mud, a protruding boulder alongside the road that always made snow plowing difficult, trees that grew straight as an arrow, some so big I couldn't wrap my arms around them, or water flowing through culverts, indicating how wet the forest was, are all memories gleaned from my walks.

The trek began through a stand of cedar, which upon rounding a 90-degree bend in the road, transitioned to a mixed deciduous forest. One long straightaway had a canopy of large poplars with overhanging branches, which, in summer, formed a shaded archway. Towering spruce and fir were mixed in, and I always had the feeling I was striding through a special place. Just as rain, snow, and sleet don't stop the delivery of the U.S. mail, nothing stopped me from my daily walk to retrieve it. Since this was before the days of Internet, email, and cell phones, written letters were the primary method of communication with family and friends. As you can imagine, I was always anxious to walk out to pick up my mail. Usually! The majority of the correspondence was happy news, but there were a few times I had to deal with the inevitable sad news too.

The day came when modern progress slowly started to creep towards my little sanctuary. One day, when I walked out to get my mail, I saw heavy equipment working on the narrow road. A major widening project was underway complete with drainage ditches on either side.

Wow! What a difference.

They might as well have been constructing an Interstate highway since now the road was wide enough to accommodate two vehicles headed in opposite directions. The terminus to this was still the head of my driveway. The road became a favorite drive for the locals who would turn around at my mailbox. It was surprising how many people went out for a leisurely cruise in the car, especially after dinner, to see what wildlife could be spotted. To a point, in my own way, I did much the same thing whenever I went out for a walk, run, or a bicycle ride to get some fresh air and see the sights.

The locals accepted me into the community immediately and I still remember many of the old timers I went to for advice. Over the years, many of my new friends walked or drove down my driveway and we'd sit and chat for a while. The hustle and bustle I was accustomed to was replaced by the slower pace of small town America. I remember being taken aback the first time I drove down the secondary road, which led to my property. Passing the first car, the driver waved.

What was that all about?

Then I passed another car, and that driver waved too. Gee, they're friendly around here; random waving to strangers wasn't something I'd ever encountered before, but it certainly was refreshing and it added to the sense that I belonged.

My property was located far from power poles or telephone lines, so it was many years before I heard the jingle of the phone. It was only because my neighbor eventually decided to get power and phone that I took the opportunity to have a phone installed. The phone company was willing to run an extension down to the dead-end turnaround. It then would be my responsibility to dig a long trench alongside the driveway, all the way to the house, for burying the wire. Once done, they would come back to make the final hookups.

Digging almost a half mile of trench by hand was a real chore. I tried using a single bladed plow pulled behind the tractor, which worked well until the point snapped. In the end, a shallow trench was all I could muster, but at least the cable was buried and out of sight. I welcomed the phone since that now eliminated the 4-mile drive to town to make a call on a pay phone. Since I had lived for years without a phone, I'd have to peel myself off the ceiling every time the phone rang for the first few months because it was so startling.

One day, during the first winter I had the phone, I went out to plow snow.

Can you guess what I did with my snow plow?

After returning to the house, picking up the phone, and hearing dead silence, I was rather dismayed to realize I had cut my phone line with the plow blade. Totally oblivious to the buried phone line, I had been plowing merrily along and had cut right through it. When I pushed the snow off the road in that area, my blade had dug down in the dirt and severed the line. The ground was frozen, so it took me a few days to thaw and expose the area to wire in a new section. I never made that mistake again!

Although my neighbor decided to get conventional electric, I still shunned the power line and remained committed to being off grid. To this day, I've heard tell of people paying a power bill, but I don't know what a power bill is. I've never had one. I've been off grid since my move to Maine around 1980.

Being in so far off the road presented challenges. Not only did I get stuck in the mud before my driveway was well graveled, but it was also a chore trying to keep it open in the winter. Maine gets many feet of snow throughout the winter season, and although my little tractor had a small snow plow, there came a time when it just couldn't keep up. There was too much accumulated snow to push. When that happened, I parked my truck at the head of the driveway, out by my mailbox, and I would have to snowshoe the 4/10ths of a mile in and out with groceries and every other needed item. More than once I lugged car batteries, 50-pound sacks of dog food, and luggage up and down my driveway, snowshoeing making it all the more difficult. I was my own beast of burden!

The early days of my life in Maine were filled with satisfying, non-stop work, from sun-up to sundown. I immersed myself fully in this new lifestyle. There was so much to learn. I learned how to use the tractor to safely plow and disc a field. A plow cuts the sod and turns the soil over. A disc harrow, the next implement I used, has a series of large discs that cut and churn the soil into smaller pieces as it is pulled behind the tractor. It may take a few passes over the ground to adequately chop things up. Finally, I used a spring tooth harrow to do the fine chopping and smoothing of the ground. Like any farming community, there's a lot of old, outdated equipment lining the field roads, and it was just a matter of searching to find needed treasures.

Until my move to Maine, I had never worked a garden. What joy I had that first year, plowing my garden spot in front of the house and preparing the soil, planting seeds, and watching my first sprouts pop out of the ground. I learned how to grow a large garden with an assortment of the typical vegetables. Everything from potatoes, carrots, Cole crops like cabbage and broccoli, tomatoes, beans, and the list goes on. It really isn't that difficult. There may be a year when a certain vegetable does poorly, but usually this is balanced out by something that does exceptionally well. Keep things weeded and watered, and nature does the rest.

A small field located a short walk behind the house is where I planted apples, plums, pears, grapes, and raspberries. Many of these plants died off over the years. Those that didn't die needed another tree as a pollinator in order to bear fruit, and since I was unable to grow the pollinator, I never did get any fruit. Disappointing, but OK. Growing what I could would have to do. Fortunately, I found a few wild apple trees scattered on my property, and there were so many apple trees growing in abandoned fields and along roadsides, I was able to pick several potato barrels worth in an evening. A potato barrel holds roughly 165 pounds of potatoes; I don't know what the equivalent in apples would be, but a barrel held a lot of fruit.

With the approach of autumn, outdoor chores and filling the larder took on a new urgency as the shorter days and bone-numbing temperatures drew near. Clear crisp mornings, mature garden plants with a touch of frost, and the forest raining leaves of red, gold, yellow, and orange signified the approach of winter and meant it was time for apple picking and cider making, a fall tradition, one I looked forward to every year.

From the barrels of picked apples, I sorted through the majority, with the best going into storage; the lesser quality apples I ground up and ran through my homemade cider press. Each fall, I canned gallons of cider for the upcoming winter, but my overall choice was always to drink it fresh. There was nothing like having a glass of freshly pressed cider, especially when the apples I used were a blend of different varieties free for the picking. I also designated one gallon of cider for conversion to cider vinegar. The apple pomace, the material left from the apples after pressing, became animal feed. Highbush cranberries and chokecherries also grew wild, and as long as I was willing to make the effort to harvest them, there was a wealth of free, wild food to supplement what I grew. I wouldn't starve.

I learned to root cellar what vegetables I could, and I canned the rest. After all these years, I still have my original pressure canner and the books I used to guide me in the proper way to can food. There's something innately satisfying when you have a pantry fully stocked with jars of yummy you processed yourself. Add in the fact I had grown most of what was contained in those jars, and I was doubly satisfied.

Sticking with the self-sufficiency theme of this lifestyle, I had the garden down pat but needed to work on the meat side of things. This required an animal house! I'd need to build a fairly large barn with stalls for various livestock. I had no desire to be a Noah's ark and inventory two of everything. I just wanted appropriately sized stalls for some chickens, turkeys, one beef cow, and one pig. There also needed to be enough room for supplies and equipment and a loft to store hay.

Using paper and pencil, I laid out the design and planned to use the natural materials from my property for the construction as much as possible. I used cedar, a rot-resistant wood for the vertical posts sunk into the ground and spruce and fir for the rafters and joists. I would need to cut these in spring, which is the easiest time to peel the bark. Bark peels the easiest when the sap starts to flow and the trees are coming back to life. My tractor and chainsaw got a workout as I carefully selected and cut trees that were within easy reach of the field and driveway. One would think that by being surrounded by thousands of trees, it would be an easy task to gather all the stems needed for the barn. But the trees needed to be a certain diameter, and they needed to be as straight as possible; therefore, it took a great deal of time to select the best trees. I made a couple of saw horses to rest the trees on and, with the aid of a drawknife, I tediously peeled the bark off of all the logs that would be used for the structure.

For the most part, I built the barn by myself, but occasionally I'd swap labor with a neighbor or friend when a task required another person. One of the memorable moments when building the barn was putting up the ridge pole. I was alone, and I needed to get a full sized spruce tree about 34 feet in length and 12 inches in diameter on the butt end, up to the second story of the barn. This was an instance when I needed to be creative and figure a way to do this by myself.

I had built the basic ground level structure, so I fashioned a ramp from the ground to the second story. After orienting and lining up my ridge pole with the barn, I put the smaller diameter end on the ramp. All I needed was a way to slide the tree up the ramp and get it to the second story. I positioned my trusty tractor on the opposite side of the building and threw a rope across to the small end of the log. Once I secured the rope, I was able to use the pull from the tractor to slide the whole large tree up the ramp to the second story. It required moving the tractor forward in small increments and me running around to reposition the log so that it stayed on the ramp, but it all went as planned. Throughout the process, I used a peavey, a long handled tool with a hook made for rolling and maneuvering logs, as the leverage it can exert on a log is unmatched. It's impressive what can be done with the right tools. The logger's peavey was an invaluable tool, and I used it many times during my stint in Maine.

Getting the log ridge pole up to the second story was the easy part. Now I needed to raise it up about five feet and set it on top of three vertical support posts that were lined up. By using a handyman jack, I was able to gradually jack up each end, put supports under the ridge pole, and work my way back and forth, end for end, until I got it up close to the proper level. From there I manhandled the log into position on top of the posts. I struggled hard with the large end of the log to get it over, and in doing so, strained my back. But the ridge pole was in place, and it was time to rest. I worked on the roof rafters, the metal roof, and the exterior over the remainder of the summer, and by fall, the barn was complete.

The barn would be home to various animals over the years. I started out gradually with chicks hatched, for both meat and eggs. The local animal feed store would have a spring sale on a wide array of poultry. Smart, since the company figured most people would be forced to buy their feed from them. The spring peepers had to have a warm place to stay. The best I could come up with was a towel-covered cardboard box placed close to the wood stove. A feed tray and water bottle kept them company.

Chicks do three things: eat, poop, and sleep, not necessarily in that order. They aren't known for their cerebral acumen, and even though the waterer was a commercial product made for small chicks, they still managed to plop themselves into the water and get soaking wet. In the middle of the night, if I heard shrill peeping emanating from the box, I knew something was wrong. I'd have to get up, make a fire, and get them dried off and warmed up; otherwise, they wouldn't survive the night. This meant getting the house hot enough to bake a cake. If it was uncomfortably hot for me, it was just right for them. Although I constantly changed their bedding and kept the kids tended to, they had a tendency to smell and I was always glad when their first real feathers came in and they were old enough to go out into the real world: the barn! They are rapid growers, and by mid to late summer, the meat birds were ready for the chopping block. The Rhode Island Red layers would inhabit the place year round for egg production.

Once I had gained my first experience with animal husbandry through chick raising, I graduated to buying and raising a piglet from a local pork producer. Everything at this point was new to me, and a learning experience. Want to raise animals… read a book on the subject. Talk to those who have some experience. This urban boy was getting an education on a way of life common to his predecessors, but was and still is foreign to the newer generations, including my own.

Part of being as self-sufficient as possible was raising my own food. Meat comes from animals, and there's no getting away from that fact. I was going to have to raise, slaughter, and process my own meat. With a how-to book at my side for reference, I dressed and cut up animals. The first time I processed a beef critter, I had the help of a local friend who had previous experience.

Taking the life of any animal was a hard thing for me to do, and I always had an apprehensive demeanor on "game" day. I was able to efficiently do the job, but it was a huge relief when it was done. One of the tricks I found useful was not to get attached to the animal. To that end, livestock were not pets, and as a reminder of this, the pig was named *Porkchop*, the beef cow was named *Hamburger*, and the one time I had a lamb, any guesses? It was named *Lambchop*.

Having animals required taking care of them. Feeding, making sure they had clean water, and assuring they had dry bedding were daily chores associated with raising an animal. I planted part of my field with grain, thinking I would be able to supplement the feed I purchased. Wheat and rye were two grains I tried to grow for my personal consumption.

In reality, grain production is hard. Preparing soil and planting is easy, it's the harvest that is problematic. At least if one is harvesting by hand. I used both a grain scythe and hand sickle to manually cut the stalks. I bundled, tied, and then stored the stalks until they properly dried. I then spread a blanket on the ground and flailed a bundle of grain on the blanket, meaning that I used a bat, stick, or flail to beat the grain until most of it was released from the stalks. This was a good activity if one was having a bad day: whack some grain to get rid of the stress. Now I had a blanket full of grain and small pieces of chaff. I would wait for a windy day and then pour the grain from one bucket to another, letting the wind blow out most of the chaff, leaving relatively clean seed behind. Only problem was: that was a whole lot of work for a gallon of seed. I spent the summer growing and then harvesting the grain, and spent hours flailing and winnowing out the chaff, but I had so little to show for the effort. Whether I grew and harvested rye, oats, or wheat, the process and the results were the same. Too much work for too little in return. I concluded that it made more sense to pay the farmer the money for a sack of grain. Nevertheless, at least the chickens were happy when I threw the threshed stalks into their pen. They would find any grain I had missed and would have clean bedding at the same time. Nothing went to waste.

In those early days, the normal routine was to plant the garden and raise as much food as possible. Many of the daily chores that take no time at all with modern conveniences took a lot of my time since I was doing things the way they were done in the late 19th and early 20th centuries. Doing my wash by hand in tubs, hand pumping my water, heating water in pots for dishes, cooking on a wood stove, maintaining kerosene lanterns--these are all examples of time-consuming tasks that occupied my normal day. The tasks were simple, but in many respects, they were more involved and required considerable effort on my part. After all, I couldn't just turn on the water faucet or the stove burner like a typical person. Yet, this was an excellent learning period for me. Although I worked and did

things the hard way, the education was invaluabl
booster. If all the modern day gizmos ever s
survive just fine.

In my spare time, I set out for walks in the woods to assess and explore my new surroundings. One hundred twenty acres is a good chunk of land, and it seemed I always encountered something interesting. To this day, forests are a source of wonder for me.

Although I was constantly on the go, I was reminded at nights, when the day was done, that it was a lonely affair without some female company. Unfortunately, it was a tough chore to find someone who wanted to live that lifestyle. My wife Johanna didn't come along for a number of years after I was fully settled in. Once she was part of the team, I shared all the chores and rituals of daily life with her. But, in the meantime, a dog and cat would be my companions.

I was introduced to an older gentleman from across town who had a few dogs. The man was elderly and had vision problems, and I went over a few times to visit and keep him company. It was during one of those visits that he expressed an interest in getting rid of one of his dogs. The timing was just right since I was now settled in and could use some company. He told me that I could take a male black lab concoction. He seemed like a friendly enough dog, and we became quick friends.

The dog and I settled into a routine, and he took well to the homestead. However, it wasn't too long after I brought him home that he didn't seem quite right; he appeared to be moving slower and getting a bit chunkier. At night he stayed inside with me and slept on a blanket in the living room. It's been so long ago, I don't recall what alerted me to the fact my buddy was about to give birth, but shortly thereafter, my male dog spit out six pups. I never questioned the man nor looked for any tell-tale clues on the gender of my new friend before I took him home. Surprise! This was truly an immaculate conception or my *dude* was a *she-ude*.

I built a box on the living room floor that served as a nursery, and the mother and pups stayed inside with me. I eventually picked a spunky puppy to keep, one that kept leading the charge over the barrier. I named her Snuffles.

As a kid, I had watched a cartoon show on Saturday mornings that had a dog named Snuffles who loved dog biscuits. That's how I came up with the name. Still immersed in my cartoon world, I found a cat and named it Felix. So Felix the cat and Snuffles the dog were my companions. Jinx the cat would be the feline replacement when Felix left for greener pastures.

Much of my life revolved around the seasons, with each season having its associated chores and work. But there was always time to take a break or have some fun.

One time, my parents were up for a spring visit, and I thought we would all go out and pick an early spring green called fiddleheads. Fiddleheads are the early shoots of Ostrich ferns that make their first appearance in May. They are generally found in wet areas and, once cooked, are very good with salt and butter. A friend showed me how to pick them, and they were delicious. So my parents and I went out and picked lots of "fiddleheads," and I told them we were in for a real treat. After a few bites, it was obvious they weren't as delicious as I remembered. In fact, they were awful. As it turns out, we had picked a pot of bracken fern, not ostrich ferns. I never made that mistake again, and my parents and friends made sure I didn't by occasionally teasing me throughout the years.

I still needed income, so when I had the opportunity I would head back to Pennsylvania to work for a couple months at my old electronics job. I designed and built test equipment for a robotics company. Various circuit boards had to be tested, and my job was to figure out the best way to test the boards, then build and program the tester. When all was done, I would draw up schematics and put a manual together. I built some of the test equipment in a machine shop where I gained experience running a milling machine and a lathe.

This electrical and mechanical experience will be a huge advantage to me as you will see further on in the book. Once the project I was contracted for was completed, I would then be on my way home with enough money to keep me going for a while.

After one of those trips to Pennsylvania, I was back home in Maine, with money in the bank, continuing on as normal, when life had an unexpected course change for me.

That change started with a knock on the door.

Maine house in the deep cold of winter

Maine house in the autumn

Garden in Maine

Kitchen after Johanna remodeled it

Barn ridge pole

Me using the washtub

Chapter 3–

Money Can Grow on Trees

That knock on the door came from a local logging contractor inquiring whether I would be interested in having my property logged. Now the young man from suburbia had some thinking to do. The prospect of logging was completely foreign territory to me, and frankly, it came as a total surprise. But before I could make any decision regarding the future of my woodlot, I needed to understand what logging entailed.

What price would I get paid for a cord of wood?

Was this something I could do myself to put some money in my pocket?

And, finally, what would my property look like after it was logged over?

All loggers aren't created equal. There are many conscientious loggers who take pride in the job they do, but, likewise, there are some who thrash and bash, leaving a decimated waste land in their wake. These are the horror stories people hear about, stories of the land being ravaged. Would that be the fate of my property if someone else did the work? These were some of the questions I needed answers to, and as it turned out, those answers determined the course of my life over the next 20 years.

Although it is a nice concept to live 100% off the land, in reality, it's a pipe dream. You can go to extreme measures to get close, but there are some things you have to have that the land can't provide. Some of those items include tools and equipment, such as a chainsaw and axe, supplies such as rope and nails, food that you can't grow yourself, and clothes, which we can't forget about unless you are willing to run around in animal skins and fig leaves. Health care, vehicle expenses, and property taxes are just a few more of the many things requiring money or barter. I had an asset of 120 acres of woodland, but I had no idea of the value of the timber. Perhaps my money needs could be met through the proceeds from the harvest of my woodlot.

To get answers to all my questions, I initially enlisted the aid of the Maine Forest Service. After all these years, I can still remember the first forester who came out to visit and walk around the property with me. We wandered around enough of the woodlot for him to get a good sense of what timber resource was on the property, and then he gave me suggestions on what my next steps might be.

The results of that first visit were a determining factor in my decision to work in the woods. After his initial consultation, I gathered all the financial numbers: what the logger would pay me for a cord versus what the mill would pay me per cord if I did the work myself. Once I considered that data in conjunction with the forester's advice, it was easy for me to reach a decision. I concluded that if I was willing to do the work, my paycheck would be many times greater than if I allowed the logger who knocked on my door to cut my trees. As it turned out, this was one of the best financial decisions I've ever made.

I formulated a grand vision. If I logged the property myself, I could turn an unmanaged, dense forest into a parklike sanctuary. I would banish bugs and mosquitoes to beyond the property lines, deer would prance through, and animals would knock on my door to see if I was free to play.

It takes some serious effort to cut and yard wood. It also takes some special skills with a chainsaw and specialized machinery, like a skidder, neither of which I had. The two big industries in northern Maine are logging and potato farming, and I had seen the "skidder" that the logger uses to harvest trees. It is a large 4-wheel-drive, articulated machine with a blade on the front and winch on the back. Articulated means it pivots in the center for greater maneuverability. What a cool toy that would be, but, alas, it was out of my price range.

Instead, I bought a bigger farm tractor, an International 656, and I became a two-tractor household. The farm tractor would be the machine I would use to harvest trees. I mounted a winch that ran off the power take-off shaft onto the rear of the tractor. This combination was far from ideal, but it gave me the opportunity to get some experience and confirm whether logging the property myself was the proper decision. I bought the last item I needed, a larger chainsaw, and was ready to log.

My education began on day one when I went out to cut for the first time as a "professional" logger. I started cutting one of my first trees, looked up, and was promptly hit in my eye with a branch that had fallen from above. Perfect timing, and I was done for the day. But I was given a second chance; the branch was big enough that it hit my eye orbit without any serious damage to my eye. It sure smarted though, and I had a black and blue eye for a while.

Foolishly, I had purchased a new chainsaw, but didn't buy any safety gear. Logging is one of the most dangerous occupations, and to be safe, it requires steel-toed boots, Kevlar pants, and a helmet with eye and ear protection. Not long after the eye injury incident, I paid a visit to the local logging supply store and got properly outfitted. It's always good to have the proper safety gear so you don't end up cutting the *wrong limbs.*

Countless people have been injured working with a chainsaw, and I was fortunate to have learned my lesson early on without any permanent injury. Nowadays, it drives me crazy when I watch television news or a TV show and see someone operating a chainsaw without any protective gear. Life doesn't offer second chances to everyone. Those same news and TV programs show people felling a tree the wrong way. When the tree falls on the house, it's rather obvious there was an error in the execution of the plan.

At this point, I officially became self-employed as a tree farm business. I had the new responsibility of record keeping and filing tax returns as a sole proprietorship. I spent hours entering numbers into a simple accounting ledger. I learned about the tax code, and what I needed to do to file a simple business tax return, and now depreciation became part of my vocabulary. I was still committed to my off-grid homesteading lifestyle, but by starting my tree farm enterprise, I went from a no frills, uncomplicated way of life to a small businessman. A one-man show.

To a degree, I'm a perfectionist, and although I haven't hit perfection yet, it isn't due to a lack of effort. With that in mind, every decision I made through the years, what tree to cut down, or how to winch the tree out without damaging the surrounding trees, revolved around my quest for the perfect woodlot.

To that end, I abhorred conventional logging and became determined to create a model forest. A small clearcut patch of an acre or two to salvage diseased or blown down trees, or to create wildlife habitat I could understand, but to clearcut large swaths of forest was rather upsetting and shortsighted to me. I felt the best approach was a selective harvest, meaning I would selectively cut only the mature or diseased trees, or thin out a dense section, thus improving the stand and leaving the rest for the future.

Wood is a finite but renewable resource, and a forest properly managed will continuously provide a crop and a source of income over the owner's lifetime. Additionally, a healthy forest provides a home for a diverse set of flora and fauna, helps clean the air, and prevents soil erosion. Forests are an integral part of our environment. Once clearcut, the land takes a long time to recover before another harvest is possible.

Silviculture, the science of growing and managing a forest,

would have categorized my woodlot as an "uneven-aged stand." It's a fancy term that basically means the forest is composed of a mixture of young, intermediate age and mature trees. Ideally, any stand should be a mix of species and tree diameters. Aesthetically, it looks much better, is excellent animal habitat, and the forest has a better chance of surviving disease and insect damage.

This is the key to a sustainable woodlot. Because trees are of different age classes, there are always trees ripe for harvesting, which in turn frees up the remaining middle-aged and younger trees to grow. This continual rotation makes for a steady stream of income, and by the time the middle-aged and younger trees have matured for cutting, there's already a new batch of seedlings established from natural regeneration, the process of seeds falling to the ground and germinating. Therefore, the woodlot always remains productive without ever having to be replanted.

It may help to think of a woodlot as a big garden. Some species are weed trees, and I wanted to cut them out to make room for the more desirable species. Although the weed trees had some value, I wanted to encourage the higher value trees to flourish. Poplar was a weed species I made good money from, but if I sold the same volume of spruce or hardwoods, I might have doubled or tripled my return for the same effort. So, in the long run, it was in my best interest to take out the poplar and let spruce, fir, and hardwoods dominate the areas.

The word "dominate" is important here. I'm not advocating the extermination of the poplar or other weed trees. They have their place too. But I wanted to relegate them to a minor part. And, much like a garden, one needs to thin the trees so there is less competition for light, nutrients, and water. I weeded and thinned thick stands of trees to help encourage the growth of a better forest. Over my logging career, I cut thousands of cords of wood off of our woodlot. Even after 20 years, I never accessed the entire property to selectively harvest it. But the areas I did work became a better forest.

When logging any woodlot, it's impossible not to have some damage, but I mitigated the risk as much as practical. Taking down a large mature tree required expertise. It's one thing to notch a tree properly and make it fall; anybody can do that. But to make it consistently fall where I wanted it to, or make it fall in a direction other than its lean, required additional skill. Otherwise, undue damage would happen to the remaining trees. Normally trees are dragged out full length. But, if I needed to buck the tree up into six pieces to prevent injury to the remaining stems, that is what I did. I then winched each piece out one or two at a time so little harm was done to the nearby trees.

Like anything else, the more practice, the better one becomes. The more trees I cut down, the more accurate I became, so that rarely did I miss dropping a tree exactly where I wanted it to go. If the tree was leaning in the wrong direction, I employed techniques to ensure the tree still fell in the desired location. One of the advanced chainsaw skills involves using the tip of the bar to make a bore cut. Not recommended unless someone is proficient with the saw. It's dangerous because of its high potential for kick-back.

During the time-frame when I was logging, I took advantage of any opportunity to return to Pennsylvania for the electronics job. It was during one of these trips back to Pennsylvania to work that I met my wife Johanna. A desire to homestead, camp, and garden were some of her interests, and she was the perfect mate for me to complete the dream. Since we had a shared purpose in life, she became part of my life, and the "I" will now shift to "we." By this time, the commute to Pennsylvania was getting a bit overextended, my electronics career was concluding, and it was time to focus on deriving income from the homestead.

Because Johanna had the same interests and goals as me, she took to the homestead well. She was taught at an early age many of the necessary skills, and was competent in many facets of the self-sufficient lifestyle: growing a garden, preserving food, cooking and baking, knitting, and sewing for example. Homesteading together came naturally, with each of us having complementary skills. Subjects I had little knowledge of were her strong suit, and vice versa, and although much of our knowledge base overlapped, in reality, very little was completely new to either of us. We made a formidable, well-rounded team when we combined her expertise with my ability to problem solve and fix things. During our time in Maine, we not only added to our basic homesteading skills, but we honed and perfected those abilities so that we had the confidence we could survive in almost any situation. Meanwhile, I continued to pursue logging as my contribution to the household coffers, and Johanna worked part-time for many years.

While adding that woman's touch to the place, Johanna made improvements to the quality of our lives through the years. We still remained off grid, but the house had some major rearrangements with her on the scene. I had 1x8 unfinished boards as my floor. Over time, they shrunk and gaps formed between the boards allowing debris to collect there. I kept the house swept, but it was never truly clean. Eventually, we either carpeted or covered the bare wooden floors with vinyl. What a difference the new flooring made! We redid the kitchen, and instead of open shelves for dishes and a wooden counter top, I built base cabinets, had a real counter top made, and installed wall cabinets above the counter. Johanna was quite pleased. We redid the exterior of the house, originally finished with board and batten, with cedar shingles, a tedious project.

Although it took some time, the functional house was transformed into a lovely small home.

While house improvements were ongoing, I still focused on the woodlot. For many years I logged with the farm tractor, but it wasn't the right piece of equipment. It really had too many limitations. Bogging down in wet ground, load size I could haul in a trip, and the small winch were all limiting factors in determining what I could do with the machine. If I was going to be a pro, it was time to up my game and get a used skidder.

Finances were limited, and we hemmed and hawed at the decision to go into debt. Staying out of debt and owning everything outright has been our life's mantra. If we needed to go into debt, we did whatever was necessary to get out of debt as fast as possible. By its very nature, debt is anti-freedom. What I mean by that is, as long as we were in debt to someone, we weren't truly free. Owing money is an obligation we take seriously, and having to make loan payments alters every day decisions.

Do we go away for the weekend, do we buy a new TV, and can we afford this or that were questions that always came into play as long as we were in debt.

Never in our lives have Johanna and I been indebted to any bank for more than a few years. Freedom is making the last payment long before it was due. So this skidder purchase was a big deal and would be the first of many tough decisions we faced when trying to decide what equipment to buy that would enable us to extract the most value out of the timber resource.

We made the decision to buy a used skidder and found one at a local dealer. It was delivered with great anticipation, as I was really climbing up in the world. Mostly because the machine sits high and has steps up to the cab! But nonetheless, it was an awesome machine and I was able to log more safely and efficiently. Now that I had the proper tool for the job, instead of dreading the day's toil with the farm tractor, I was excited to go out and work our forest each day. It was a John Deere skidder and "Johnny" and I were inseparable in the woods.

Although I could have jumped on the machine and headed to the woods for an on-site education, I thought it was more prudent to head out in the truck and visit a few logging friends to see what tips and tricks I could pick up from them. A couple of hours spent with those guys gave me so much useful information. They taught me safety tips, proper operation, and maintenance during my visits with them.

I carefully laid out every road and trail through the woodlot so that I could access the most wood with the least amount of damage to residual trees. I had a main trail heading into the woods, and then off of that main trail were side trails arranged in a herringbone pattern. Generally, I winched out full length trees from those access trails.

With "Johnny," I was able to access more of our woodlot, including the wet cedar areas, although sometimes I'd have to wait for winter and frozen conditions to reach the wettest sections. It was better to be patient and wait for optimal conditions than to go out too soon and rut up the woodlot with those big skidder tires. Although the machine had 4–wheel-drive and chains on the tires, it was still possible to get it stuck in the mud. When you get a big machine like that stuck... it's really stuck.

I recall one occasion when I had the machine at a hard tilt with one side on firm ground while the other side was buried in muck. It takes a lot to tip a skidder on to its side, but I was a little nervous I was close to doing that. The more I tried to free myself, the more the side in the mud sunk down and the more the skidder listed to that side. By applying downward pressure on the blade, I was able to raise up the front end enough so I could throw chunks of wood and tree brush into the rut. That filled up the channel so when I released the blade pressure at least my front end was now stable. The rear was still a disaster, but I was able to use the winch to pull the skidder back enough so that I could throw more debris into the rut and eventually extricate myself from this dilemma. That was by far the worst pickle I was ever in with the skidder. The powerful winch on the back of the skidder was a great piece of engineering, and as long as I had a long enough cable and could find an anchor point I was always able to winch myself out whenever I got stuck.

I mentioned previously the large quantities of snow a typical winter season brings to northern Maine. There was never a depth of snow "Johnny" couldn't wade. With chains on, it struggled and churned its way through anything I was ever faced with, but it was a long process. It was hard on the machine to bust a new trail through the deep snow, but once the trail had tracks, a good night of freezing made all the difference with traction the next day.

Although I could get the skidder to create access trails through the woods in deep snow, it was a lot harder for me. There were winters when the snow was so deep in the woods, I'd wade snow that was nearly up to my waist, and at times I would have to crawl on hands and knees on top of the snow to get to a tree. With the chainsaw in one hand and the winch cable slung over my shoulder, I would throw the chainsaw ahead a little and struggle toward the tree. Then it would take me a while to kick and stomp the snow around the base of the tree so that when I cut it I wasn't leaving a 3-foot stump.

Winter logging had definite disadvantages: deep snow, difficulty starting the machine in sub-zero weather, and having to plow the driveway and landing so the log truck could get in to pick up a load of wood. But there were just as many advantages: the ground was generally frozen, the temperatures were more comfortable for working hard, and there were no bugs, including bees. I had to be careful of bees in the summer, since they like to make nests in the ground or in a decaying tree. Several times I found myself merrily cutting away, and suddenly bees were furiously buzzing around me. Even in summer, I wore long-sleeve shirts and was well-protected, so a sting or two was all I received. Logging sure was a tough way to make a living.

We bought a used standard highway plow, and rigged up a way to attach it to the skidder's front blade so I could really move the snow. Now I could keep the driveway open year-round. The trick was to try not to plow a foot or more of snow at a time. Instead, we kept up with the storms and plowed every time a few inches accumulated. If there was a big snowstorm raging during the night, we got up several times to plow the driveway.

Johanna drove the truck and followed behind me to provide light, while I plowed with the skidder, since there were no lights on "Johnny."

She had the "hard" job. Nice warm cab, relaxing, slow motion drive with the music playing.

I had it "easy." Completely exposed to the cold air, my gloved hands were always cold and wet. As I struggled to discern the driveway in the headlights beam, wind-driven snow pelted my face and I squinted my eyes to protect them. As I brushed past tree branches laden with new fallen snow, the snow cascaded into the open skidder cage, plastering me, so that by the time we were done, I looked like the Abominable Snowman.

I felt bad for Johanna!

In retrospect, I can say I safely logged for about 20 years, but I had a few close calls. The one that sticks in my mind was when I was cutting a large poplar tree. With the thousands of trees I'd cut over a 20-year career, this was one of only a couple of trees I misjudged. This tree was perhaps 22 inches in diameter and quite tall. A skidder is designed with a blade on the front that can be used to push trees over once they are properly notched. For safety, a skidder also has a heavy protective cage that surrounds the operator when seated in the cab. I had notched the tree and was trying to push this tree over.

Timberrrrr! Uh Oh!!

Instead of the tree falling away from me, it came straight back at me. I sat in the skidder and watched this poplar come back and fall on top of the machine. It sat right above me on the roof of the skidder cage.

Phew, that was a close one!

Glad the cage held. Worst thing I could have done was panic and try to get out of the skidder. Protection of the operator is what the cage is designed to do, so have faith it will do the job. I was simply able to drive out from underneath the tree, but it was eerie seeing that big thing teetering up above me. I believe in this instance, my miscalculation was on the wind direction. Regardless, it all ended well.

Our woodlot was a nice mix of poplar, spruce, fir, and cedar. Poplar went to the local pulp mill for wafer board, spruce and fir to the sawmill, and cedar to the fencing and sawmill company. The nagging question was, how can we maximize the return on our timber resource by adding extra value? This was partially answered when we invested in a post peeler. The peeler makes a fence post or rail from smaller diameter cedar trees. The machine peels off the bark so what is left is a smooth piece of wood.

This was a great way to utilize our many dense, small-diameter cedar stands. Because loggers generally get paid by the cord, and it takes a lot of cedar trees that size to make a cord, very few loggers would have bothered to harvest such small cedar since there is so much work involved. While it wouldn't have been economically feasible for them to cut such small diameter stems, we, as the land owners, could get a good return on our efforts.

In fact, very few people would have managed our cedar stands the way we did. To give you a sense of what I consider dense, cedar stems were generally 3 to 7 inches in diameter and were spaced, on average, every 3 feet. Many times, trees grew thickly in clusters of 2 or more. The cedar stands were always dark; no sun ever got to the ground.

I had a main road leading into the cedar areas but no secondary offshoots. Walking into the stands, I selected the best trees to remain and cut down a few stems immediately adjacent to give them some breathing room. Because the forest was so thick, there was no room for the cut trees to fall; they just remained standing. I had to take a set of hand-logging tongs, manually grab hold at the butt of each tree, and manhandle them until they fell. Once the trees were on the ground, I limbed them. Most trees were 20-30 feet in length. Then using the hand tongs again, I dragged each tree out, one by one, to the road. From there, I was able to use the skidder to yard those trees to a central landing for further processing. A physically grueling endeavor. Over the course of years, I was able to release the best trees so they could grow for the future, while at the same time utilizing the small trees I thinned out. I harvested thousands of trees in this manner, and the remaining stand was quite the source of pride.

We added an additional piece of equipment to our collection when we purchased a large front-end bucket loader, which came with a set of forks. The loader and forks allowed me to load bundles of finished product onto a flat bed, which meant I could hire a local trucking firm to ship large quantities of fencing to customers. A tractor trailer would come down to the dead-end turnaround, and I would load bundle after bundle of our finished product on to the trailer. How satisfying it was to see a full tractor trailer load of post and rails drive out to market! That satisfaction wouldn't have been possible had we not invested in the post peeler and loader.

Our woodlot had abundant quantities of Balsam fir trees,

which I logged, and the fresh boughs were wasted by being left in the woods after I limbed the trees. Johanna was taught at an early age how to make Christmas wreaths by her Dad, and she thought she could fashion wreaths out of the fir boughs I left in the woods. If so, we could make money from something we normally wasted. It doesn't get any better than that! After some experimentation to perfect the technique, we added wreath-making to our business plan. Each November would find us out picking wreath greens. Because of this, we were getting more value out of every fir tree cut. Additionally, we picked tips from areas that had high concentrations of young fir trees.

Harvesting wreath tips was an enjoyable activity--going out into the cold, crisp morning air, wandering randomly around in the forest, and snapping off branch tips, which was made easier by the cold temperatures. Eventually, we would accumulate an arm load of brush, which we dumped into a central pile. Once we had enough greens, we would haul the large pile to the house. In later years, we made the wreaths in an outside shop, but the first couple of years, we made the wreaths in the house, and the scent of Christmas lingered throughout the season. We also hung a thick fir wreath every Christmas on the porch by the door, decorated just the way we did for our customers, with sprigs of cedar cones and greens and a big red velvet bow. By word of mouth alone, we got orders for 80 to 100 decorated Christmas wreaths each year. These were mail-ordered to customers throughout the United States and brightened the doorways to many homes. Wreath making made for an intense 3-4 week period of time, but it was a nice change of routine for us.

What else could we do to increase the value of our timber resource?

Wouldn't it be great if we could saw our logs ourselves and produce lumber to sell locally? Why send out all of our saw logs to a mill when we could perhaps double or triple our money by sawing the logs ourselves?

After another agonizing decision, we decided to buy a small, portable sawmill. We had researched every small band saw on the market, and we took every opportunity to attend loggers events featuring these sawmills. The more I studied them, the more unimpressed I became with the quality of the components and engineering, and yet they were quite expensive. But one sawmill seemed like it would work for us, and I drove out of state to pick it up. The deal turned into a fiasco, and I ended up coming home empty handed.

It's said that necessity is the mother of all inventions, so perhaps it's fitting my frustration would be the father of inventions too. As my dad would say, I know just enough to be dangerous, and I thought I could design a band sawmill that would be as good as, if not better than, the commercially available products. I had no formal mechanical engineering or physics training in school. I knew nothing about band sawmills other than what I had observed, and yet I was planning on designing a gizmo that would be better than what teams of engineers and companies already had in the market?

What in the world was I thinking!?

This was really going to be a challenge, and I was stepping well outside my known comfort level. I say "known" comfort level because none of us really know what those bounds are until we try. Nevertheless, this was going to be a $30,000 gamble that I could indeed engineer a better mousetrap, or should I say sawmill, than what was on the market.

I had a few things working in my favor. The mechanical and

machine shop experience I had from my electronics career would come in handy. Also mechanics and mechanical principals are easy for me to understand.

In fact, my first memory of doing something mechanical was as a little boy. Cars were fascinating to me, and I had thoughts of becoming an auto mechanic, but I was quickly discouraged from this occupation when I had an industrial accident. My parents had bought me a pedal-powered car, red and fire engine like. Being a solidly built, metal vehicle (they don't make them like that anymore), a youngster could get in and pedal around the yard or down the neighborhood sidewalk. Not being satisfied with the performance of my little car, I brought it into my make pretend service center and straight into my imaginary service bay. Supporting both ends of my car on kitchen chairs, I slid under to take a look at the whatchamacallit while it was on the "lift." I was wrestling with the thingamajig when one end of my car fell off the chair and landed on my face.

To this day, I have a scar on my forehead and, if memory serves me right, I needed a few stitches. Fortunately, the injury was minor and wasn't a big deal. With the passage of time, the scar merged into one of the many wrinkles on my forehead and is barely visible. Regrettably, I never did file a make pretend law suit against the repair shop! Funny, the things we remember from childhood.

Before committing any drawings of my sawmill to paper, I spent time in the local college library researching the principles of mechanical engineering. At home, I poured over structural steel tables and consulted with engineers and component salesmen and, as a result, was ultimately able to design a fully hydraulic band sawmill powered by a Ford gas engine. My machine was portable and capable of cutting a tree 36 inches in diameter by 24 feet long. It was able to hydraulically lift the log from the ground, compensate for the tree taper, hold the log in place as it was being sawn, and turn the log when needed.

Not only did I design a machine that could take a log and produce lumber, but if the log was turned and cut enough times, I could whittle the world's longest toothpick!

I spent months drafting a set of mechanical drawings any machine shop could work from, with full dimensions for every part of the sawmill. Paper and pencil were my designing "tools," and in place of fancy CAD (computer aided design) computers and software, I cut out full-sized, cardboard templates I could hold in my hand when I just couldn't mentally visualize a problem and its solution.

To fabricate my contraption, I found a machine shop in the middle of the state of Maine that was willing to work with me. It was my hope I could work at the machine shop assembling the pieces as they were machined. By late spring of 1994, the shop had the steel on order and I had all the components ready to go.

It was time to build us a sawmill!

I headed down to the shop where I began work immediately. I had paid for the steel and placed a substantial deposit with the machine shop, so we were committed to seeing this project through. How exciting it was to have a couple of their employees dedicated to the fabrication of something I had conjured up. They welded heavy steel rails and crossbeams in place, and as the machinist finished each piece of the puzzle, I was on hand to assemble it.

It wasn't long before things started taking shape. Sitting on heavy duty saw horses, the long frame of the saw didn't look like much until they built and mounted the carriage. The carriage was really the saw assembly. The log would remain stationary, and the carriage with Ford motor would straddle the log and ride down a set of tracks. The saw head, which had a set of large wheels for the saw blade to ride around, had a very accurate screw assembly to raise and lower the head. This controlled the depth of cut, allowing me to cut any thickness of lumber I desired. Because I had a background in machine control, I designed the sawmill so I could computerize the operation in the future if I wanted.

As it was, all I had to do was stand at a control panel and tweak switches and knobs to cut a log. The hydraulics was set up so I could control the carriage up, down, forward and backward as well as control the speed of certain operations. The machine shop did a marvelous job fabricating the mill, and in roughly six weeks it was ready to paint and travel home.

After I got it home, I finished the wiring and hydraulic plumbing. What a thrill it was to fire it up for the first time and watch it actually cut a log. Standing at the controls, I could turn a knob and watch as the saw head went up and down or turn another knob and the sawmill advanced down the tracks. Turn another control and the sawmill sped up or slowed down. It pretty much worked as planned right out of the gate. I needed to do a few minor tweaks and adjustments, but the overall design was solid.

The machine shop was impressed and invited us to make a proposal on building this as a commercial product for market. Johanna and I made a presentation to the company's engineers and president, but they ultimately decided to focus on in-house projects of their own.

Over the years, I was able to enhance the value of our woodlot by sawing lumber from the logs I had previously sold to the big mills. Because my sawmill was capable of cutting large trees, I was able to efficiently cut standard sized boards and framing lumber, as well as large timbers like 8x8s. I sold much of my sawn lumber locally but was also able to sell and ship cedar lumber to the same customer who bought my peeled post and rail products. Once the local folk became aware of my sawmill, I had additional business from them when they brought their own logs to me to custom saw.

For younger readers still in school, I'd like to pass on my personal experience to you. You just never know where or when you will need some of the things being taught in school.

For example, I never thought I'd need basic trigonometry to figure the roof line and rafter length for the house I designed or geometry to calculate the length of a band saw blade that rides around two wheels. Or English for writing and vocabulary skills needed to write a business plan or a future book. I want to offer you some encouragement in absorbing what's being taught. Although I never mastered any subject, I came away knowing the basic fundamentals, and it's served me well. I was no whiz in any subject, but I retained just enough of the principles to be able to go back to books and cipher out the problem at hand.

Being the high tech guy that I am, I'd just pull out my handy abacus or slide rule from the desk drawer to do my figuring. I write that in jest, and use a simple calculator now. But back in my electronics schooling, I was taught how to use a slide rule and still remember how to use it to some degree.

When time allowed, Johanna worked the woodlot by pruning trees, offloading lumber from the sawmill or helping with fence posts. She was an integral part of keeping things going. If she wasn't out working the woodlot, she was working at her job or toiling to keep me well fed. The kitchen stove was always busy, and I never lacked power foods to keep me going.

Throughout my logging career, professional foresters came out to visit or inspect my work, and had nothing but positive feedback and encouragement for me. I learned a great deal about logging and forestry from them, and I always took to heart the practical advice they offered. Johanna and I took a great deal of pride in our stewardship of the land. We joined the National Tree Farm program, and ultimately were twice named the County Outstanding Tree Farm.

For my part, I turned into a workaholic and was either logging or sawing lumber seven days a week from sun up to sun down for weeks on end until I physically couldn't go any more. I'd take a day off and then repeat that work schedule. I did this for years and had created my own homemade rat race. I was working myself to death. The curse of the type "A" personality.

But there were a few times when we took extended vacations. Being self-employed gave us flexibility in our lives, and we were fortunate to be able to do a few special trips. Like the time I spent six months of my life on the Appalachian Trail.

Why don't you take a walk with me for a while.

"Johnny" hauling a load of poplar trees

Heap of wood headed to market

Johanna on the Massey Harris tractor

Spruce log ready to be sawn

Loading lumber for market

The sawmill I built

Selectively harvested spruce and fir

Set to do some serious plowing

Chapter 4–

Wandering for 165 Days and Nights

Lost on the mountain, I was enveloped by thick gray fog and wind-driven snow. I was wandering in a meadow surrounded by sparsely spaced, stunted trees with gnarly snow-encrusted branches. The scrubby, weather-beaten trees were a testament to the harsh environment through which I was hiking. The white markers I was using to guide me along the trail were gone, merged into a seamless background obscured by the strong winds and heavy snow that created near whiteout conditions.

I was near the highest peak in Virginia, in proximity to the summit of Mt. Rogers, when the snowstorm had hit. I had made it to the top of the mountain and found myself in a white surreal landscape, having no idea which way to go. It was unsettling, but I had food, gear, and winter camping experience, so if need be, I could hunker down somewhere under a tree for the night.

Since beginning the journey at Springer Mountain, Georgia, I had been relentlessly following the white blazes painted on the trees which were my guideposts along the Appalachian Trail. For several months now I had been hiking, and had contended with some snowy trails, but this was the first serious weather obstacle I'd encountered.

From my pack I pulled out my handy compass along with the guide and map for this particular section of the trail, and oriented the map northward. Using map and compass, I ascertained that if I headed in a westerly direction, I would eventually intersect a blue blazed trail that would lead to shelter. Off I went, tramping through the snow, faithfully following the bearing indicated by my small magnetized pointer. Once I knew the direction I wanted to travel, it was a simple matter of pointing the compass to take a bearing, sighting on an object, such as a tree, in line with my intended route and walking to my target. By continually repeating this process, I was able to travel in a more or less straight line.

Although I have confidence in my orienteering abilities, I find

I always have a hint of doubt. Is the map right? Did I orient the map correctly and set the compass properly? And where is that trail anyway? I should have intersected it by now!

From my perusal of the map and the map scale, I had a vague idea of how far I needed to travel, and the important thing was not to panic. Eventually my orienteering skills enabled me to find the blue blazed side trail that led to a shelter, where I remained for the duration of the storm, in the safety of the lean-to. To this day, I am quite confident that if I have a map and a properly set compass, I can find my way out of anything. Later, I heard about a Boy Scout troop that was up on the mountain during the tempest, and they had to be rescued. It was quite the storm.

Being the outdoors, adventurous types, Johanna and I decided we would thru-hike the Appalachian Trail together. The Appalachian Trail is a foot path starting at Springer Mountain, Georgia and ending at Mt. Katahdin in Maine. At approximately 2,180 miles long, it winds its way through 14 states and generally sticks to higher ground along mountain ridges, although there is plenty of valley walking too. The highest point on the trail is Clingman Dome in The Smoky Mountains National Park, Tennessee, at an elevation of 6,643 feet; the lowest point is the Hudson River in New York at 124 feet.

A thru-hike means starting at one end and walking until getting to the other end. No trains, planes, or buses would be allowed to shorten the hike. This trip would be accomplished solely by our own two feet, by repeatedly placing one foot in front of the other countless times. Late in the 1980s we formulated a plan on how we would accomplish this feat. There were so many things to think about.

When would we attempt to do this hike, what gear would we need, how far would we hike each day, and how would we handle the food needed for each day? These were just a few of the many questions that needed to be resolved before the big journey could begin.

It was one thing to sit in the warmth of the living room fantasizing about making the final push to the summit, trudging the final steps northward--arms raised in celebration--but quite another to cope with the reality of all the logistical planning that needed to be done before we initiated the first footsteps from the southern terminus.

In the weeks leading up to our trip, we prepared for our hike by getting out and walking the local roads with fully weighted packs to get our bodies used to the activity. As it turns out, you really can't prepare for the trek unless you are hiking and carrying a loaded pack on your back for hours each day. You can't imagine how sore your hips and shoulders get once you saddle up and walk day after day with a full pack. A full pack for me was about 45-55 pounds, depending on the food load, and Johanna's was about 36 pounds.

Our plan was to start at Springer Mountain in January and walk north through the spring season to end the journey in Maine sometime in June. We left Maine in December 1989, made a stop in Pennsylvania to visit family, and then, after final hugs and well wishes from them, resumed the long drive down the interstate highways bound for Georgia. We drove our old Ford pickup truck with the intent of selling it to a local car dealer in exchange for cash to help fund the trek. We made the rounds in the area, and were fortunate to find a small used car dealer who was willing to pay a fair price for our vehicle and give us a lift to the trail head.

On January 15th 1990, we arrived late in the afternoon at Springer Mountain. There's no direct access to the summit of

Springer, so earlier in the day we were dropped off at Amicalola State Park, and from there we made the 8-mile hike to get to the official trail head.

We found the shelter easy enough with its two commemorative plaques cemented into the nearby rock. We had come a long way, and we were brimming with excitement. I'd like to say we had the shelter to ourselves that night, but we shared it with an abundance of mice, which made for a poor night's sleep. Mice, as it turned out, would be a constant nuisance at shelters.

How nice it would have been to have packed a cat, a piece of equipment we overlooked.

It's fairly customary for a hiker to have a trail name they use to sign registers at the various shelters along the way. A hiker can write their thoughts and comments in these books, and it's also a way for others on the trail to keep in touch to a degree. I chose the trail name *Steadyfeet*, and I also kept my own journal, which I tried to write in daily.

We were aware of the statistics regarding successful thru-hikes, and the numbers were clearly against us. For the many people who attempt to thru-hike the trail each year, only a small percentage of them actually complete the trek. Many hikers show up physically and mentally unprepared for the rigors of the mountains and the trail. Numerous stories are told of hikers with optimistic dreams, showing up at a terminal end laden with the best gear, who, in order to lighten their load, jettison stuff along the way, or who completely bail out in the first week or two. We were certainly surprised at how rugged and tough the trail was right from the start. For the first week, we were both stiff and sore until we started to adapt to this new regimen.

Back in 1990, I knew of only one successful winter thru-hiker, so we were fully aware we were bucking the normal routine with this attempt. There were many factors we considered when we decided to do this as a winter hike. We weren't gluttons for punishment, but we knew if we started with the masses, as is typical in the spring, we would be walking with crowds and competing for shelters. By hiking in the winter, we figured we had several advantages. We would probably have the shelters to ourselves and, because the foliage was off the trees, we would have unimpeded views from mountaintops and scenic overlooks--views the typical thru-hikers never get to see.

Of course, the downside was that we needed to lug winter clothes and equipment for each of us, which included a set of snowshoes and small ice crampons. We also packed heavy clothes, a heavy coat, hat and gloves, rain gear, cookware, stove, sleeping bag, survival gear, and food. We came prepared, ready for the worst the trail could dish out, but all this gear required large backpacks in which to stow our stuff.

We chose our backpacks for our individual anatomic frames, and each wore a shoulder harness and waist band in order to distribute the load onto our bodies. Numerous means of adjustment allowed us to tighten or loosen a strap throughout the day's hike to seek the most comfortable position. If the hips started to ache, we would loosen the hip belt a little and cinch the shoulder straps a bit more so the shoulders carried more of the load. Then reverse that order when the shoulders needed a break.

As luck would have it, we were blessed with unusually warm weather those first weeks in January, and we quickly grew tired of lugging around the snowshoes. To lighten the load, we sent them home when we arrived at one of our first mail stops. We didn't carry tents--instead opting for bivy sacks. A bivy sack is a waterproof over-sized bag designed to protect the hiker and his or her sleeping bag from the elements. In practice, the sacks didn't work as well as we hoped they would. The head area was the weak spot, and it was hard to keep out the rain. It was also an ordeal to get into the bivy/sleeping bag combination, and even more of an ordeal to extricate myself in the middle of the night when nature called.

Another negative of a winter's journey was that many of the stores and hostels normally open for the hiking season were closed for the season. Keeping our footwear dry was problematic too. We frequently had wet hiking boots, and with night time temperatures below freezing, they were inevitably frozen the next morning.

Thawing them out was a ritual where we wedged our feet into frozen boots, left laces either loose or untied, and walked until the boots started to soften up. We looked like Herman Munster hoofing the trail until the boots got back to conforming to our feet. I'd like to say that one gets used to soggy and frozen boots, but each morning, there was a moment's pause as we contemplated immersing warm, dry feet back into those receptacles of misery. Our boots were high quality, but they could only take so much abuse and punishment before wearing out. We had planned on using two sets of boots with the intention of swapping boots in Pennsylvania, which was the half way point of the trip.

Foot care was paramount since our feet would be taking the brunt of the abuse. Difficult terrain, long mileage days, and wet feet would be constant problems with which we had to deal. Even in the best of circumstances, hotspots and blisters can be debilitating. Many times throughout the trek, we took advantage of a stream, washed our feet, and then aired them out for a spell. As much as possible, we didn't allow hotspots to develop into blisters. We used a combination of foot wash, dry socks, and protective layers of moleskin, or a similar commercial product, to keep the blisters at bay. After the first month, blisters weren't much of a concern. Our feet toughened up, and at the same time, with each step taken, our boots became more broken in.

Nevertheless, our feet were either overheated and tired in dry weather, or shriveled, cold, and wet in rainy weather. Our feet always had some challenge to contend with, and it was prudent to keep them as happy as possible.

If our feet could talk, they would have said, "There was never a dull moment!"

I wore a 35mm camera around my neck and had to get used to it bouncing off my chest with every step. If I put it away in my backpack, I would invariably come upon a scenic overlook and would end up having to stop to retrieve my camera from my pack. I found it best to keep it out and let it beat my chest into submission.

During the first couple of weeks of our hike, we broke our bodies into the routine by taking it slow and only walking 7 to 13 miles a day. The trail has three sided, lean-to type shelters, generally set a day's hike apart from each other, which provided a roof over our heads and a sleeping platform to keep us up off the ground. We utilized these shelters especially when rain threatened. On poor weather or overcast days, the next shelter was always the carrot stick dangling in front of us, the target that we greeted with a sigh of relief when we threw our gear and tired bodies under cover, safe from the elements. I found myself playing a mental game of noting how far we had walked each day, how many miles we had accrued since Springer Mountain, and how many miles left to the big prize, Mt. Katahdin. It was part of my goal-oriented psyche.

We found the trail in Georgia to be surprisingly rugged. To us, mountainous terrain meant the peaks and valleys of New England with the well-known ski runs and famous mountains. Killington and the Presidential range in the White Mountains come to mind. By contrast, in Georgia, it seemed as soon as we arrived at the top of the mountain, we were headed right back down again. This section of the trail was actually hilly, as opposed to mountainous, and the only thing beyond one hill was another hill. Even with the foliage off the trees, I don't remember many viewpoints. Right out of the gate, this was a grueling test of how fit we were and how strong our desire was to hike for the next five months.

White 2x6 inch paint marks on trees delineated the trail. These blazes were our visual guide and constant companion, and as long as we followed them like optical breadcrumbs, they were confirmation we were on the Appalachian Trail. Double white blazes signified a potentially confusing change of direction. Any blue blazes on trees denoted a side trail where water, trail access, scenic overlook, or shelter might be found. At trail junctions, there was usually a sign post to denote mileage to other significant points, much the same as mileage signs on a highway.

The trail skirted the North Carolina/ Tennessee border and remained a challenge. Although we planned to do this trek together, Johanna's knees and feet gave out, and sadly our dream of a joint hike fell apart. After limping the trail for days, and then hiking for a day in wet snow, her misery factor increased exponentially, and we made the decision for her to leave the trail. I would carry on solo. She rejoined me for a hike through the Shenandoah's, but I hiked the remaining 1,800 miles alone. It was certainly a big disappointment that we wouldn't complete this together, but it cemented my determination to see it through to the end.

I enjoyed hiking in North Carolina. The Great Smoky Mountains National Park was an easy hike, and was literally "a walk in the park." Gentle grades, nice open forests, and stone shelters with a chain link fence across the front to keep bears out, or perhaps to keep the hikers in, although I never saw any signs "please don't feed the hikers" posted anywhere. The only stone shelter I used in the park was shared with the company of a group of guys who kept me well entertained for the night. Being stone, it was cold and damp, but it had a fireplace in which to build a warming fire on that rainy night.

Hard-working volunteers maintained both the trail and the shelters, and were devoted to making the trail a pleasant experience.

Sometimes, despite the trail crew's best efforts, some sections of the trail became almost impassable after a storm went through. Hurricane Hugo made a mess in a few locations in both North Carolina and southern Virginia. The crews had their work cut out for them clearing sections of the trail. Trees were piled up like match sticks, which made for slow progress. The blown-down trees forced me to veer off the trail and bushwhack around them, while other times I was forced to crawl under and over tangled masses of wind-damaged forest, which was made all the more difficult with a large pack on my back.

The woods at morning, noon, and night was the perfect place to encounter wildlife. Deer, porcupine, and a few stray and friendly dogs became company. Johanna was with me in one of the earlier shelters, a beautiful stone building on top of Blood Mountain, when we had a memorable animal encounter. Since this particular night was relatively nice, we decided to sleep outside, but close to the shelter in case the weather turned on us. In winter, I found any stone building was damp and cold, and I would choose to sleep outside unless forced inside by weather.

Not long after we settled into our sleeping bags, we became aware of an animal scampering by. I grabbed my flashlight, and in the probing beam of light, I saw the characteristic white stripe of Pepé Le Pew. One would think with the sleek white racing stripe, he would've been anxious to leave once we were on to him, but he was in no hurry. We made the wise decision not to bother him, and in return, he left us alone. Later that night, we did have to move into the shelter when a passing shower came through and sure enough, Pepé was rain-averse too and joined us in the stone building. He didn't stay with us long though and we had a restful night's sleep.

Another animal we encountered more than we cared to was mice. Many shelters were infested with them. The last thing we wanted to deal with was mice after we had just walked 15 miles and were dead tired. They were the friendly type though, and thought nothing of making you and your gear their personal playground. I made a note to buy mouse traps and vowed to do some mouse trapping at the other shelters where we stayed. Many times we hadn't even drifted off to sleep before the snap of the trap kept me busy. I caught dozens and dozens of the varmints.

While Johanna was with me we tried to utilize the shelters as much as possible. But when I was hiking on my own, I used them only when it looked like I might encounter poor weather. Most days I hiked until dark, found a spot to lay down wherever I was at that moment, threw my sleeping pad and bag on the ground, and quickly went to sleep. There were a few occasions, while daylight ran out on me, when I was forced to sleep in the middle of the trail with steep grades on either side of me. I recall sleeping on a couple of scenic overlook ledges where the next step out would have required a parachute. I could sit snug in my sleeping bag and look out over a valley of scattered farms, and see the glow of civilization's lights. First one light would appear, and then as dusk progressed, more joined in, dotting the plain like stars in the sky.

Several times I was offered a place to sleep by kind locals in the areas through which I hiked. I remember being in a Virginia post office, picking up my mail drop and inquiring about local lodging, when a gentleman overheard the conversation. Next thing I knew, he invited me to his home where I stayed overnight. He refused to accept any payment for his hospitality.

I remember sleeping behind a store where the anxious owner was worried for my safety since night time temperature was expected to be zero, and I also have memories of a pleasant stay at the Graymoor Monastery in New York, with many kind monks.

One of my more memorable nights was spent on a North Carolina "bald" mountain, where I was exposed to the direct force of high winds.

A bald mountain is one that has no trees and is mostly grass. The winds were so strong that night, it was all I could do to keep my gear from blowing away. If I'd had a dog named Toto with me, the little guy would have been blown into the next county. I can still recall being in my nylon bivy sack, on my nylon sleeping mat, and struggling to stay on the mat because both surfaces were so slippery. I was buffeted by wind all night and didn't get a lot of sleep. Between the din of the blowing wind, and the constant flapping of my bivy sack, I knew I had made an error in choice of my nighttime bed. As soon as I had enough daylight, I carefully packed up my gear and got off the mountain.

You've probably driven down an interstate or other road where there were lots of bridge overpasses and wondered as I have, "What would it be like to sleep feet from overhead traffic?"

There was one section of the trail that was a "road walk." I was cold and wet from a day of rain, and I'd had enough walking. The road wound its way under an interstate highway bridge. I saw an abutment and climbed up the steep slope to a large concrete footing that was out of sight, and feet from the above road. What better way to be serenaded to sleep than by the thump thump of trucks rolling by so close to my ears!

It was an auditory delight, and I was lulled to sleep *dozens* of times through the night. Very peaceful!

So far I haven't mentioned food. The majority of our food was prepared ahead of time, before we ever stepped foot on the trail. It would have been an expensive journey if we had bought prepackaged, freeze-dried food, or shopped along the trail in nearby food stores. We tried to be as frugal as possible, so Johanna dried all kinds of nutritious food, much of it from our own garden. This way, we would not only save money, but the dried food was much lighter than what could be purchased fresh at the store. She carefully prepared and packaged each day's meals. Then the packaged meals were boxed up and made ready for mailing.

Along the trail, there were towns generally within easy walking distance, where you can pick up mail, get a meal, or do some shopping. In advance, we selected certain towns for mail drops and ended up with 29 boxes that were mailed to us. My mom mailed the packages at predetermined times. Bonus points from having her do this came in the form of fresh cookies or candy my mom included in the package.

You would be amazed at the amount of food and calories consumed by someone walking the trail. I learned that man can only eat so much dried food before man gets sick of eating it. Although Johanna did a great job of putting everything together, there was only so much dried food I could eat before my body rebelled. I approached the local grocery store lusting after any food that wasn't dried.

Wasn't I breaking one of the 10 commandments? "Thou shalt not lust after your neighbor's supermarket."

Anyway, going into a town after being on the trail for a week was always a treat, and I consumed copious quantities of food on those occasions. Generally, I'd eat a large meal and then have a half gallon of ice cream for dessert. One small restaurant I stopped in was serving chili dogs. I ate five chili dogs on buns, a quart of tomato juice, and almost a pound of cookies.

I sought out all-you-can-eat buffets but rarely found them. When I did find one, I made the most of it. What really would have been wonderful was to find an all-you-can-eat "take out" buffet where I could pull in with something like a trash can on wheels and really tank up. Such are the dreams of the long-distance hiker.

Amazingly enough, I actually put on five pounds of weight during my trip. I had little body fat when I started and little when I finished. I put on extra muscle, which was unexpected. I thought I'd be a string bean when I was done from all the exertion, but it turned out to be good exercise and I came away in great shape.

Which brings us to a bit of biology. As you probably know, the food cycle starts with food intake through the mouth, then progresses through the lungs on its way to some squirrely chamber deep in the bowels of the body, where magic happens, and then the fertilizer comes out through the exhaust port.

Believe it or not, we actually knew someone who believed food went through the lungs on its way to the stomach. Good thing chummy was a mechanic and not a doctor. Anyway, that cycle pretty much applies to all living animals.

Does a bear go potty in the woods? Indubitably.

As a hiker out in the woods, one is faced with the daily ritual of having to "lighten the load," so to speak.

Being originally from the Philadelphia area, I am a big Flyers hockey fan. As it so happens, the Flyers team color is a bright, vivid orange. Since this was a winter's hike and the weather was chilly, I often wore my orange Flyers hat as I walked along. It was late morning, and I was making a detour into a nearby town for my scheduled mail drop. Walking along on a quiet country road, I was surrounded on both sides by a forest that was still devoid of all foliage. On this desolate stretch, that natural biological urge triggered and needed to be dealt with promptly. I decided this was as good a place as any to take care of business.

There wasn't a soul to be seen, and I wandered off the road a considerable distance into the woods, where I dug a nice hole. Squatting over my freshly dug hole, I saw someone in a jeep slowly driving up the road. The driver came to a stop and was peering into the woods in my direction.

I thought, "You've gotta be kidding me."

I might as well have had on a flashing neon sign since there was no hiding my orange hat at that point. There was no cover, and there was nothing for me to do but *sit tight* and not move. My only hope was that the man was a visually impaired driver out for a joy ride.

After what seemed like an eternity, he drove off towards town. To make matters worse, once I was done with my paperwork, I realized I had an untied shoelace, which unbeknown to me, had draped itself in the hole.

Wasn't that just special!

The topper for all of this was, once I was back on the road hoofing towards town, that same man passed me again returning from his trip. How embarrassing. I was glad to get out of the area and back on the trail.

To this day, I have been so traumatized by the event, I lug a sleigh full of lumber with me whenever I'm out in the woods, so when that next urge comes, I can build me a proper outhouse!

On another occasion, the "need" arose at night, and I had to dig a hole in the dark by flashlight. I was off in the woods, had taken care of business, and then carelessly dropped the flashlight into the hole.

What a klutz!

I assure you, it wasn't because I was so proud of my accomplishment that I needed a bright, illuminating beacon in the bottom of the hole so I could admire my work, but at least the flashlight was easy enough to find. I still have that flashlight for sale if you know of anyone looking for a good, slightly used flashlight. Cheap!

I was making steady progress and was well on my way into Virginia. A scheduled rendezvous with Johanna in Shenandoah National Park helped keep my focus and drive going. By this time, the day spent on the mountain in the whiteout was a distant memory, and I was enjoying the walk through the state. The mountains were beautiful, and I was walking through valleys primarily composed of large farms with fenced fields and pastures. Animals were out grazing and didn't seem to mind as I walked through their territory. Many fields were fenced to keep the animals in, and stiles and gates were set up, which allowed a hiker to pass through, but which restricted the farm animals. Although there were hints of spring, I was still dealing with doses of snow and a lot of cold rain, but temperatures were warming and the vegetation was starting to green up, a sign spring was finally ready to burst forth.

Johanna and I met in Shenandoah Park at the appointed time, and we hiked about 100 miles together. That was the maximum amount of mileage we had planned to do, and it was a nice break for me. I appreciated the companionship. The Appalachian Trail paralleled the highway through the park, and it was easy hiking.

Compared to the southern Appalachians, this central part was very easy and I was able to make good mileage each day. There was one day when I walked out of Virginia into West Virginia, and then on into Maryland. It didn't take a lot of mileage to make that claim, but it was fun to be able to say I had hiked in three states in one day.

According to the trail guides and comments I had read, the trail through Pennsylvania was rocky and supposedly hard on the body, in particular, the feet. I was apprehensive as I approached the state, but I had no problem navigating the course. I found my footing easy, using my good foot-to-eye coordination to quickly go from rock to rock. But I could understand how easy it would be to twist an ankle.

Crossing state borders was always a thrill, and I loved to come across any such trail marker or signpost. They were "signs of progress" for me, and the information the sign gave was usually significant and pertinent–the mileage down a side trail to a shelter or to a scenic lookout, for example. Comparing this information to my trail guides, I could easily figure out exactly where I was and what lay in store further down the trail. The guide books were very detailed. Everything of importance was noted in the book.

When I came across the marker for the halfway point, I didn't know whether to be happy or dismayed. I had churned out a lot of miles and would have to churn out an equal number more if I was to complete the journey. Pine Grove Furnace State Park in Pennsylvania was the half way point. The marker pointed north and south with wording which read: 1,069 miles to Springer, 1069 miles to Mt. Katahdin.

Upon reaching Pennsylvania, I had come full circle. Our last visit had been in January, when we visited family as we passed through on our way from Maine to Georgia, and now I had walked all the way back to Pennsylvania. It was right around Easter, and I was just in time to decorate some eggs with my family. I was ready to take a little break from the trail to refortify. Refortify was synonymous with putting a hurting on the family refrigerator and freezer. I had pushed hard and had walked 300 miles in 13½ days to get there. I was cold, exhausted, and starving. It was a joyous reunion with my mom and Johanna at a restaurant parking lot, the rendezvous point, where a highway crossed the trail.

How was I to know the cruelty about to befall me? I was handed a small ice chest. Drool was running out the corner of my mouth as I opened it in anticipation of...*an ice chest full of dried food?*

Oh, that was mean! After all of us had a good laugh, the real ice chest appeared and I was an eating machine for the rest of the day.

As long as my carcass was relaxing at my parents, I was making no progress towards the conclusion of this trek. I was having such a good time; I definitely had a serious bout of inertia to overcome. When it came time to say our goodbyes, my parents dropped me off at the point where they had previously picked me up.

The goodbyes were hard, and my family decided they would accompany me down the trail for a little while. I threw my pack on, and we had a leisurely walk on a pleasant, sunny day. As we hiked and chatted, my dad teased me by saying how easy this hiking was.

For some reason though, he wouldn't wear my backpack when I offered it to him.

As we strolled along on this warm day, I drank from, and emptied, one of my water bottles. Drinking water is scarce in this section of the trail, and difficult to access, so we took advantage of a nearby water source. A long, steep descent down a rocky side trail was required to reach the spring below.

I said "Come on Dad. Let's go down and get my water bottle filled."

I had the last laugh as dear ol' Dad came back up huffing and puffing, commenting how crazy that was. My stay with the family was a wonderful break from the trail, and now I attacked the remainder of the trip with renewed vigor.

Walking alone gave me ample time to think and reflect. If only the mountains could talk. To a degree, I was walking back into history and geologic time. I found some of the geological formations and the handiwork of the glaciers to be fascinating.

For example, a car-sized boulder suspended in air with nothing but a few smaller rocks supporting it was a marvel. I observed how the Earth heaved and folded to create the mountains. Rock layers, deposited as sediment, were once flat, but are now buckled and pushed up at an angle. The Delaware Water Gap, easily accessible by vehicle, is a good place to see this feature. When there, I saw a jutting, exposed hill face clearly showing layers slanted at an angle.

Walking along the trail and coming across a grave or marker was a sobering experience. I still have clear memories of coming upon a soldier's grave, a hermit's grave, and a child's marker.

The hermit's grave read, "Lived alone, suffered alone, died alone."

I can't explain it. It was an eerie reminder of one's mortality. No one else was around, and I had an opportunity to reflect on that life as well as my own.

The remainder of Pennsylvania, all of New Jersey and New York were more of the same, easy walking and gentle grades for the most part. Once I was back on the trail, after the family visit, I was excited to be northbound again and ready to churn through the remaining states. Spring was in full bloom by this time, and I relished the warm days and greening vegetation. However, the further north I walked, the more the seasonal weather battleground became apparent, as evidenced by a greater frequency of clouds and rain. Spring was still duking it out with winter, and summer was fighting with spring. The weather couldn't make up its mind. Eventually summer would win this battle, but in the meantime, I was often wet. Bugs were making their first appearance and were a reminder I would need to prepare for their unwelcome company.

Other hikers I encountered on the trail were always friendly. Most were day hikers, although a few were out for weekend excursions. So many people went out of their way to help me or share their food with me once they learned I was hiking end to end. I always liked showing up at a shelter when other people were there, since a thru-hiker was unexpected, especially during the winter months. People were always fascinated with the concept of thru-hiking. Fellow hikers I met were inquisitive, and I was happy to answer all their questions. I was the crusty old hiker walking in to camp, ready to entertain and spin a few yarns of trail life.

I have many memories of people I met, including a few who were on the unusual side. One afternoon I was headed to a shelter after my day's hike, and there was a young college guy inhabiting the place. After hellos were exchanged, in the course of conversation, I found out he was a sociology major. We chatted for a while, and then he asked me if I would be interested in a bong hit.

Well call me a square, but I had never heard the term before and was a bit baffled. Turns out he was offering to smoke some pot with me. I declined his kind offer, and to this day, I can say I still have no idea what it's like to be high on drugs or alcohol. He was also into LSD. I didn't hang around to see what "tripping" was all about. I took a short break and then pushed on to the next shelter.

Another memory I have was of two guys I met somewhere in New York who wanted to chat. It was obvious the pair weren't hikers and had no idea what path they had come upon. They were curious how far I was going and asked me, "Where does this trail go?"

I told them it went all the way to Maine.

It was apparent they weren't geography savvy when one asked me, "What's that--about three days hiking, camping out?"

Possible I guess if one had a portable transporter beam, but otherwise, for us mere mortals, it's a couple months of walking.

Another character I encountered was a guy who likely lived on the streets of New York City and who had decided to walk some of the trail. I was talking to a couple of other hikers when he showed up with what he said was 80 pounds of stuff on his back. He was proud to say he was averaging 6.45 miles a day. He had it down to hundredths of a mile. I didn't have the presence of mind to ask if he was accurate to plus or minus half a foot.

Can you imagine the long-distance hiker keeping track of the hundredths of a mile?

"Dear diary, I took an extra 10 steps today and peeled off another .01 mile. That'll get me to Katahdin 13.4 seconds earlier than anticipated."

This guy talked right over, or flat out interrupted, the other guys. Fortunately, all of us realized we were dealing with someone with impaired social skills, and we were good sports about it.

Once I got into Connecticut, the forests were filled with tree species I was more accustomed to, and the quaint towns I visited had a New England look and feel to them. Although I was exhausted and was ready to see the end, I had impetus to keep plugging. But, truth be told, there were times when I was ready to call it quits. I was tired of the rain, I was tired of being tired, and one of my knees was giving me a great deal of trouble. Going uphill wasn't a problem, but when walking on flat ground, I was limping, and going down a mountain caused me a lot of pain with each downward step. I had not used a hiking stick up to this point, but now that I was back to mountainous terrain of Massachusetts, Vermont, New Hampshire, and Maine, I adapted a stick to function much like a crutch, and used it as an aide to take some of the pressure off of my knee when I walked.

Although I seriously wanted to quit at that point, in reality my personality wouldn't have allowed me to bail out. There was no way I wouldn't complete the goal. I'd crawl across the finish line if I had to.

Along with the elevation of the New England mountains came

the return of chilly weather and snow. Patches of snow in the woods reminded me I was walking north with the spring season. Summer hadn't quite arrived yet. Although I was walking in some pain,--Massachusetts' terrain, with its rolling, moderate climbs-- proved easy enough to navigate and was an enjoyable state through which to hike. I arrived at the state's highest point, Mt. Greylock, as the crew was opening the lodge for the season. I was fortunate to avoid the sleet and snow that night by staying at the lodge and working in exchange for my night's stay.

I have no idea what a normal weather pattern is for the areas I traversed that year. Regardless of whether I was in the south, central, or northern states of the Appalachian Trail that winter, I spent a high number of days walking in the rain. I wore my rain gear quite often. But it really didn't matter very much because I still showed up at a shelter mighty wet. Not only from the rain, but also from sweating. I guess you could call the wet, changeable weather another disadvantage of winter hiking. In fact, once I got to the Long Trail in Vermont, rainfall was 7 inches above normal for the area, and I renamed that section the Long Wet Trail. I slogged down trails that were literally running rivers, my feet sloshing in my boots with every step. Later, I heard that section of the trail was unofficially closed.

Speaking from experience, I can say it is one thing to hike in the rain for a day but real misery to have to eat in the rain, go to the bathroom in the rain, and walk in the rain day after day, and not be able to dry out clothes and equipment. Many times when I got to the shelter after my day's hike, I stripped out of the wet clothes and replaced them with a set of dry clothes from my pack. The next morning, with a grimace, I got back into the cold, damp clothes, which I had hung on a line or handy protuberance for the night, and stowed the dry clothes safely in my pack. I was always grateful to see the sun after a prolonged wet spell, and it surely gave me an extra spring to my step.

How excited I was to cross the border into New Hampshire knowing I had only one more state to traverse, and then the trip would be over. Thirteen states down and one more to go. New Hampshire had some hard, long climbs from the valleys up to the high peaks. For a week, on sunny days, from high elevation vantage points, I was able to see Mt. Washington in the Presidential range as a distant but welcoming beacon. I knew I would have to surmount that obstacle if I was going to make it into Maine.

New Hampshire was my favorite state to hike on the Appalachian Trail. Being above treeline, where you had long range panoramic views, was something I had looked forward to. The grind up the mountains was grueling, but by this time, I was in such good shape, it was more a case of putting my head down, keeping my feet moving, and, like a machine, walking nonstop to the top. My knee was less of a problem at that point, and I no longer hobbled along. Using a hiking stick during the previous month had given my body enough time to heal.

From the summits, without any trees to block the view, I had the sense I was standing atop the world. And, to a degree, I was. On a sunny, clear day, with feet firmly planted on Terra Firma, I had a bird's eye view of nearby mountains, valleys, and distant peaks set against a backdrop of blue sky. On mountain sides, I could clearly see a meandering line of demarcation where the forest grew no higher, the tree line ended, and, above were bare, rock capped mountain peaks. Looking behind me, I could see where I had been the last few days, and a forward look gave me a clue as to where I was headed and what lay in store for me.

Throughout my hike, I tried to walk anywhere from 14 to 20 miles per day, with 28 miles being my longest distance walked in one day. That long 28-mile day, I was feeling miserable from a cold and had stopped somewhere along the trail in New Hampshire to sleep for the night. Sometime during the night, it started to rain, which caught me off guard. I had no choice but to pack up and hike a nearby road in the dark. I walked until I eventually came to a closed local park, where I slept protected on the outside of a covered bathroom pavilion. By pure chance I found this park. The park staff wasn't happy when they found me the next morning, but once I explained the situation, they were very nice. I continued on into the nearby college town of Hanover, New Hampshire, and recovered for the day at a hostel before resuming my walk.

My timing was impeccable as I got into the Presidential Range just as crews were opening some of the lodges, and I was again able to exchange work for overnight stays and hardy meals. Mt. Washington, the highest peak in the Northeastern United States, is well known for its weather extremes, and I was anxious to get past it and continue on.

The highest recorded wind gust on Earth, 231mph, was clocked on this summit, and hurricane force winds of 75mph occur more than 100 days out of the year on this mountain.

There I was, standing atop Mt. Washington, with no wind, merely overcast gray skies, admiring for a brief time the building at the summit--a building that had thick chains to hold it in place, chains going across the roof down to anchor points on the ground. And then onward I marched.

That's one way to keep a building from escaping, wrap it in chains!

I knew I had been very lucky to have crossed the summit without having had to deal with severe weather. If I had been there one day later, I would have faced sleet, snow, and wind gusts to 102mph.

Maine was the last state of the hike, and I was exhilarated to finally cross the state line from New Hampshire to Maine. There was a number of challenging sections in this state. Mahoosuc

Notch, a notorious section, is a mile-long, boulder-filled ravine. The term boulders might be an understatement. Car-sized blocks of scrambled rock, which needed to be crawled over, under, and around, is a more apt description. Many times I removed my pack and pushed it through ahead of me as I squeezed through some tight spots.

I didn't mind this place, though, and found it to be an interesting part of the whole trail experience.

Further into Maine, I encountered a couple sections of the trail where I needed to transform myself into a Billy goat.

I'd come to what looked like an unnavigable route, look up with a puzzled look on my face, and mutter to myself, "Seriously, the trail goes up there?"

As I used my hands to crawl up, I was aware this was not a section where I wanted to lose my balance. The heavy pack on my back was throwing off my center of gravity, and I needed to focus on keeping my body leaning in towards the mountain.

There were some wonderful sections of trail in Maine that skirted lakes and crossed rivers. The last stretch of 100 miles is known for being as close to wilderness as the trail gets. This 100-mile section goes through the Maine woods, and has a few logging/forest service roads, but otherwise it is remote. I needed to be fully stocked with provisions because there were no towns or supply points. There were only a couple times while walking in that isolated stretch when I met other hikers or campers. I had the shelters all to myself, sort of.

Sort of, since anybody familiar with the Maine woods in June knows they are never alone. I had the company of swarming mosquitoes and black flies. It was sport for me to sit in a shelter and thin out the population by constantly swatting at my legs or by plinking them out of the air with my hand, thus perfecting my hand/eye coordination.

On June 28th, 1990, I climbed Mt. Katahdin in northern Maine and realized I had reached the end. I had dreamed of this moment for so long, and yet when the moment arrived, it was anticlimactic. Thru-hiking the trail in the winter was an accomplishment I was proud of, but I was relieved that it was over. It was now time to move on to the next chapter of my life. The next day, family and some friends celebrated with me, and we camped at Baxter State Park for the night.

Days later, a good friend of mine asked to borrow one of the stainless steel cook pots I had used on the trail. When he returned it to me, the lid had been engraved denoting the accomplishment, with the dates I started and ended.

It read "Ron Melchiore A.T. Thru Hiker 15 Jan 1990 28 June 1990" It's a memento I will always treasure.

Hiking the Appalachian Trail was by far the hardest thing I've done in my life. Over 2,100 miles walked in rain, snow, sleet, cold, sun, and heat. A terrain that changed daily, that took me over rocks and roots, through wetlands, and up and down mountains as well as nice flat stretches. I viewed magnificent vistas, which left indelible impressions in my mind and also walked boring trail that offered little to see. Mixed in with the sheer drudgery of having to walk many miles day after day were days when I was anxious to walk. At times my pack felt like the proverbial anchor, while other times I didn't notice I had anything strapped to my back. The occasional stumble and fall, sore, tired feet, twisted ankles, and a knee that was close to failing me were challenges I faced and conquered. Although it was physically demanding, the mental battle to get up each day and walk was the real challenge, to will the body down the trail, mile after mile.

The Appalachian Trail is a trail of contrasts, and I am grateful I was able to complete it. It wasn't until years later, when I smartened up and found an easier way of traveling than walking.

Johanna and me at Springer Mountain, Georgia

A bald mountain

A hard day on the Appalachian Trail

One of the many geological wonders along the trail

Chained building atop Mt. Washington, New Hampshire

Halfway point trail marker

Mt. Washington ahead; note the cairns as trails markers

Stone shelter in Smoky Mountain National Park

My dad lugging a massive load of water

Rocky trail in Pennsylvania (note the white blaze on tree)

Some tough winter hiking

Priest Mountain in Virginia (the trail goes over the summit)

Upthrust of a mountain at the Delaware Water Gap

Winter camping

Me at the summit of Mt. Katahdin, Maine, the northern terminus

Mom, me, and Johanna at Baxter State Park, Maine

Chapter 5 –

Sure Beats Walking

Years had passed since my Appalachian Trail hike, and I was itching for another escapade. Not that it took me seven years to physically recover from my walk, but time has a way of slipping by. A calendar on the wall near the phone cycled through the months and was replaced at the turn of the year by a new calendar. Before we knew it, seven long years had elapsed since the big trek. In those intervening years, the homestead had kept us busy and the quest for the almighty dollar had occupied our life. We were overdue for a vacation. Time for a road trip!

As a kid, I always enjoyed bicycling. As an adult, there's something to be said for new technologies and being able to effortlessly glide down the road on a touring bike. Stronger, lighter frames, better wheels, and superior components make a bicycle ride immensely enjoyable. Johanna had always dreamed of visiting national parks, so we conjured up a road trip, where I would bicycle across the United States and Johanna would do some sightseeing.

With a bit of advanced research and discussion, we decided which would be the best season to go and, in general terms, what route we would take. Logistically, much less planning was required for this trip compared to the Appalachian Trail hike. There was no food preparation, no meticulously planning out mail drops, no fretting about the type of equipment to take, nor its weight. Having a vehicle along for the "ride" gave us wide flexibility with our equipment choices and our itinerary. The ice chest we carried allowed for grocery shopping along the way; no dried meals for this biker, nothing but fresh food on this adventure!

The summer of 1997 we packed our camping gear, stashed the bike in the truck, and started the drive west. I had decided I would start my bicycling tour at the ferry terminal in Anacortes, Washington State. Starting in the West and bicycling to the East meant I could take advantage of the westerly wind flows, which would provide a tailwind, although there were many times I biked with stiff headwinds.

As you can imagine, my cycling took me on every kind of road: easy flat riding as well as the inevitable long climbs with the subsequent runs of downhill coasting. My bike was made for the distance tour, and I had a range of 18 gears to help propel me down the road. Each gear had a purpose, and I utilized every one of them depending on the terrain. Although we took interstate highways westbound to get to Washington State, the bicycle route east was on secondary and tertiary roads. Biking guidebooks and maps gave a choice of several different routes, and we ultimately chose the northern route for cycling across the country. Sticking to the northern states was more in my comfort zone, as the heat and humidity of southern states really had no appeal. Northern states can get plenty hot as it is; I didn't need to choose a route that would subject me to more hot weather than necessary. Plus we had never seen that part of the United States. All this would be new territory to explore.

On the way west to Washington State, we visited several national parks and monuments. Two of the most notable were Yellowstone and Little Big Horn Battlefield and National Cemetery. Both parks were magnificent, each in their own way.

Yellowstone was amazing to us for the variety of surface formations and oddities. It's a strange world of both lush and fire ravaged forests, set against a backdrop of mountains. Bison and elk grazing in the surrounding forests were a frequent sight. But a gaze around revealed bland, gray/white dead zones of treeless, barren flats, which were devoid of plant life, other than a few species that have adapted to the harsh growing conditions.

Because of the geothermal activity Yellowstone is known for, the ground temperature is higher than normal, and the soil is laced with minerals and chemicals. The air even has a sulfur smell to it. These dead zones are where most of the geological features are located: the mud pots, hot springs, and geysers. These areas looked like a cross between large salt flats and a moonscape. Interspersed with various geothermal features, the ground in these zones had a thin, flaky pie crust appearance, and people have lost their lives breaking through the surface and being scalded to death.

Boardwalks built for the public's safety allow visitors to safely venture into the middle of these areas, and gave us an opportunity to view the mud pots, hot springs, and terraces of deposited minerals up close. The skeletons of unwary animals that had wandered into these active areas were reminders to stay on the boardwalks, or else risk an unpleasant demise. What looked like areas of smoke were actually pockets of steam released from vents deep in the Earth. With proper timing, we were able to see jets of hot water shoot out of the ground as geysers--the most famous being Old Faithful.

We've all heard of the geysers, but the boiling mud pots and hot springs were geothermal wonders that were unexpected and fascinating to me. Mud pots, a bubbling area of viscous material, much like cake batter, slowly plopped and erupted as heat and steam from below escaped. Cones, which had the appearance of tiny volcanoes, were left behind as remnants of old activity.

Hot springs, pools of blistering water, randomly pockmarked the dead flat zones. One hot spring was noteworthy for the terraced structure it had built. I had no idea hot water steadily flowing up out of the ground could create a step-like configuration from the deposition of the dissolved minerals in the water. These large formations grow over long periods of time from water slowly flowing upwards, seeping over the sides, and continually depositing layers of minerals in its wake. They are works in progress since, as long as the water flows, the structures continue to slowly build.

Rainbows of color are found throughout the park. It's hard to believe that some of this color is created by microorganisms that have adapted to this hot environment. Other colors are caused by the minerals themselves. All of these features combine into one colossal landscape, which, once seen, is impossible to forget. A person could make the argument: you've seen one tree, you've seen them all. You've seen one mountain, you've seen them all. But this place was extraordinary, and I can't imagine anybody stating: you've seen one geyser, you've seen them all. Yellowstone was an unforgettable place.

Little Big Horn Battlefield/National Cemetery was a disquieting place with gravestones visible in the fields. We arrived on a hazy, blue-skied day. Looking out across gently rolling fields, for miles in the distance we could clearly see the previous year's brown stubble, mixed in with the spring season's first greening shoots. The randomly scattered gravestones marked where a man had fallen. Clusters of markers denoted where groups of men had fought and died. An organized cemetery plot nearby had gravestones neatly aligned in rows. The desolate landscape left me with the sense there was a tragic loss of life on both sides of a conflict, and as the name suggests, it has the feel of a solemn, forlorn burial site.

At Lewis and Clark State Park, in Montana, we encountered an interesting windstorm. We arrived in the afternoon, set up camp, and were enjoying the scenery. After finishing dinner, Johanna took a shower while I hung back to watch over our stuff and putter around the area. There was very little air stirring, when all of a sudden, a strong wind started howling. Unbeknown to us, this phenomenon occurs when the wind rips down into the valleys. I had no idea what triggers these winds, but we were caught in its cross-hairs.

The wind storm came on so suddenly, it was all I could do to hold down the fort. Everything on the picnic table blew off, including the Coleman stove. Not much I could do about it since our tent was ready for lift off. There was a frenzy of activity on my part since I didn't know what to protect first. A quick look at the tent, which held all of our sleeping gear--its sides deformed by the buffeting wind--suggested that was a good place for me to start. I unzipped the tent door, jumped in, and put my back to the wind, arms spread eagle, doing my best to brace the side from being pushed inward. All I could envision was me, in the tent, being blown across the field like a tumbleweed. After 10 minutes, the big blow was over and it was like nothing ever happened.

Despite my best efforts, a tent pole did bend, but it was fixable. When Johanna got back from the bath house, she had no idea what I had just gone through, but mentioned that she had heard some strange noises while in the shower. We spent time recovering our items and, as I recall, we never did find a few of our things.

We arrived at the Ferry Terminal at Anacortes, Washington, on May 18th, and I was anxious to start my journey east. I dipped my hand into the Pacific Ocean and vowed the trip wouldn't be over until I dipped my hand in the Atlantic Ocean in Rockport, Maine. Symbolically, I liked the concept of being able to say I had touched two oceans and cycled the distance between both of them.

My odometer, the only electronic gadget on my bike, was set to zero, and I was on my way. Pedaling through farm land initially, I began with short mileage days to get my posterior used to this new regimen. Even though I wore padded cycling shorts and had a gel-filled bicycle seat, I still needed to get off the seat every 60 to 90 minutes to take a break and stretch my legs. I started out riding 20 to 40 miles a day, and thereafter, increased to 45 to 80 miles a day, depending on road conditions. On a few occasions, I pedaled even further, with 115 miles being the longest distance I cycled in one day. On the one hand, we had no set schedule, but I didn't want to make a career out of biking across the continent either. The mileage I set out to do each day was a good balance. On my downhill runs, the fastest I dared go was 40mph. Seemed like the prudent thing to do; that was fast enough. This was a tour after all, not a race.

Johanna carried the bulk of the gear so I could ride relatively unencumbered by not having to carry the typical, fully loaded touring panniers. I did have small panniers on the rear rack and a handle bar bag where I stashed lunch, tools, spare inner tube/patch kit, and some extra clothing. I mounted an air pump as well as two water bottles on the bike frame. The bottles, filled every morning before departure, were within easy reach so I didn't have to stop to get a drink. My easily accessible handle bar bag carried my map and guidebook.

I marked campgrounds, motels, and other notable places on route maps, which made planning very easy. I'd look at the map in the evening, decide how far to go the next day, and select where we would camp for the night. Then Johanna would look at the road atlas and decide what was of interest for her to visit within an easy drive of my route. We each had the freedom to explore for the day and always ended up at the same place each night.

She would break camp in the morning, drive ahead to a prearranged destination, and I would roll in later that day to a camp already set up. I had it made! If there was a site along the way she wanted to explore, she had enough free time to divert and still make it to the day's campsite in plenty of time. This arrangement worked out great. I was able to bicycle and make distance, while Johanna satisfied her desire to sightsee and visit places that interested her.

This is probably a good place to elucidate a special quality I seem to possess. It's a curse really. For some reason, I have an innate, unfortunate allure such that regardless of whether I am on a plane or bus or in a hotel, motel or inn, or campground--whether state, provincial, or federal park, in the United States or Canada--I invariably end up right next to a screaming child or loud boisterous neighbors who believe they are the only ones within a country mile of anybody else.

And so it was right on cue, when we showed up at the campground after my first day's ride, that the neighbors carried on well past a reasonable time. Listening to the lady next door barfing away late at night was just an added treat. We always try to select an out-of-the-way campsite or room, but the charismatic magnetism I possess seems to draw near the obnoxious ones. I seem to be a statistical anomaly, since I end up next to these inconsiderate types far more than probability would suggest.

I ran into considerable rain throughout the trip. Sometimes I chose to ride in it, and other times I bagged it for the day. Unfortunately, if I encountered rainy weather when I was biking through mountainous terrain, the views were obscured by cloud and fog. The clouds were frustrating because I knew I was cycling through some spectacular scenery, yet I was unable to see it. Very disappointing! Pedaling through the western states, I relished times when it was sunny and I had unimpeded views of the mountains. I never tired of seeing jagged mountains with their snow-capped peaks, rising off either side of the road.

Just as walking in the rain was no fun, riding in the rain wasn't any better. Despite wearing rain gear, I inevitably ended up wet, the spray from passing cars and trucks always managing to splatter me. This, combined with the fact there wasn't a whole lot to see because of poor visibility, made for a lousy day's ride. Rarely did I choose to start pedaling if it was raining when I got up. In that event, we'd stay in camp and I would get a day to rest. Once on the road though, if it started to rain or shower, I had to deal with it, as I was committed to making the next campsite. Depending on how bad the weather was, we would sometimes bypass a campsite in favor of a motel room to dry out, which was a real treat.

I wore riding gloves and a safety helmet with an attached

rearview mirror, so I always had a sense of what was approaching. I wore gloves not only to protect my hands from road rash in case I fell off the bike but also to cushion my hands on the handlebar. The padding in the palm of the gloves dampened any vibrations and made for an easier grip on the handlebars. I generally wore sunglasses, not only to combat glare but to keep bugs and debris out of my eyes.

Just as there are rules of the road for vehicles, bikers have many of the same obligations to which they must adhere. Bikers ride on the same side of the road as traffic, and they need to obey all traffic signs and lights. I guess if I lived in a city it might have become second nature, but I couldn't get used to being at a light, in a traffic lane, with cars lined up behind me, especially if I needed to make a left turn. I would be in the left lane, both feet firmly planted on the ground, waiting for the light to turn green, thinking "OK, don't fumble around for the pedals."

The pedals had toe clips, which I needed to slip my feet into, and sometimes getting my feet into those clips was a tricky maneuver. Toe clips make for a more efficient ride by allowing the rider to not only push down on the pedal but also to lift it up with each leg stroke, a feat made possible only because the rider's foot is securely attached to the pedal by the clip.

In one Midwestern town, I encountered a detour while following the bike route. I hate detours when I'm in a car, and since I was on a bike, I thought I could ignore the detour sign and bike on through. The road had been stripped down to a wet, clay mud. The further I went down the road, the more the mud collected on the tires, chain, bike frame, and me. It wasn't long before I had such a buildup, I needed to deal with it.

This muck was the stickiest, dirt-related goo I had ever encountered. I found a stream and tried to give the bike a bath. I had a devil of a time cleaning off enough accumulated mud so that

I could backtrack and try a different route.

My bike never forgave me for that blunder!

For the most part, the car drivers were excellent and moved over as best as they could. Same for the tractor trailer drivers. They gave me a wide berth, but even then, at the speeds they were traveling, a solid wall of air would always hit me as they sped by.

I can still remember pedaling merrily along on the highways and frequently stealing a glance into my rearview mirror. The approach of cars didn't faze me, but to see a tractor trailer approaching at high speed, filling up the view in my mirror, unnerved me and I'd brace for the blast of wind every time. Semis were really only a problem when they were unable to move into the passing lane because of other traffic. Several times, however, despite my best efforts, I was blown right off the road. Fortunately nothing serious as I was always able to veer off, plant my feet, and catch myself before going belly up. I never had any close calls with other traffic either, although a carload of upstanding young citizens (doofuses) threw a can and shouted at me as they went by, which gave me quite a scare.

A run-in with a dog that came charging off of a property was my closest disaster. Because I was on a downhill slope, I was able to out-distance it. The only other annoying canines were a couple I wasn't able to outrun. They forced me to stop and I pulled out a can of pepper spray I carried as a deterrent.

Years previously, I had been bitten by a dog when I was on my bike, so I knew dogs were potentially dangerous. Fortunately, these were more bark than bite, and I never had to dispense my repellent. When the owner of the dogs drove up to me on his ATV, I thought

I'd have an extra confrontation, but to his credit, he had come out to apologize and get control of them. Surprisingly, in all the miles I traveled, those are the only dog confrontations that come to mind. I suspect I was fortunate in that respect. I had more dog encounters bicycling around northern Maine while preparing for this escapade.

Out West, there are wide expanses of road with sparsely spaced towns, which made for nice riding. I thoroughly enjoyed the ride through the western states, and when I look at pictures of the bicycle trip, I am flooded with good memories. Washington, Idaho, and parts of Montana are forested and mountainous. Along the route were places where the road hugged the side of a mountain. Beyond the guardrail, there would be a steep drop off down to a river valley below. Brown, muddy water capped with white froth raged through the river system, swollen from the combination of spring rains and snow melt in the mountains. Always an eye-catcher, running melt water from the snow pack would funnel into steep mountain ravines, creating waterfalls that flowed down a mountain and cascaded off and out into space toward the abyss below.

We crossed into Idaho from Washington and set up camp in a forest service campground, not noticing anything unusual weather-wise. After spending several hours shopping in a nearby community, we departed from town and noticed the sky had a most unusual look to it. The sky was black with turquoise coloring. As lightning flashed, we sensed that the sky was signaling the coming of a major event. We had never seen this color of sky before, nor have we since. We hurried back to camp just in time to meet the camp ranger, who had driven to our site to warn us that 50 to 60mph winds were on the way. We were able to secure the tent and throw gear in the truck just before a downpour of rain and hail hit.

That was a close one, and there's no telling how our equipment would have fared if we had not gotten back in time. The brunt of the storm missed us, but some areas got a thrashing with numerous twisters dropping from those ominous clouds we had seen.

I have a special affinity for mountains, and Glacier National Park in Montana was the highlight of my ride. Since we were only in the month of May, most mountain passes still had residual snow. From afar, we even saw the remnants of some old avalanches. One notable pass had massive banks of snow on either side of the road. The sides of the snow banks were straight up and down, making it obvious a snow blower had been called in to keep this pass open. Chugging up the mountain was work, and when I took a break, I pulled my bike off the road shoulder and rested it against the handy wall of snow.

Chugging up the mountain is just as it sounds. A long, slow grind in low gear. My 18-speed touring bike came with a set of low-range gears. The lowest is called a granny gear. The toughest climbs could be done with the granny gear, but it was still a big effort to summit the hill. On flat ground, if I selected the low gear, my legs would rapidly spin the pedals while my forward motion would be quite slow. Very easy pedaling, but my speed would be minimal.

When I got to Glacier Park, Johanna was waiting for me and we took some time to explore the area. I stowed the bike in the truck bed and we drove the truck around to see the sights. Through breaks in the clouds, we were able to see the vast range of snow-capped peaks. To be at a scenic road overlook, standing at the edge of a sheer drop-off, and have a commanding view of a deep valley with its sweeping panorama of craggy mountain peaks, was magnificent. The one mountain road I had planned to take through the park was still closed due to snow, so I took another, lower altitude route to continue.

Near Glacier Park is Marias Pass, which is still in Montana. This was where I climbed up and over the Continental Divide. This was significant for me because now I was getting somewhere, and it was significant as a geological feature too. To the west of the Divide, water drained to the Pacific Ocean, and to the east, water flowed to the Atlantic.

One memory that will always stick with me is how the terrain changed, from rugged mountains to flat and gently rolling ground once I got out of the Rockies. As I biked along, I would occasionally stop and look back at the beautiful mountain range towering majestically, jutting into the sky. Truly awesome!

Coming out of the forested western states, the softly undulating landscape transitioned to prairie, which was fairly featureless other than the occasional ranch or farm house with wide open cattle ranges and farmland. Now that I was on flatter ground, I was able to do a bit more mileage each day.

A railroad, the lifeline for moving goods and freight east and west, paralleled the road I pedaled for long stretches, so it wasn't unusual to see a number of trains go by on any given day. What a thrill it was to see the long freight trains, or even the speedier Amtrak trains chugging along the tracks. It was equally thrilling for me to wave as a train rolled by and see the engineer wave back while he tooted his horn. Several times this happened; it was a friendly gesture that made the next few miles easier to pedal.

An occurrence like this was all the more memorable when I was on a long desolate stretch, with no traffic--a tiny figure on a bike going one way, and a colossus of a freight train, no end to it in sight, headed the other way.

When pedaling on flat ground, I employed a technique called spinning. Spinning is when the legs are pumping at high rpm's and pedaling is almost effortless. The higher cadence is made easier by being in a lower gear. With little effort, I may be pushing 20mph and not breaking a sweat.

In all activities, there are times when a person gets into the "zone," and cycling is no exception. The body is effortlessly firing on all cylinders, the energy level is high, and the mind is along for the ride. There is no thinking, just pedals being cranked by legs that have turned into pistons, driving the bike forward. Perhaps a tailwind is blowing and, with a lower gear, I would feel little resistance to my leg strokes. Bike and man are in harmony and, much like a runners high, I am able to "crank" out the miles.

A glance down at my speedometer shows my speed, a rate fast enough so that a tiny outline of a house far down the road rapidly grows larger as I approach and then quickly becomes smaller in my rearview mirror as I leave it behind. My focus turns to a new pinpoint in the distance as a target.

Of course, I faced the opposite extreme too. Strong headwinds! Take it from me, it was no fun to be fully exposed in the prairies with a gale in my face. When this happened, I was forced to lower my gearing, but instead of feeling little resistance, it was all I could do to rotate the pedals and push against the wind to make headway.

Along with being able to see great distances in the prairies came the ability to see vast expanses of open sky and vistas of cloud formations. Coming from the forested East Coast, I found the prairies to be a foreign landscape, with cloud displays taking more prominence in the sky. They had a different look than what I had ever previously seen, as if dabs of fluffy cotton candy were dolloped across the sky, floating on an unseen medium. Whereas in the East, the only visible sign of an approaching thunderstorm would be the arrival of an ominous, dark sky, out West, we could see the entire cell forming and taking shape, since trees didn't impede the horizon.

Drinking water, which we normally take for granted, was something we couldn't get used to in the western states. Growing up, we were accustomed to clear, tasteless water, and the same was true from our well in Maine. We weren't prepared to drink the foul-tasting liquid that westerners called water. The taste comes from minerals and local elements that dissolve in the water supply. One place we stayed had water with a brownish tint, and I don't think it was because ready-made iced tea was being piped in.

Having lived in the woods of northern Maine for years, we had ample experience with black flies and mosquitoes. At least we thought we did. Eastern Montana added a new dimension to the experience however. For the first time in my life, bugs gave me a scare. I was biking through a mostly treeless, barren landscape. Numerous ponds and irrigation ditches, perfect breeding grounds for abundant generations of mosquitoes in a season, dotted the countryside. Those combined features made for real misery. It seemed every mosquito within 10 miles of my vicinity had a clear bead on me and sensed the blood coursing through my veins. They were on a mission to relieve me of some of my life-giving fluid. As long as I kept pedaling I was fine. If I stopped, the mosquitoes came in swarms.

No, that's too tame. I was assailed by hordes of swarms.

These mosquitoes were well-trained and didn't hover around thinking (if mosquitoes could actually think) about what their next step would be. These guys just attacked right out of the gate, and my body was covered in seconds. It was truly amazing and ferocious, and to this day I've never experienced anything like it and hope I never will again.

One early morning, before I got going, a truck came through the camping area spraying for mosquitoes. I couldn't do much about it except hop on the bike and ride through the "fog" to better air. As kids growing up in the 1960s, while visiting grandparents on the New Jersey coast, my siblings and I saw the occasional truck come through the neighborhood spraying a foul-smelling, white fog, and

I shudder to think what fun stuff we were inhaling back then.

Once we got to North Dakota, we took a break for a few days to explore Theodore Roosevelt National Park, where we encountered a large herd of grazing bison. It's always exciting to see wild animals in their natural habitat, and this was no exception. Even though we were in a proper campsite, this site was smack in the middle of their grazing area. We were in our small, two-man tent as we watched this herd get closer and closer.

As I observed their approach through the *super strong, buffalo repelling, wispy* tent screen door, I was mentally willing the leader to turn away and take the pack elsewhere. Unfortunately, his mental willpower was stronger, and he resisted my powerful telepathy.

Approximately 50 adult bison and babies surrounded our tiny tent. They take on mythic proportions when they are at the door of your tent sniffing, snorting, and peering.

We chose not to pet the brute that rattled the tent frame.

While I make light of the encounter, in reality, this was a potentially dangerous situation. People have been killed by bison, so this was not the time or place to let out a rip-roaring sneeze and start the proverbial stampede. We could hear them roaming about our tent all night long and, consequently, we didn't sleep very well.

Upon reaching the Badlands, we encountered territory that was so varied it is tough to describe it. While the Grand Canyon is undoubtedly in a league of its own, the Badlands had a similar look, albeit on a smaller scale. Some areas had convoluted masses of rounded mounds of brown dirt and exposed rock, interspersed with gullies and steep-sided ravines, much of it covered with sparse vegetation. Other locations had jagged rock formations in lieu of the nice rounded hills. We could easily discern the sedimentary layers and colored bands of soil that told the story of ancient seas, rivers, and even volcanic activity.

The result of wind and water erosion, the arid, barren scene was fascinating, but about as rugged and unforgiving a landscape as one can imagine. Both of us found the Badlands to be very interesting and, although we would never tire of visiting them, we would have no interest in living there. We are forest people. I am thankful the Appalachian Trail didn't go through something like that. I'd rather gargle fish hooks than throw a pack on and have to hike through that tortuous topography.

Up until this point, I'd had three flat tires. It's amazing the junk you find on the side of the road. I saw scrap steel, glass, keys, rubber straps, and enough nuts, bolts, and hardware to build a robot. I even found money. Ol' eagle eyes didn't miss the money.

Thus far, I had found $2.00 and was on my way to retirement! Vehicles sped by oblivious to most of the stuff. If they only knew the treasures they were missing. The cyclist gets to pick the route through the debris field, which is the road shoulder, and there were times I wondered if the highway department paved the side of the road with broken glass.

In Minnesota, we had a planned layover as we were shopping for land in the Province of Ontario, Canada. After stowing the bike in the truck, we crossed the border into Ontario. We had previously set up appointments with several real estate agents to look at remote properties. After getting directions and info on one property, we set off to view it.

The directions were something like, "Take this road six miles, turn on the sandy road, and it's out there somewhere."

So off we went in search of this elusive parcel. The sandy, gravelly road eventually went through a section of recently clearcut forest. The area was a place of stumps, with unsalvageable trees crisscrossing the ground. Weeds and small shrubs were starting to repopulate the land. We drove as far as we dared go. It was late afternoon when we decided to set up camp. The weather was hot and dry, and we had an intense lightning storm that evening with little rain; we sure felt vulnerable and exposed with our aluminum framed tent set up in the middle of a vast clearcut area.

Three times in my life I've been within 150 feet of lightning strikes, twice when I was outdoors and once when I was sheltered in a house, so perhaps I'm a little more nervous than most when the bolts are flying across the sky. With every flash, the tent became fully illuminated, and we were greatly relieved when the storm moved away.

The following day I was able to find the property. The plan was to camp out there so we could get a good feel for it. Because it was impossible to drive to the property, I decided to try biking to it. I pulled the bike out of the truck, loaded camping gear on to the bike, and started cycling through the sand. It wasn't long before I turned my perfectly round rear tire into an "elliptical rhombus." I had just ruined my wheel from too much weight in terrible road conditions. We had to walk our gear the rest of the way to our campsite and, once back in Minnesota, we were fortunate to find a bike shop that carried a new wheel.

Montana, North Dakota, and Minnesota were my favorite states west of the Mississippi. Even when we were westbound, headed to our starting point in Washington State, I loved the feel of the wide open road. Traffic was sparser than what I was accustomed to in the eastern part of the country. The only problem was that traffic moved at higher speeds. Speed limits at that time were faster than they were on the east coast; I believe 70mph was the speed limit. So tack on an extra 5mph at a minimum, and people were whizzing by me as if I was standing still. For the most part, I had wide shoulders along the main highways, which made for safe riding. Once I got into Minnesota, there were plenty of secondary and tertiary roads to ride without the constant flow of traffic. From Minnesota to Maine, the route generally followed these quieter roads. The central part of the country was uneventful and consisted of rolling or flat farmland, which made biking pleasant. It's amazing how much corn and soybeans are grown in this country. Mile after mile, I biked along country roads with nothing but fields of corn and soybeans as far as I could see.

We had a wonderful stop in Iowa at a campground called Pikes Peak State Park. Situated on a high bluff, the park had trails and vistas overlooking the Mississippi River. River traffic was interesting to watch, since we had a sweeping view of the waterway. Barges and tugs slowly worked their way up and down the watercourse, and at night, from our high lookout, we could see the lights of homes as well as the running lights of slowly moving ships, both of which kept us mesmerized for quite some time.

The terrain got hillier as I made my way into New York. I had gone from farm fields back to mountains and forest. Fewer drivers moved over now, but there was still good biking. Along with cars and my bicycle, the occasional horse and buggy trotted down the roadside. The buggies have a red and orange triangle caution sign mounted on their rear to warn traffic they are slow-moving, and to use care. It gave me a kick to see a buggy ahead in the distance, catch up to it, and then pull out into the passing lane and zip on by as if I were a driver. The horse didn't know what had just blown by. By the time Mr. Ed figured out I wanted to race, I was long gone.

Closing in on our home state of Maine, the mountains and terrain began to have a familiar look to them and I could sense I was closing in on my destination. I could tell I was on a bicycle route when I was straining for all I was worth, in my lowest granny gear, grinding up one of the steepest climbs I had faced, when I came across big letters painted on the road shoulder that said, "What pain?"

At one point, I passed a junction where the Appalachian Trail crossed my bike route, and I realized I had come full circle, where ancient history met history in the making.

On August 18th I rode into a public boat launch in Rockport, Maine and dipped my hand into the Atlantic Ocean. My odometer read 4,158 miles. I was able to see the country at my own pace, and I came away from this trip with some terrific memories. The distance biked across the country was roughly double what I walked on the Appalachian Trail, yet my bicycling took about half the time, approximately three months. It's true… bicycling does beat walking! I had a total of seven flat tires, but I had my revenge by recovering coins from most every state I traveled across. That made it all worthwhile!

Start of my trip at the ferry terminal

Mountain pass with high snow bank

Rainy day bike ride

A typical camp setup

Marias Pass and the Continental Divide

Little Big Horn Battlefield National Cemetery

Multi-colored terraced structures in Yellowstone National Park

Scenic overlook in Glacier Park

My new invention: the wobble wheel

Some rough western terrain

Another adventure completed at Rockport, Maine

Chapter 6–

Who's Afraid of a Little Wilderness?

I confess to having a sugar high while I was sitting around the campfire. I felt gunky. I'd had one too many pieces of chocolate, sandwiched between graham crackers and perfectly toasted, golden-brown marshmallows (s'mores), and now I was paying the price.

I was certainly aware of the sharp focused reality of the lakeside campsite that surrounded me, and yet, in my mind, a blurry edged image of a homestead in the bush came into focus. In my chocolate-induced stupor, and because we were having so much fun, I was unable to pinpoint the exact moment this fantasy crept into my grey matter but...

Wouldn't it be wonderful to live by a lake and have campfires on demand?

How nice would that be!

One of the things we both enjoy is the outdoors. Camping, canoeing, and campfires. When Johanna could convince me to take a break, we took full advantage of some of the more enjoyable outdoor activities. On this particular occasion, we were camped on Scraggly Lake in northern Maine. Several hours of driving, some of it on gravel back roads, brought us to a pristine campsite situated on the lesser used end of the lake. With no one else around, we enjoyed our secluded spot, both on land and water.

In Maine, semi-wilderness areas are set aside for the public's use for camping, boating, canoeing, fishing, and so forth--and at least once each summer, we made it a point to throw the canoe on the truck and head to a remote campsite. Johanna would go grocery shopping, and then we would have an ice chest filled with treats. We loaded a tent, sleeping bags, chairs, fishing gear, and a chuck box-- which held various kitchen equipment--in the truck, and we were on our way to go camping.

Our "chuck" box is a metal, box-like container, with handles on each end, which holds most of Johanna's cooking utensils, plus cutlery and plates. It's just a convenient way to have the camp kitchen ready for action. We always had a great time on any of our Maine camping trips, so it was a bummer to have to pack up and head home after a few days.

Maine has a wonderful recreational reputation. It can be argued that there is wilderness in western and northern Maine, especially in the vast tracts of paper company land, which encompasses much of that area. But to me, it comes down to how the term wilderness is defined. Logging roads and trails crisscross most of the forest in that part of the state, and logging trucks and logging activity are prevalent, all of which are signs of human activity. But, no doubt, for someone coming from a city or even a rural setting, the woods of western and northern Maine, with their populations of moose and black bear, are the epitome of wilderness.

For me though, true wilderness is a forest with a lake or river, without any signs of human habitation or activity. Wilderness is not seeing another soul; wilderness is just the two of us with a sense we are the only inhabitants on the planet.

Because the ownership of Maine's vast tract of woodlands are in the hands of various business entities, very little private land can be purchased. Fortunately, the state had the foresight to set aside recreational areas, so the public is free to use and enjoy the forests and lakes in those areas. The corporations that own forestland are also very good about letting the public use their property for recreation and hunting.

And so it was that, during the camping trip to Scraggly Lake, it first occurred to me, maybe we could "camp" year round by finding a remote lake somewhere and start over with a new homestead. It would force me to break the work cycle I was in, and it would be another adventure. Johanna wasn't fond of the thought of starting over, so she left it up to me to research and find another place to call home. I heard the call of the wilderness.

As you know by now, my wife and I live far removed from civilization. But that wasn't our original intention when we started the search for an isolated property on a lake. All we wanted was to find a lakefront property that had neighbors at least half mile away.

With so many lakes in the northern United States, how hard could it be to find something suitable? Surprisingly hard, since I couldn't find a piece of real estate that met our criteria, even after searching in numerous states, including Maine and Minnesota. We wanted the feel of wilderness, but it was impossible for us to find anything even close to being isolated. There was no place where houses and cabins weren't lined up like ducks in a row. That kind of defeated the purpose.

We started the search in Maine and then branched out across the country. Wanting snow in our life--we needed the four seasons--we hung our hopes on finding an appropriate property in the northern states. We used the bike trip to make inquiries as I biked myself east. Around the same time, I made a search for Alaskan properties and came up empty. This was discouraging. It seemed no matter where I looked, whether in Alaska or the lower 48, the majority of the lakes were developed.

That would never do with homes so close together you could pass the sugar from one house to the next through an open window or have to hear "Barky" the neighborhood dog, noisy speed boats, and roaring jet skis.

It was pretty obvious I had struck out, so I turned my attention to Canada.

What was involved in moving to Canada?

I sent away for information and applications, and we decided to go through the immigration process. We are grateful to have been granted permanent resident status in Canada. Our search could now span two countries in North America. We wanted to stay as close to the East Coast as possible and thought Ontario had potential because of its wide tracts of wilderness with numerous lakes. After making a few trips to explore northwest Ontario, we determined the country was beautiful. One of those trips took place during my bike trip, which was the time I rearranged the shape of the rear wheel on my bicycle.

There were a few properties of interest in Ontario, but the purchase prices were high, especially considering we had to fly in or we had a long off-road drive to get to them. So I expanded the search some more. I looked at a map of Saskatchewan and was amazed at the large area of lakes and wilderness in the northern part of the province. A few scattered dots on the map showed where a few small towns were located, but the rest of the northern area was a sparsely inhabited expanse of forests, lakes, and rugged hills.

Wait a minute. This was prairie.

It's supposed to be flat as a pancake and nothing but wheat fields forever.

I don't recall learning in school about how awesome the wilderness is in the northern prairies. I must not have been paying attention to the teacher the day that was taught. Nevertheless, this was a revelation, and I did some research on what needed to be done to get permission to live on one of those remote lakes.

I talked to people in the provincial government, and found out there are lakes available for lease north of a certain latitude. All one needed to do was file paperwork, pay an application fee, and, if there were no conflicts, a lease might be granted. Encouraging some migration to the northern part of the province helps with the tax base and local economy. This encouragement was mutually beneficial to those looking for a wilderness setting as well to the province. But these lakes are in remote locations and access is tough.

For most people, a move to the bush would present insurmountable challenges. The need for human contact, the desire to shop at will, and a fear of the unknown are dissuading factors for the majority of the population.

For us, there was nothing to fear being out here alone, and we were completely at ease. The forests only become dark and scary when a person lets fantasy and their imagination get the better of them. There are no monsters behind trees. We weren't afraid of the wilderness; to the contrary, we become a bit apprehensive when we return to civilization and were immersed in the nonstop hustle, bustle, and traffic. The cacophony of noise and confusion left us shaking our heads.

We prefer the comfort of the woods!

The next chapter, "Smells Like Chicken," recounts my first visit to northern Saskatchewan. That initial exploratory trip took place in the fall of 1998 and was enough to convince me it was time to make the big move to Canada, so we could devote our full time to the property hunt. My arrival in the province was exciting but uneventful.

My departure was... well let's just say, I almost didn't get to leave the province.

Camping in Maine

Chapter 7 –

Smells Like Chicken

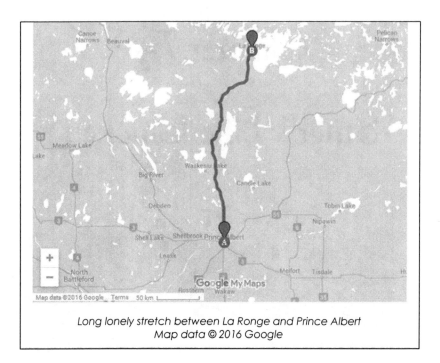

Long lonely stretch between La Ronge and Prince Albert
Map data © 2016 Google

It was a good thing I was dead to the world, sound asleep, and unaware of what was approaching. I was lucky that night; the confrontation could have ended with me being dead to the world quite literally. Not everybody lives to tell the tale of having a bear reach out and touch them. But I did. Here's how it happened.

I was on a mission to explore and get information about the La Ronge area in northern Saskatchewan. This would be my first trip to the province and, since Johanna had to work, we decided that I would fly to Minnesota alone, rent a small vehicle, divert to look at a northern Ontario property for sale, and from there, make the long drive across part of Ontario, all of Manitoba, and into northern Saskatchewan.

La Ronge is a small town located along the shoreline of Lac La Ronge, a rather large, deepwater lake dotted with hundreds of islands. The town had its beginnings as a frontier center on the outer fringe of civilization. Located about 150 miles north of Prince Albert, La Ronge, at that time, was accessible by a lengthy trip on a gravel road. Since then, this major north/south highway has been paved, making it a pleasure to drive as it winds through the boreal forest. The town's main street goes through the heart of downtown, working its way along the lakeshore, and has many businesses adjacent to the road.

It was early October, and temperatures were still warm when I made the 50-mile drive north of La Ronge to the small hamlet of Missinipe, where a float plane base is located. Missinipe is a tiny town situated on Otter Lake, a part of the Churchill River system, which in a bygone era was the main thoroughfare for trappers and local natives. Today, the Churchill River offers extensive recreational opportunities for the outdoor enthusiast. My purpose in driving to the float plane base in Missinipe was to hire a Cessna 185 so I could check out some of the vast tracts of wilderness we ultimately wished to call "home."

This was only my second experience in a float plane. For the many readers who haven't experienced a flight on a float plane, let me try to describe it to you. It's a thrill of a lifetime, and we've been fortunate to be able to fly at least twice a year for the last 16 years. No matter the size of the plane, whether Cessna 185, Beaver, Single Otter, or Twin Otter, the feelings of excitement are the same.

Once you are seated next to the pilot and buckled in, the engine is started and you putt-putt your way out from the dock. Even at an idle, the engine and propeller have enough thrust to take the plane on a leisurely cruise to an area that will allow a long unimpeded takeoff.

As the engine warms up, the pilot goes through a check-out routine, and when satisfied, looks over at you and asks if you are ready.

Your smile and thumbs up is your reply. Here we go!

He makes an adjustment to the throttle, and very quickly the engine is screaming at a high pitch. At first the plane is slow to respond, but with increasing speed, you are quickly skimming along the water and pretty soon you get "on step." This means you've reached the speed where you are still connected to the water but you are hydroplaning. Any reference point you see out the side window quickly disappears from view because of your increasing speed, and with a glance down, you notice the swath of spray being thrown off the float on your side.

Not long after, you leave the lake surface with a surge as the floats break free of the water. The pilot will follow the lake contour and make some adjustments while the craft gains altitude. Staying handy to water is safest just in case the pilot needs to make a quick landing, but eventually a change of course is required, which will take you over land, with the ensuing bird's eye view of the surrounding countryside.

The pilot and I took off that day in October so I could look at some areas my topographic maps suggested might be of interest. An initial assessment was more easily accomplished from the air, then--if I deemed the area worthy of further exploration, I could do a more thorough investigation through an on-the-ground inspection. A camp that was for sale was also on the itinerary, and we landed so I could look the place over. Occasionally, fishing camps are put on the market, but this one proved to be of no interest to us. Nevertheless, I had seen enough to know northern Saskatchewan was magnificent, offering real potential with its carpet of forest and lakes as far as the eye could see.

Landing on a lake is almost as exciting as taking off from one. From a distance, you can see the lake and, as you approach, the pilot will assess the wind direction and determine where to land on the lake.

Circling overhead a couple of times, the pilot is looking for any rocks or obstructions that would impede a safe landing. Once all the variables are known, with a wide sweeping arc, you will approach the water in a long graceful drop, the plane's nose slightly down in attitude, pointed to the lake below, with treetops getting closer as you descend. Skimming just above the surface, the pilot eases back on the throttle and the plane settles down with spray cascading off the floats, forward momentum quickly slowing as the friction of the water, combined with a reduction in engine throttle, reduces the plane to a slow taxi.

"We made it," you tell the pilot. "Nice landing!"

When I returned to La Ronge the next day, I met a local, short, older woman, perhaps late 60s to early 70s, and her daughter. They were two very nice people who had a camp for sale on Lac La Ronge. Although it has been over 16 years since the event, I have a vivid memory of me in a power boat, captained by the older woman, who had a lit cigarette, which dangled from the corner of her mouth--engine full-bore, spray churning off the sides of the boat as we zoomed past islands in the lake.

We arrived at their camp to find an older cabin in reasonable condition but built for people a bit closer to planet Earth. I'm 6 feet tall, and I had to stoop to get through the doorways. Clearly this was a problem. Somehow I would have to do major re-constructive surgery on the doorways or, at the very least, create "noggin notches" to allow my head through without bonking my cranium. I decided that while a nice location, their place was going to require more work than we were willing to do.

Although I was unsuccessful in finding a suitable place, the trip was a good one. I had learned a lot about the area, had made a few friends, and I was convinced more than ever that northern Saskatchewan would be the place we would move to and call home.

It was time to begin the long trek back to Minnesota, and then on to Maine. After gassing up the small rental car in town, I stopped at the local chicken joint in the downtown metropolis of La Ronge. I will keep the name of the chicken joint anonymous, and just say the Colonel's fine herbs and spices were a delight for a hungry palate. I grabbed the box containing my chicken dinner and headed to the car. Driving south towards Prince Albert, Saskatchewan, this starved driver ate the whole meal and I'm pleased to say that the Colonel did a fine job with my dinner.

It was evening and the sun was in the process of setting, but it was still warm, in fact unseasonably so. The 150-mile drive to Prince Albert is on a fairly desolate road with little traffic, and since it would soon be dark, I decided not to push on any further as it had been a long day and I was getting tired. I found a small campground located at about the half way point between La Ronge and Prince Albert, so I stopped to get some sleep. Pulling off the highway, I drove through the camping area, selected a site that looked good, and parked the car in a manner which would buffer me from any nighttime traffic.

This campground was nestled in the forest and was unoccupied except for me. Because this was a primitive camping spot without running water, I used the paper napkins provided with my dinner to clean my hands as best as I could. Since it was a nice night, I threw my mat and sleeping bag down right behind the car. I wrapped myself up in my sleeping bag and was off to la-la land in no time.

I had been sound asleep for a few hours when something smacked my feet. I immediately sat bolt upright.

Through the dark, I could easily see the bulk of a bear that had retreated about 10 feet from my sleeping bag. He looked at me. I looked at him. We looked at each other for a few seconds, and then in the most manly, non-threatening voice I could manage, I said, "Shoo, go on shoo."

It didn't take the bear long to realize I meant business and that he had met his match. However, I'm grateful I didn't have to do any bear "rassling." After admonishing him, he sulked off into the darkness of the woods. I threw the sleeping bag into the car, slept poorly behind the wheel for a few more hours, and then resumed my journey home.

Although I tell this with a humorous bent, in hindsight, I was mighty fortunate. That bear could just as easily have wrapped its big jaws around my neck and dragged me off into the forest.

The moral of this story is: don't go to bed outdoors in bear country, smelling like a fine piece of fried chicken wrapped in a "bag" to seal in freshness.

Chapter 8—

Searching for a Diamond in the Rough

In the early spring of 1999, we crossed the Canadian border and were welcomed into Canada!

We were officially immigrants. An acquaintance, who owned a tractor trailer, had offered to move us to Saskatchewan. So, after packing his trailer with our year's worth of accumulated luggage and furniture, we drove our pickup truck in as the last item, closed the trailer, and drove across the country for five days with him.

When we left Maine that day in May, we were sad knowing that a chapter of our lives was closing, yet at the same time, we were exhilarated to be making a new start in our dream location. It was natural to daydream and fantasize about what it would be like living alone on a remote lake, but we had no real-world experience to compare it to, other than the short camping trips we had taken by ourselves. After an uneventful cross country journey, we arrived in Saskatchewan and safely stowed our possessions in a storage facility in La Ronge.

We led the life of a couple of vagabonds, focused on the prize of finding a wilderness destination, but had no set home from which to work. Our tent, pitched in the local provincial park, or town campsite, served as our home. The town campsite was free, but had no amenities other than an outhouse. When the need arose to get a shower, we opted for the provincial park.

Further north along the gravel road that led to the float plane base, there were other provincial camping sites that we utilized for a change of scenery. When we got fed up with camping and needed a break, we spent a night at a local motel, where we met and became good friends with the proprietor. Those motel rooms were a treat, and we enjoyed the shower, sleeping in a real bed, and tuning in to the television to watch a favorite show. We were biding our time, trying to make the best out of being "homeless" while searching for our permanent home.

We purchased a number of topographical maps of northern

Saskatchewan and then started looking for lakes suitable for us. Topographical maps gave us a good idea of what the terrain of any given area was like before we ever traveled there in person. These maps allowed us to visualize the various surface features such as rivers, streams, boggy wet areas, and hills.

The glaciers had a large hand in shaping the lakes and the surrounding countryside. If you look at a topographical map of the region, you will notice how all the lakes are scoured in the direction the glacier moved. Another interesting feature you might notice is two perfectly round bodies of water, the results of meteor impacts from the past. The craters forming the lakes are visible on the map or satellite image.

Both impacts hit within the last 200 million years, so I'm sweating it out that there might be a third impact any day now! If I see a streak across the sky, it will be my early warning to run for cover.

Our ideal homestead spot needed to have specific features. Because northern Saskatchewan is part of the Precambrian Shield, there is a lot of exposed bedrock. The Precambrian Shield covers about half of Canada and has a diverse set of characteristics: thin soils, rocky outcrops, tundra, boreal forests, mineralization, and, of course, thousands of lakes and waterways.

A large garden was important to us, so the presence of bedrock was an obvious deterrent. We needed to see at least some potential for garden soil. The house foundation would also be a concern if we had nothing but bedrock with which to work. Anchoring the house to bedrock would take some creativity. We would need a south-facing exposure, not only to capture as much solar heat and light in winter as possible but also to utilize our solar electric panels fully. The last requirement was there should be no neighbors. Not only were we seeking an isolated spot, but if someone already had an existing camp or cottage, they had chosen that spot for a reason and we felt we would be intruding on their privacy.

From our study of the topographical maps, we selected what looked like the best lakes. Then we narrowed down the list by finding out if there were other occupants on the lake. Once we had a list of lakes, the next step was to assess them from the air and then visit them if they looked promising.

It was late spring, shortly after our move to Saskatchewan, when we arrived at the float plane base and chartered the smallest plane, the Cessna 185. This was purely a scouting trip, a search for the "diamond in the rough," that jewel of a lake that would glisten in the sunlight and catch our eye from above. Johanna clambered aboard into the back seat, while I climbed into the front seat next to the pilot. A set of maps and a GPS receiver occupied my lap. Both of us were giddy with anticipation. This would be Johanna's first float plane ride. We took off and followed the lake contour. As we gained elevation and swept in a northerly direction, we could make out the rapids of the Churchill River and the structure of the steel bridge that spans it. Without the bridge, there would be no road access to the north, so it's a vital link for the mines and communities that rely on this road.

Once we were in the air, I was able to follow our progress and see where we were headed by matching what I was seeing out the window to what was shown on the map. But I couldn't lose focus. If I wandered off in my thoughts, it was very easy to get disoriented and lost, and I was quickly baffled about where we were.

The wilderness all looks the same from the air. Woods, lakes, and rivers. It is possible to fly for hours and not see a community. Unless you can home in and identify with certainty what lake or river you are flying over, the situation can get dicey in a heartbeat.

Not that it was my responsibility to know where we were. I just liked to follow along and keep tabs on our progress. From a safety standpoint, if for some reason I had to make a radio call for help, I at least wanted to have a clue as to our location.

Float plane pilots are professionals and have done this enough to know where they are. Of course, if I had looked over and seen the pilot with a puzzled expression and sweating profusely, or if he was reading a beginner's guide to flying, I'd probably have broken out in a sweat too!

Seriously though, we never had a concern with any of the pilots. Every one of them has been top notch. These days most pilots use GPS exclusively, but years ago, many pilots also had a map in their lap in case the GPS failed.

Moving to the bush was atypical, and I'm not aware of anyone else living full time in such a remote location in Saskatchewan. I can only imagine some of the conversations that took place around the lunch and dinner table at the float plane base.

"Those two crazy people have no idea what they are doing."

"They think they're going to build a place to live, have a garden, and live out there year round."

"I'll bet they don't last a year out there!"

Although I'm just guessing at the chatter and giggles, I have no doubt we were quite the topic of conversation. Ironically, we never thought of this move as too extreme, but I can understand how people would be taken aback by what we wanted to do. For us, it just seemed like a natural thing and wasn't a big deal.

Narrowing down our choices to three lakes showing the most promise, we decided to camp out at all of them so we could do a more thorough assessment. We loaded our gear into the plane, flew to each lake, and were dropped off with the promise the pilot would be back at the appointed time a few days later to pick us up.

I always felt relieved when the pilot showed up because I wasn't keen on sending Johanna bushwhacking 40 miles for help.

Since it was just the two of us, I would have volunteered to stay back to protect our camp and cook the steaks!

Once Johanna returned with the rescue crew, I would have patted my stomach, let out a polite little burp, and pointed to the grill while muttering that I had saved her a piece of meat, albeit a bit dried and charred.

Of course, I say this in jest. If anyone was going to thrash through the bush, it would have been me.

As much as we liked bush-camping, it was costly to fly to a remote lake to camp for a few days. Additionally, by midsummer we were feeling some pressure to find a home site as soon as possible. Fall comes early here, so time was running short. Plus we knew there would be a delay while the government dealt with our application. Assuming the application was approved, an environmental law officer would then fly out to our selected site to do a quick survey for the deed. Then, once it was all formalized, we could proceed to do some work on the property before the onset of winter.

By July, because none of the lakes we investigated felt like the right place for us, the next step was to expand the search area and look at more lakes we had selected from the topographical maps. We hired the Cessna 185 again and flew north with nervous anticipation to begin the new search.

Would we finally find a place to call home?

En-route, I noticed we were flying over a body of water we hadn't planned on viewing. As fate would have it, a sandy beach caught my eye and I immediately asked the pilot to circle back. He did. We made a few passes over the lake, and I asked if we could land and taxi to the beach. The lake was placid as the plane taxied into a slight cove where the sandy beach was located. After the pilot cut the engine, we slowly drifted up onshore, the floats stopping the plane's forward momentum when they came to rest on the sandy shore.

As Johanna and I got out of the plane, on to the float, and then made the short jump to the beach, a feeling of peace and tranquility overcame us. After walking for a short period of time through a well-spaced pine-spruce forest, we turned to each other, smiled, and knew this was going to be home.

It was magic!

This was one of those rare occasions in life when a series of chance events led to the overwhelming sense Hockley Lake was the right place for us at this time in our lives. We had found our "diamond in the rough," and we had grand plans to polish it into a cozy homestead in the bush.

With an unplanned, spur-of-the-moment stop at a lake not on our itinerary, the search was over. As soon as we returned to La Ronge, we applied for a lease. It seemed like it took forever, but in reality, Saskatchewan Environment Resource Management (SERM) was outstanding to work with and we were granted a lease in relatively short order. What a relief when we received word our lease was approved. Once we had the lease in hand, we began the next phase of the project.

We were heading to the wilderness and were almost home!

All worldly possessions packed and ready for Canada

Hockley Lake, our new home, awaits!

Chapter 9–

Sort of Homesteading

Welcome to Hockley Lake!

A huge weight was lifted off our shoulders when our lease application was approved, and we knew we had a place to call home. By mid-July of 1999, we were eager to start building. Now we had the daunting task of converting the leased plot of woodland into a homestead. This was when the fun and the hard work began. Although we had high hopes and expectations, we knew it wouldn't go as smoothly as planned. We'd run in to snags and battle bugs and would have to deal with the weather gods. For the duration of the summer, we expended a great deal of effort to make a start on our new homestead. We were dead tired, but we also experienced a true sense of physical accomplishment.

Once permission was granted in midsummer to settle here, we immediately flew out to start clearing the lot. We pitched our small, two-person backpacking tent, set up the kitchen area complete with fire ring, and settled in for a lengthy stint of work. This would be the first of several work trips we made to Hockley Lake that first summer. After working for a few weeks, we would fly back to town for supplies and a brief rest, then fly back to the lake to work some more. Each time we flew in, the plane was filled with building materials and equipment. Our motto was to utilize every plane to its maximum extent. We maintained this schedule until October when the snow arrived and covered the ground.

Our first priority was to open up a trail from the beach to our camping site, then on up to where we would build the house. Starting from the beach, there is a flat shelf of land a few feet above the high water mark and then the terrain rises steeply to a sandy knoll that sits 15 feet above the lake surface. We chose to locate our homestead on this high hill.

This was virgin wilderness, and the forest was dense. Using nothing but a chainsaw, we cleared a path from the lake to the house site. I cut down the trees, sawing them into firewood as I went, and

Johanna removed the brush and collected and piled the firewood. Because the trees were very small in diameter (4- to 5-inch average) compared to what we were used to in Maine, we mistakenly thought we could have the house site completely cleared in two days. What we failed to take into account was how numerous these small trees were and how long it would take to deal with them. But we cleared the house site within the first week. To break up the monotony, we alternated clearing work with other chores like lugging lumber and supplies from the beach.

Initially, the weather was stiflingly hot, so after working up a sweat, a dip in the lake was a welcome relief. But by the time we left in October, we were dressed in multiple layers, beginning with long underwear. A swim in the lake was the furthest thing from our minds.

Because there were so many things we wanted to accomplish, at times it was a difficult decision about which task should be the priority. Meanwhile, it was exciting to visualize what the homestead would ultimately look like when we were finished with our work.

SERM had granted us two leases. One for the house and one for a large garden plot. We slowly expanded an opening in the woods towards the borders of our leases, letting the surrounding forest and its standing trees serve as the boundary line markers. Slowly but surely, we made progress in creating a large opening in the canopy, allowing the sun to shine in, making for a bright, cheery home site.

We were driven to clear this parcel as soon as possible so we could move on to building. My logging and chainsaw experience came in handy. I continued to buck all trees into firewood while Johanna hauled and stacked the pieces. We moved the brush to the edges of our lease and, at first glance, one would have thought we were building the great wall of Hockley, since there was so much piled up brush. A few years after the house was built, we flew in a rented chipper to deal with all the brush, and ultimately purchased our own chipper.

The chips make a great addition to our gardens, and we added them to our compost pile as well as mounded them over our buried water line as insulation against freezing. It was a relief to get all the brush cleaned up. Not only did the place look much better, but more importantly, our home was no longer ringed by a large, dry pile of brush that would become a circle of doom if it ever caught fire.

We flagged out the borders of the gardens and pulled out each tree, and its roots, within those boundaries. Through trial and error, we found a way to clear not only the trees but their roots all in one shot.

With the aid of a chain and a two-ton come-along, I was able to anchor to the base of one tree, put a chain on a nearby tree as high up as I could reach, attach the come-along to the chain, and then topple the tree. I continued ratcheting the come-along until I pulled the tree free, roots and all. I repeated this tedious process many times until I had our garden areas cleared. The cleared garden areas are approximately 75x35 feet each. Quite an accomplishment.

We had flown in a new rototiller to work our gardens, and I plowed the lower 40 after the trees were removed. I disced in all the forest duff, and after I went over the areas a few times, our gardens actually started to look like gardens. The first pass was the most difficult as I had to make frequent stops to clear the tiller tines of small roots and debris. Many small roots wrapped themselves around the tines like pieces of twine. Tilling became easier with each subsequent pass, and now, years later, tilling is a breeze.

Progress was slow, and I had a good sense of how the first pioneers must have felt converting forest land to farm land. It is not easy work. The pioneers had horses and oxen to help, whereas I had mechanical tools and 'Ron power,' but fortunately I had relatively small areas to clear.

One of the characteristics of the Precambrian Shield is poor, thin soils, and our sandy knoll was no exception. As soon as I started rototilling, it was evident that a thin layer of moss and decaying organic matter was all that covered our new garden spots. At most, 2 inches of top soil existed.

Thanks to Johanna's hard toil over the last 16 years, we now have dark loamy soil 8-10 inches deep. Over the years, she has collected wheelbarrow after wheelbarrow of forest duff and rotting log material from the surrounding area to improve our garden's soil. I bet she's hauled a couple hundred wheelbarrows of organic matter to our gardens by now. And it shows by the type and quality of produce we ended up with.

Early on, we wanted to increase the soil fertility. To do this we opted to use manure, a traditional choice. We made the mistake of flying in a large quantity of store-bought, bagged manure. In hindsight, this was a big error because the product was never composted properly and, as a result, we imported many non-native weed species. We have been weeding the garden of these pests ever since. Unfortunately, they are a prolific bunch.

Included with all the supplies and gear we flew in was a nice aluminum boat and motor for fishing and exploring the lake. In July, before departing from La Ronge for Hockley Lake, we went on a frenetic shopping spree and bought all the things we would need for the summer's excursion. The boat was one of the many items we purchased. Our boat is a no frills 17 footer with a 9.5HP four-stroke Yamaha motor. We also brought our canoe, a white, fiberglass, two-person vessel. We loaded the canoe inside the plane, but the boat was much too big to get through the doors. Much to our amazement, we watched the dock hands strap our boat to the struts of the float.

From the dock, they rolled the boat onto its side and positioned it along the plane's left strut. Then, they secured the boat with numerous ratchet straps. This was a 17-foot aluminum boat, and it was being flown on the outside of the plane. It was quite a sight to see.

Obviously, it was critical that the strapping be done perfectly, lest our boat get free and start flapping in the breeze, or worse.

Although we worked hard for the remainder of the summer, we took time to explore our new water playground, and we stalked the creatures of the deep with rod and reel. What a thrill it was when I pulled up my first trout from the depths!

Like a true fisherman, my arms and shoulders ached as I struggled for hours to pull in that mighty fish. The boat and I were dragged up the lake and then down, and even with my motor on full throttle, in reverse, I couldn't stop the fish from giving me its personal tour of the lake.

I finally got the *2-pound* trout to the surface, where I rested and caught my breath.

Okay, maybe I embellished my fish tale a little. But, really, it was a thrill to catch the first fish, and a relief to know there were actually fish here. Lots of them. But until we caught one, there was the concern we had just settled on the Dead Sea.

That summer, we flew in enough building materials to build a firewood and a storage shed. We bought and hauled in pieces of actual telephone poles. These pressure-treated posts would last a long time, becoming the posts for our woodshed. I've lugged around a lot of posts and timbers in my life, but those telephone posts were some of the heaviest material I've ever had to move by hand. While it's very nice to sit high on this knoll with its wonderful, panoramic views, I should point out that everything had to be manually carried or dragged up the hill. Manhandling the telephone poles up the slope was about the limit of my abilities. Once we had snow, the snowmobile could do the work, but that summer and fall, it was all people power.

It's not like we live on Mount Zeus, but a sharp, 12-foot rise is a strenuous obstacle. Think of it as walking supplies and lumber upstairs from the first floor to the third floor, but without the steps. Just sandy dirt, where a loss of traction or a slip was a common occurrence. Eventually we were able to get the construction materials for the summer's projects moved to the building site, all the post holes dug for the woodshed, and a shed built that would hold 12 cords of firewood.

Now Johanna had a place to stack the wood she had been collecting to allow it to dry. Completion of the woodshed also helped immensely with tidying up the place, since firewood wasn't strewn all over the yard.

We were also able to build a small storage shed so that when we left in the fall, we had a sturdy, protective home for all our tools. In addition to getting the firewood and tools under cover, we started digging the trenches for the house foundation. Where we intended to build the house, we drove stakes into the ground at the corners, ran string from those stakes, and then dug a shallow trench using the string as a guide. We made a wooden frame and attached a mesh screen so we could sift out the small gravel from the sand we dug out of the trenches. Eventually, the gravel went back into the trench to act as a solid base. We laid pressure-treated 2x10 planks in the trench, on top of the gravel, and by placing a level on the planks, we could gauge whether we were indeed digging a level trench.

By the time we were able to start working on the foundation trench, cold weather was settling in, so this task would need to be resumed next spring when things warmed up again. When we left in early October, snow was on the ground and some of the nearby ponds were starting to skim over with ice. We'd had enough playing and camping in the cold for now. It was time to leave for the winter, but the new homestead was well underway. All in all, it was a productive couple of months.

Communication in those early days at Hockley was unique--at least unique to us. Many hunters and trappers worked in the bush on their trap lines and lived in cabins they built. Their communication system included a battery-operated transceiver. Voice could be transmitted as well as received. The antenna consisted of a long wire that they hung as high as they could get it, between trees. In the town of La Ronge, an operator was stationed 24/7 near a high-powered radio. Someone would call in from the bush and would want to place a call. The operator would dial the call to a landline and then acted as intermediary between the caller in the bush and the person receiving the call on the landline. The operator listened in and, depending on who was talking, either broadcast or received the voice.

It was like the days of walkie-talkies. "Blah blah blah *over*," with "over" being the key word.

Acting as the go-between, the operator directed the voice traffic back and forth between the two parties using a simple foot pedal switch. Depending on the switch position, voice would be transmitted to the receiving party or their voice was sent to the caller. This banter went back and forth until both parties had said all they wanted to say, and the communication ended with *over and out*, thus enabling the operator to know the conversation was completed. Anyone tuned to the frequency being used could listen to the ongoing conversation. There was no such thing as a private chat--quite reminiscent of party lines from long ago.

Several times during the day, the operator would broadcast the weather forecast to those in the bush. The system was truly a lifeline to those who were isolated in the wilderness. Not long after our move to the bush, the provincial government disbanded this communication system; now all communication is via satellite.

We rented one of those units the first year we were out here. I strung the antenna wire as instructed, as high as possible, yet my voice was barely audible to the base station in La Ronge. Weather conditions had a huge effect on how well one could send and receive a transmission, with every day being different. Not only that, but every hour in the day could be different.

My parents made a prearranged phone call for my birthday. From Pennsylvania, they called the base station in La Ronge, right on schedule, and then the operator contacted me. Here I was, out in the bush, and I heard my name called over the radio. Although there was just as much static as there was voice, I was able to carry on a semblance of conversation with my parents. But, I'm kind of a private guy, and having birthday wishes and my personal, private conversation with my parents broadcast to every radio throughout the north, which was tuned into my frequency, including the operator, was difficult for me.

Although that conversation took place long ago, I have a faint recollection of how it went.

Operator: "Victor Echo Echo 840 are you by?"

Me: "Yes, I'm here, over."

Operator: "Your parents are on the line. Standby!"

Then I heard my parents singing, "Happy birthday to Ron, happy birthday to Ron, happy birthday dear Ron, happy birthday to you."

Me (a slighter darker shade of red): "Well thank you. Don't forget to say *over* so the operator knows to transfer us. Over!"

And so it went. I remember the static was a bit much that day, and we didn't carry on much longer.

At this point in time, the Maine property hadn't sold yet, and as long as we owned it we would continue to go back to earn money from the forest resource through logging. Once the snow and cold came, we left our lakeside camp and returned to Maine for the winter. Johanna finalized the floor plan of the house, and I designed the structure, laying out on paper where every piece of lumber was to go. I developed a materials list and ordered exactly what was needed to construct the home.

Remember, we can't run to the hardware store. Once the plane leaves us, we're on our own. It was essential to have everything we needed on-site!

We returned to Canada the following spring, March of 2000, and had all the building supplies delivered to the float plane base. The ice was still several feet thick. Temperatures were cold, at around zero Fahrenheit. In order to efficiently move the mountain of construction materials to our lake, we hired the biggest plane on skis, the Twin Otter. The maximum load the Twin, or any plane for that matter, can carry is determined, in large part, by the distance it has to travel. The further the plane has to fly, the more fuel it has to carry to make the journey, and the less payload it can haul.

Under the right circumstances, the Twin can transport 2,000 to 2,900 pounds worth of payload.

That's a lot of stuff!

With some additional manpower supplied by the airline, we

were able to fill and fly in 10 full plane loads of materials over the course of two days.

Another way to look at it is this: In those 10 plane loads, a snowmobile and an entire 1,500 square foot, two-story house were flown to Hockley Lake over that weekend.

By the time everything had been transported, the lake ice was littered with piles of things: lumber, insulation, stoves, windows, doors, plywood--you name it.

We used the snowmobile, also flown in on one of those trips, to move the lumber uphill to our building site. It was a tedious process getting all of it up the hill, since we could only take a little bit at a time. As an illustration, we bundled together six to eight 2x8s as tight as we could, cinched them with a strap, and then attempted to haul the bundle behind the snowmobile, up the hill, without losing any of the load.

Many times our strapping came loose and the trail up the hill was strewn with scattered pieces of building materials. One could easily follow the path we took; just follow the trail of ejected lumber, much like following a trail of bread crumbs. But we did ultimately get all construction supplies off the lake, piled in a central location, and protected by large tarps. It was quite the job, and even with the cold temperatures, we were sweating by the time we were done.

The following month, in early April, with the lake still solidly frozen, we flew out with lots of food and supplies, including an expedition tent, which we called home for the next 4 months. The float plane owner kindly loaned us the expedition tent, and it was a godsend. We had to shovel a couple of feet of snow before we could pitch the tent, but luckily the pilot and the crew helped in setting it up. Temperatures were still going down to the -20°F range at night. We were relying on a kerosene heater and heavy down sleeping bags to keep warm.

Four days after our arrival, we heard a plane off in the distance. We knew we were going to have some company when the plane buzzed by and circled overhead. We weren't expecting anyone, so this was an exciting development. The pilot who had initially dropped us off returned with a small wood stove and chimney pipe made for expedition tents. The guys at the airline had worried about us since the temperatures were unusually cold for that time of year. The stove improved our comfort level and quality of life, and was greatly appreciated.

We shoveled off the house site and did what we could until the snow melted and the ground thawed. Between Johanna and me, we were framing the second story, when, in early June, my brother came to lend some muscle. He was here long enough to get the roof and most of the siding on and even lay some vinyl flooring. Later in the summer, my parents came to help. They came in on a flight that also brought the kitchen cabinets. This was our family's first trip to see our new place and, of course, their first flight on a float plane.

We needed a well-designed, insulated home to deal with the extreme temperatures we would face. One winter, our big yellow thermometer, mounted on a tree visible from our living room window, registered -57°F.

That's 57 degrees below 0, which has been the coldest temperature here to date.

That day, the closest weather station to us, Key Lake, was officially the coldest place on the planet. No other location in the world with a recording station, including the Arctic, Antarctic, or Siberia, was as cold as we were.

You might have a mental image of Johanna and me, with heavy parkas on, huddled around the stove, teeth chattering, hands outstretched to the heat of the warming fire, but in reality it was just another day. It was a novelty we hit that temperature, but otherwise, no big deal. Although, I confess, it was fun to write to family and friends, if nothing else than for the shock effect: it went down to *what??!!*

Because of the potential for such extreme cold, when I was engineering the house years ago, I wanted the home to be super insulated, so I searched for appropriate construction methods. After spending time researching the topic in the construction trades section of the library, I was uninspired by what I found. The basic principles for a warm dwelling are insulation, minimal thermal bridges between inside and outside, and eliminating drafts and air exchange as much as possible. The concepts are simple enough, but incorporating those various elements into a building would be more involved than I expected.

We ended up with a house with ten-inch-thick insulated walls, with minimal studs. Even wood conducts heat, albeit poorly, so the fewer studs reaching from the inside of the wall directly to the outside of the wall the better. Our walls have very few studs making direct contact from interior to exterior. The vast majority of the studs in the wall are made up of pairs of studs with an insulating strip of blue board between their narrow face (two 2x4s arranged this way to create one 2x8 equivalent). That strip of blue board breaks up the direct transfer of heat from the inside to the outside. We inserted fiberglass insulation in all the wall voids and then sheathed the interior wall with a layer of blue board Styrofoam. In my research, I couldn't find anyone designing or constructing walls the way I did.

One of the smartest things we did was to properly install a plastic vapor barrier. This is just heavy gauge plastic that comes on a roll. Extra hands really help to hold the plastic in place during installation, especially when covering the ceilings. We taped all seams of the plastic barrier with a special ultra-sticky tape made for that purpose.

In a typical house, a great deal of air infiltrates the dwelling through all the outlets, so we installed plastic inserts into all the outlet and switch openings located on the outside walls. These plastic inserts were manufactured products made for just this purpose. We also taped and sealed their seams. Windows and doors also have some leakage, and the trick is to minimize all of this air flow. The end result is that we now are basically living in a large plastic bag. With a house so tight, there are no drafts, and interior temperature is constant regardless of room or corner. At -57°F, it was easy to keep the house warm that day.

However, ventilation is necessary. It's nice to be airtight, but we still need to breathe. We don't live out here with a permanent tinge of blue on our faces due to a lack of oxygen.

To that end, we installed ventilation tubes through the walls, both upstairs and downstairs. Ventilation tubes are a commercial product that allows a homeowner to control the venting of their house very easily. They're adjustable, so you have a great deal of flexibility with how much outdoor air comes into the house. It's better to have a tight house and be able to control what air enters than to have a leaky house over which you have no control.

Another key for a warm house is the attic insulation. Normally, the roof rafters come down and rest on the top wall plates, tying into the ceiling joists. The weak link in the attic insulation is down in the area where the roof rafter meets the wall, the space in the attic right over the exterior walls. In order to create more insulating space, we put another plate on top of the ceiling joists and then put the roof rafters on top of that. Doing this allowed us to stuff insulation into the area uncompressed, which gave full insulation value.

This technique wasn't my idea and may be standard practice in colder climates, as it makes a huge difference in minimizing heat loss from this area. We can have 18 inches of snow on the roof and have no icicles. Seeing icicles hanging off of a roof eave is a sure sign of heat loss from a house. The escaping heat melts the snow, which starts to drip off the roof, only to refreeze forming the familiar spikes of ice.

Nor do we have ice dams anywhere. After a snow, you may have noticed a ridge of ice along the length of the eave. This icy ridge signifies heat loss through the roof, which has melted the snow, but because of cold temperatures, the water quickly freezes into an icy mass at the edges of the eave. Further up the roof, snow in direct contact with the roof melts but doesn't refreeze because the layer of snow on top of the melt water acts as insulation. Water trickles down to collect and back up at the dam. If there is enough water, it can infiltrate under the shingles and work its way into the attic. Once water starts seeping into the attic, there is no telling what damage can be done.

Our attic has almost 20 inches (R 65) of fiberglass insulation.

Is it overkill?

It all depends on the heating and cooling bill one has. Just as fiberglass insulates against heat loss in winter, it also insulates against heat gain in summer. It is amazing how cool the house is when the outside temperature is 80-85°F. The flip side is how remarkably toasty the house is at -57°F.

All windows are triple-glazed, meaning that each window is composed of three sheets of glass, which improves energy efficiency. We have two large, south-facing picture windows, which are great for taking in the outdoor views and capturing the heat of the sun. The angle of the sun is low in the winter months, so the sun shines directly in. It's surprising how much heat value is gained from those front windows, even on the coldest days.

Between the combination of a sunny day and the heat of a small fire in the morning to cook breakfast, the upstairs maintains a comfortable temperature, and at times, can even get a little too warm. We opted not to have any north-facing windows on the back of the house, although if we had to do it again, we would have one on each floor. It would be an advantage to see any happenings to our north.

There were two really dicey tasks during construction that were a huge relief when we safely completed them.

First, we had a wood cook stove weighing roughly 500 pounds which needed to come in from outside and make it to the second floor. Attaching our come-along to a reinforced beam in the ceiling, we winched it up through the open stairwell. In other words, before any stairs were in place, there was a rectangular opening in the second floor through which we were able to sneak the stove.

Installing our two 5x5 foot triple-glazed picture windows on the second story was the other trick. My brother was on one ladder, I was on another ladder, and each of us held part of the window with one arm. We used brute force to walk the windows up the ladders and in to place. Johanna had a safety rope on the windows to help support and lift. They were mighty heavy windows, and I'm glad we didn't build a third floor. As I write this, I am in view of those big picture windows. I don't know how we ever got them installed.

Ceilings are lower in our house, meaning our walls are non-standard height and a little shorter. This means less wasted space above us that needs to be heated, which contributes to the ease of heating our home. We have a wood stove downstairs, which is the main heater.

By design, Johanna put the shower close to the heater stove, making it a warm place to stand and dry off after coming out of the shower. Unless temperatures are -10°F or colder, there is no need to run the heater stove constantly. One good fire in the morning and one good fire at night generally keeps us comfortable. Because of the tightness of the house, wind makes no noticeable difference in heating the dwelling.

Shortly after the house was framed, we hand-dug trenches for our greywater waste disposal system and installed three lateral lines. The laterals consist of 4-inch perforated pipe, which we laid on a bed of gravel in the trenches. We carefully sifted through all the material we had shoveled out, to separate the stone from the sand. Then we covered both the water line and leach field with layers of insulating blue board before backfilling with the sifted sand.

I plumbed our kitchen sink, utility sink, and the shower together, allowing them to drain into this leach field. To prevent clogging of the leach field lines, I installed in-line filters with a screen in all the drainage pipes, just beyond the trap, so before any greywater headed out of the house, it was filtered. Every month, we take apart the filters and give them a good cleaning. This preventive ritual allows us to capture the majority of solids before they have a chance to go out and clog our field. Cleaning the filters is a simple maintenance chore that has worked well and should prevent our system from having to be dug up to be fixed.

Initially, we hand-dug a 34x18-inch-wide trench, 200 feet in length, to the lake for our water line. The digging was time-consuming but relatively easy in the sandy soil.

During the first winter we had a problem with our water line freezing. It froze even though the line was insulated with Styrofoam and buried. The following year, we installed a water line heater cable, which would keep it ice-free, but we had to run the cable a little each day and it was an energy hog.

Many years later, we hand-dug a well closer to the house and shortened our water line by 100 feet. By cutting the length of the line in half, we eliminated 100 feet of water line that could potentially freeze. We also installed a new heater cable, but because it was half as long, power consumption was cut by a large factor. These days, with all the insulating wood chip mulch covering our well and water line, all we need to do to keep our water line ice-free is to run the heating cable five minutes in the morning and five minutes in the evening.

In the summer of 2010, we decided to dig the well, which happened to coincide with the most recent fire. For anybody who has tried to dig a deep hole in the sand on the beach, you know it's pretty futile. The walls constantly collapse and the hole fills in with sand.

Our digging ordeal was compounded by two facts: first, I was in a lot of pain, and second, I had one eye watching the fire.

Before I could start the well, the first thing I needed to do was to dig up the original water line to expose the pipe. Since the plan was to cut our water line distance in half, I needed to shorten and pull some of the tubing up and out of the trench. Because I could easily see where we had originally dug the trench for the water line so many years ago, it didn't take me long to dig up the last 100 feet, which went down to the lake. I now had our trench reopened and the insulated water line exposed.

Lying flat on my stomach, my plan was to reach down into the trench and pull up the pipe to ground level. I was aware I was lying on a small rock around the area of my chest but was focused on the task at hand and chose to ignore it.

After all, it was just a little, itsy bitsy rock. Maybe one inch in diameter.

From a prone position, I tried to lift the pipe.

Snap, crackle, and pop.

Broke a rib just like that. I couldn't believe a little rock did that to me. Of course it hurt, and I knew I had tweaked my rib, but I was in denial it had actually broken.

At this point, the house had no running water and wouldn't have any running water until we dug the new well, installed the well-casing, and reattached the line. There wasn't much choice but to grimace, bear it, and keep on working.

So in spite of a broken rib and the threat of a nearby fire, this is how we managed to dig our well. We had a plastic PVC culvert 30 inches in diameter and a little over 6 feet in length, which would be our well casing. That length needed to be buried in the ground, which required a hole in the sand at least 6 feet deep and 4-feet wide. I dug what I could until I hit water, about 3 feet down. Now the walls started caving in, so we stood the culvert on its end and set it in the hole. Then I got inside the 30-inch culvert and bucketed out sand and water for hours, broken rib and all.

Every time I bent down, my rib let me know it. I handed one bucket at a time to Johanna, who was stationed at the edge of the hole; she dumped it out then returned the empty bucket to me for another load. We kept this up until I couldn't stand the pain from my ribs any longer; my hands were numb from the cold water, and I needed a break.

We were a true bucket brigade.

After several rounds of the bucket detail, I eventually couldn't dig down any further. At this point, I ran a rope around the top of the culvert and hung heavy sand bags around the perimeter. I fired up the gas-powered water pump we use for our sprinklers and attached a pressure nozzle. By running a high-pressure jet of water around the inside base of my pipe, I was able, with the aid of all the attached weight, to slowly sink the culvert into place. Now we have a safer water supply since we aren't drawing from the lake, and we have the freezing problem essentially solved. We were without running water for 11 days, but it was worth it.

We have a hand-dug root cellar, a big hole in the ground 7x7 square and 4 feet deep. It's plywood-lined to keep the walls from caving in. This root cellar is under the house and is accessible through a trap door in the floor of my shop. This is where we store our root crops, like potatoes and carrots, through the winter. The water pump and pressure tank are also located here. If we need to go away for an extended period in winter, we run down all of our canned goods. All the jars are stacked neatly in cardboard boxes, and then we go through an insulating procedure, which safely protects our food from freezing. We store some canned goods and staples like sugar, flour, and eggs year round in the cellar.

If you were here visiting and overheard Johanna tell me she's "going shopping," what she really means is she is headed down to the root cellar and will bring up the needed items.

We sure have done a lot of digging here. Fortunately, being on a sandy knoll made digging quite easy. But, alas, we've never found any buried treasure. Not even an old gnarly dinosaur bone. One thing we found interesting was how stratified the ground was. There would be layers of different colored sand, then a layer of pea-sized gravel, and then back to pure sand. It was obvious there had been some real forces at work here in ancient times to sculpt this landscape. It is fascinating to us but probably ho-hum to a geologist.

I completely designed our power system with a large solar array, initially, and not long after added a wind turbine. The electronic controllers for all this stuff are state-of-the-art. Seldom used, a small diesel generator provides backup power for those extended cloudy periods with no wind. The short days of November and December rarely have a day without some clouds or haze and are usually the only two months of the year the generator would need to be used. At this time of year, due to our latitude, when the sun does shine, it is at such a low angle, our total daylight is inadequate to completely replenish the energy we consume each day. But one good windy day or night and we can be fully charged, and even have excess power. As a general rule, regardless of the season, we don't like to waste spare energy, so we'll utilize that power by running on the treadmill, vacuuming, doing laundry, or plugging in the Christmas tree lights.

When engineering the system, I had to factor in a multitude of variables. What did we want to power? How much power was consumed by each device, and how long was each device expected to run in a day? How many days of battery storage did I want? Did I want a 12VDC, 24VDC, or 48VDC system? Did it make sense to power some things direct from the batteries? So many decisions. I began by making a list of all the appliances and gadgets we needed to power. I also considered what possible items we might want to buy for the homestead in the future and made an allowance for those things.

Next, I estimated how many hours each day the item would run and then added a large fudge factor. I calculated battery size so that we would have lots of power even if the sun didn't shine and/or the wind didn't blow for a lengthy period of time. Because nothing is 100% efficient, I needed to take that fact into account. So, for example, if I drew 100AH (amp-hours) out of the battery, it might take 110AH of solar/wind power to recharge the battery.

This gives you an idea of the decisions that need to be made for any off-grid system.

You may wonder how the sun actually powers the house. Solar panels produce direct current (DC) voltage, a form of energy batteries can accept. In effect, the solar panels recharge the batteries. We have a couple of appliances that can run directly off the DC from the batteries, but the majority of our appliances run off of standard 120VAC.

The inverter, an electronics box, enables our batteries to power all the electrical items we use on a daily basis which require alternating current (AC). It takes 24VDC battery voltage and converts it to 120VAC, so we can function like any typical house. Sensing when the generator is running, the inverter then becomes a powerful charger to replenish our batteries.

We flew in and installed almost a ton of deep cycle batteries. Because I never want to fly in and manhandle 300-pound sets of batteries again, I baby them and allow only a 20% discharge before fully recharging them. Although the batteries are made for a deep discharge, meaning you can drain much of the power out of them before recharging back to full, we prefer to shallow discharge only, and, as a result, we anticipate a much longer life expectancy before they need to be replaced. They are still going strong after 16 years. Of course, proper maintenance is essential too. Keeping the battery tops and terminals clean of acid and encrusted sulfate is a priority, as is keeping them full of distilled water. A little care will go a long way towards battery longevity.

We love being off-grid and cannot imagine living in a home that is tied to the utility company. Alternative energy gives us independence from traditional energy sources, whether nuclear or fossil fuels. It takes us out of the loop of escalating energy costs. It puts us, the energy consumer in control. If/when the power grid fails, we have peace of mind we won't be affected. Furthermore, living off grid gives us the freedom to live anywhere--even 100 miles in the Canadian bush. As a salient bonus, we are doing our part to reduce carbon emissions and are helping to keep the planet green by living an environmentally friendly lifestyle.

Occasionally I come across an article and read about someone who is being persecuted and threatened with prosecution by municipalities who have the misguided belief that it should be illegal for anyone to live disconnected from the grid. If true, it's a nefarious attempt to impose control and limit people's freedom on how they choose to live. Any decree by any government entity to restrict our choice of power, water source, or self-reliance would be a serious threat to our way of life--a way of life that is, in a small way, an answer to the pollution problems, water shortages and squirrelly climate changes and weather patterns that are taking place.

Within one year we had our home completed. All framing, plumbing, electrical, and finish work was done. I mentioned how simplistic our Maine home was, and by comparison, our new castle is deluxe.

You would be hard-pressed to know you were 100 miles out in the bush. Satellite color TV, internet, hot and cold running water, and a shower. Big kitchen with maple cabinets and large countertop workspace for Johanna. She has most of the typical small kitchen appliances, including a nice sized refrigerator/freezer. Would you believe she even has a portable electric dishwasher? I had it flown in as a special surprise for her. If I do something to irritate her, I head over to where the dishwasher is parked, tap on its top lightly to remind her what a great guy I am, and all her irritation disappears.

Best purchase I've ever made!

Where we had one tiny refrigerator/freezer in Maine, we now have a full-size appliance in the kitchen, plus two chest freezers outside. We put the freezers outside for a number of reasons. We didn't want to dedicate floor space to them inside the house, and more importantly, we use winter temperatures to our advantage. Our winters are long and cold, which allows us to turn the freezers off, thereby saving large amounts of power. At least five months out of the year, temperatures are cold enough so that our freezers can remain off.

Both the refrigerator and the freezers are special highly insulated appliances that are very energy efficient. For off-grid homes, energy efficiency is a priority. These appliances are a little more expensive, but the savings in energy consumption are significant. It costs a lot of money to fly in diesel fuel to power the generator, so the less the generator is used, the better. Compared to the Maine house, we now have far more freezer capacity to inventory and store food, a must since we only shop twice a year.

Because the commute on a plane makes it impractical to shop every week, it should be no surprise we don't shop very often. The couple of times a year we go shopping are the times we also receive mail and see other humans for a few days. Then, it's back home again. Every time we fly home from shopping, the plane is fully loaded. Planes are expensive and since we're paying for both legs of the trip, regardless of whether the plane is empty or full, we try to be sure we fully utilize those planes. When a plane comes out to pick us up, we try to have supplies on board. When the plane departs, we try to make sure the outbound plane has something on it too, such as empty fuel cans or bags of garbage we've accumulated.

We don't generate much trash here. We compost organic matter. We use paper and cardboard to start our stove fires. Since we don't buy many prepackaged commercial products, we don't generate many empty metal cans, glass, and plastic containers. Finally, we try to utilize things fully before having them go to the landfill.

For example, we reuse our empty one-gallon plastic milk jugs in a number of ways. Many times Johanna will cut off the top of the milk jug and use the bottom for seedling containers. Another use is filling the jugs with water and setting them in the greenhouse each spring and fall to act as thermal mass. Thermal mass in this application refers to the large amount of water in the milk jugs, which absorbs heat from the sun and then releases that heat over time. This released heat is transferred to the greenhouse, which helps moderate the temperature inside. When outside temperatures get chilly, this method helps keep the interior warmer. A wood stove is another example of thermal mass. Long after the fire is out, the metal is still warm and radiating heat to the room. Only after the plastic jugs start breaking down from age do we send them to the dump. We only send 10 to 12 bags of garbage to the dump each year.

As a safety net, we inventory a couple years' worth of food staples. This includes all of our canned goods, sacks of wheat, which Johanna grinds by hand for fresh flour, and other staples like my 50# sack of cocoa powder--for me an essential nutrient and building block of life.

Shopping for food is more ordeal than fun. Forget those wimpy shopping carts that run the typical grocery store aisles. The store we buy most of our food from sells in bulk and has large, flat, roll-around carts. We generally fill two of those to overflowing, and then it's a challenge to get everything in the car. I swear I hear the car groan when it sees us come out of the store. Buying in bulk is cheaper for us in the long run; sacks and case-loads suit us better.

We get our dairy by flying in roughly 35 gallons of frozen milk, along with various types of cheeses every six months. In Maine, we used to raise our own meat animals. One would think being surrounded by wild game, we'd fill our freezers and have a smorgasbord. Many people do hunt moose, bear, and caribou. We don't, but it's not due to any philosophical reason against hunting. I simply have no desire to eat wild game. I grew up on traditional beef and pork and don't care to eat anything else. However, if we had to, it would be easy enough to hunt for our meat source. We certainly know how to dress the animal and cut, wrap, and process the carcass into various products such as sausages and cured meats.

Nowadays, we just fly in a side of frozen beef and a whole pig and do the cutting and wrapping of the meat ourselves. To make various types of sausages, we work with cubed meat, which is partially frozen, mix in spices, and then grind it in a small electric grinder. It's easier grinding when the meat is partially frozen. Our grinder has a sausage stuffing attachment and, while one of us is feeding the machine, the other is tending to the sausage casing to make sure it slides smoothly off the stuffing attachment so the final product looks like a sausage, and not some disfigured, bulging wreck.

We cure hams and bacons and then smoke them. To cure the meat, we rub a mixture of salt, sugar and various spices over its surface. Then, we place the meat into sterilized buckets; the length of curing time is determined by the weight and thickness of the meat pieces. Bacons might be in cure for a few days, while hams might be curing for 30 days. Once cured and smoked, our finished products have far more flavor than what is normally purchased in the store. If you are familiar with the term "country ham," you will have an idea of how our hams taste.

We simmer batches of meat bones in a large stainless steel pot. Johanna then cans the soup stock for later use as the base for various types of fine soups. One year she canned 80 quarts of stock.

A full canner load is 7 quarts, so it was a lengthy process to get the canning done.

This whole routine will give us a two-year supply of frozen and canned meat as well as soup stock. As a side bonus, we render much of the fat and then make it into soap so we are thorough in utilizing everything.

One of the things we have a hard time dealing with is the dramatic difference in the amount of daylight throughout the year. It's tough to get used to. By midsummer, it's already evident the days are getting shorter. By fall, the loss of daylight is accelerating and the sun is lower in the sky. At its worst, we are losing 4 to 5 minutes of daylight each day. In December, the stars are still out at 8:30 am, and it doesn't get light until about 9:00 am. Officially, on December 21, sunrise is 9:33 am and sunset is 4:23 pm. That's only six hours and 50 minutes of daylight. Amazingly, we don't suffer from the dreaded "cabin fever" of winter.

By December 21, the days are the shortest, but mentally, we know the worst is over. We've gotten over the hump and are headed to spring. This is a big deal for us. The trend is ready to reverse, and happy days are here again. Day length increases slowly at first, but then increases rapidly as spring approaches. It doesn't take long to notice the days getting longer when you add 4 to 5 minutes each day. The angle of the sun is now getting higher in the sky. In June, it gets light at 3.30 am, and it is still bright enough to see at 11:00 pm. Officially, sunrise is at 4:09 am and sunset is 9:54 pm. We enjoy a 17-hour and 45-minute day.

The difference is "night and day" between the seasons.

During the days of June, the night is never pitch black. We need a curtain over the bedroom window to block the incoming light so we have a sense of night. Surprisingly, we have more trouble dealing with the excess light of summer than we do dealing with the excessive dark of winter. It's hard to feel sleepy when the sun is out. The ol' body's biorhythms get out of sync.

Inevitably in October, the weather turns chilly and we'll have our first fire in the heating stove. In the month of May, we'll likely have our last fire, making for a lengthy heating season. Per year, we figure roughly three to four cords of wood for the cook stove and four to five cords for the heater stove.

Several times we have had forest fires rage through this area. We utilize the burned forest for our firewood. Ready-made, mostly dry spruce and pine, free for the taking. Over time, as we cut the dead, fireburned trees, the forest is getting cleaned up and it looks better aesthetically. Plus, the buffer of open ground between the homestead and the forest gets wider each year, which makes us safer in the event of a future fire. While not as good as hardwood, the spruce and pine throw heat and are fine. As long as we burn the stoves hot once a day, we have minimal creosote buildup and we only need to clean chimneys once or twice a year.

The only downfall to wood heat in this environment is, if we go away in the winter, we have to drain the water system completely and put our jars of canned food down in the root cellar to keep them from freezing. Not a big deal, since we don't leave home that time of the year very often, and over the course of a couple days, we can be ready to close the house if need be. Small inconvenience for wood heat in our book. If we went away more often in the winter, we could easily install a small propane heater as backup. But then we would have the added expense of propane as well as the cost of flying it in, so we'll stick with wood heat.

The annual chimney cleaning and mounting of sprinklers for fire suppression are two chores that require roof access. Safety is always paramount since we are a considerable distance from medical help. Therefore, whenever I get on the roof of our two-story home, I wear a lineman's belt and am tethered to an anchor point on the roof. I also have a wooden ladder mounted to the roof to aid in getting to the peak. The metal roofing is slippery, especially when wet, and a fall over the edge would be catastrophic.

Our method of doing the weekly laundry is considerably different than most. While the majority of people throw their clothes in an automatic washer followed by a tumble in a dryer, we run a reliable, old wringer washing machine from years past. Although it's an antique, we wouldn't care to use anything else. It does a great job, is ultra-reliable, utilizes water efficiently, and is simple to use. Johanna says it certainly does a better job than those "modern pieces of crap front loading machines." I guess she doesn't like front loading washers.

She washes the least dirty clothes, the whites, first and then, with each succeeding load, she progresses to the dirtier stuff. Once all the clothes are washed, usually three loads worth, she drains the washer, adds fresh water, and puts the clothes in a rinse cycle. She rinses articles in the same order in which they were washed, least dirty to dirtiest. Then she wrings everything through two closely spaced rollers under high tension from a spring mechanism to squeeze out as much water as possible (*everything but her fingers!*), which is a real time-saver.

To dry, Johanna hangs the laundry outside on a clothesline on warmer days, and in winter, she hangs it inside on wooden clothes racks made for drying. An electric clothes dryer is out of the question due to its high energy consumption, and although propane-powered dryers are available, it doesn't make sense to fly in cylinders of gas to power a dryer when the heat of the house in winter, or the sunshine and breezes in summer, do a fine job for us.

Our chosen lifestyle is one that is environmentally friendly but, equally as important, is just plain fun and satisfying. Although there are times when we still need to work hard, such as when we collect firewood or plant the garden, life here is like being on a permanent vacation, and who wouldn't want a little more vacation time. It's one big adventure.

Many people have the fantasy of picking up and heading to the bush. For most, it remains a dream. We aren't anti-social, but we are comfortable with ourselves and don't feel the need to be surrounded by people. We each have our own space when needed, are able to depend on each other, and can live for months and months with no one but our own company. We are confident in our abilities to live, adapt, and thrive in circumstances that would be uncomfortable for most.

If everybody wanted to live in the bush… *it would be called a city*.

So fortunately, there are some of us who head to the less populated countryside, thereby doing our part to keep the cities less crowded. To a degree, it's ironic we live off grid and are so remote, yet a writer and a videographer managed to find us, and we had a wonderful visit with them. They came to interview and film us for part of a book and documentary film they were doing about off-grid Canadians.

We are sort of homesteading out here. We still do many things the old-fashioned way, and we do provide for much of our needs. Even when there are chores we don't "do" the old fashioned way, we have practical experience and knowledge of how to do them that way if we had to. Except for the rare times when we need to utilize the generator, we are completely self-sufficient for our power. We provide our own fuel for heating and cooking. Our monthly bills are minimal. We grow our own vegetables and a lot of our fruit. We use a blend of the old-fashioned techniques along with the newer bells and whistles of modern society.

In a sense, we have picked and chosen what amenities we will take advantage of to make our quality of life better. We are content with our chosen life, and even when we are out here for a long spell, there really is no overwhelming desire or need that can't be filled. Any desires are satisfied by having the items in stock. We make sure we have a good supply of food items on hand. For example, I love ice cream, so we make sure we have a supply of it. Let me rephrase that: we make sure we have the ingredients to make ice cream. There's nothing like homemade ice cream, especially on a hot summer day. No point going without and being semi-miserable. This approach can apply to anything. Bottom line: We have a modern house with all the conveniences, and we're happy to call this place "home."

As is true of most things in life, we have learned from past experiences. We have adapted well to life in the wilderness, and we've struck a balance between remoteness and civilization. To step outside gives me the sense we are the only two remaining humans on the planet, and yet with a flick of a switch, the computer or television instantly connects us to the rest of humankind. The portable radio we employed initially has been replaced by voice over Internet (VOIP), and we have a real phone on the wall that uses satellite technology. As backup, we also have a true satellite phone. It's imperative we have backups and plan Bs in the event our primary systems fail.

We've improved and refined our quality of life immensely from those early days in Maine. Although our bush existence isn't what I would deem "homesteading" in the truest sense, we still live our lives with a pioneering spirit and a determination to "sort of homestead," a lifestyle that gives us a great deal of freedom and satisfaction. We've paid our dues with the hard work, and it's nice to settle into a more leisurely existence.

Another Twin Otter load of materials

Johanna clearing the site of snow in early spring

Chilly!

Firewood shed holds about 12 cords

Clearing the land

First floor framing

Clearing brush and firewood from the home site

Second story framing

Our trusty wringer-washer

Tilling the new garden area

Hand-winching out every tree stump with roots

Johanna in the camp kitchen

Sifting gravel from the sand for house foundation

Johanna digging the root cellar (note the full woodshed)

Our garden hoop houses in early spring

Our temporary home

Our boat being strapped to the outside of the Single Otter

Snowmobile used to move supplies from lake to house site

Chapter 10–

Do Bush Planes Serve Pretzels with the In-flight Movie?

Sadly, the answer is no. There are no pretzels served during the movie. In fact, there is no in-flight movie. Flying in a bush plane is a no-frills means of transport to get from point A to point B. I don't fly first class when I sit up front next to the pilot, nor does Johanna fly second class when seated in the rear. But I do end up contorting my body like a pretzel to get into the Cessna 185.

Because the plane is sitting in the water, tied to the dock, the passenger door is inaccessible. The only access is through the pilot's door. It's a matter of climbing in and scrunching my body across to get into the passenger seat. There is very little room to maneuver, and I have less flexibility as I get older. With the Beaver and the Single Otter, there is more room to scoot across and it's much easier to get settled into my seat. In winter, access is easy, since both sides of the plane can be reached by simply walking around the plane.

Once we're all seated and secured, the pilot will go over where the survival gear, fire extinguisher, first aid kit, and flotation devices are located. After a quick check of the mechanical function of the plane, the pilot starts the engine and the trip is underway.

How we love to fly in a float plane!

I monitor our progress by glancing at the digital readout of the GPS, which is mounted in the dash. Miles to our destination and time left to travel are the two key pieces of data I watch. Even without the GPS, I have a good idea where we are, and, from afar, as soon as I see the familiar shape of our lake and pick out the two islands in the bay, I know we are close to home.

Although flying in a float plane isn't as safe as flying in a commercial airliner, we're very confident in the pilot's abilities each time we fly. As you can imagine, after all the flights we've taken in bush planes through the years, we have a few stories to share. Thankfully, we've never had any death-defying experiences. Safety is paramount; the planes are well-maintained, and the pilots are well-trained. In fact, there have been several times when we have loaded the plane and taken off, but after a few minutes, had to turn around and return to the base because weather conditions were too bad.

It's amazing what a difference there can be in the weather over a distance of only 60 miles. We can take off with good visibility and see only a veil of clouds in the distance. Those clouds can become denser and lower to the ground the closer we get to them. The pilot will look for an opening and, if he finds one, we'll zig-zag our way through, flying not far above the treetops. Otherwise, we are forced to return to base and wait for the weather to clear. Frustration happens when we've been away from home for a while, are anxious to get home with a plane load of food and perishables, fly to within 15 minutes of home, and then have to turn around and head back to the float base because of poor visibility. Fortunately, that has only happened a few times.

Because the seasons we travel are notorious for fog and snow showers, we always schedule the plane for a day or two earlier than needed so we have a window of opportunity to get out to make our appointments. On numerous occasions, this foresight kept us from having to cancel or reschedule due to a weather delay.

The closest call we have ever had, if you want to call it a close call, was the day we first landed on Hockley Lake. It was a warm, sunny day when I had noticed the sand beach and asked the pilot to land. It was an uneventful landing and the rest is history. We loved the place as soon as we pulled up onto the beach. Although we were convinced we had found the right place to call home, we still wanted to continue with the day's itinerary, and view the other couple of lakes on the list. We took off from Hockley and made a beeline for the next couple of lakes. We never landed at any of them, but rather we got a sense of the lakes purely from viewing them at altitude as we circled overhead. Nothing caught our attention, so on our way back, we decided to take one more look at

Hockley, since we were still "in the neighborhood."

The north end of Hockley has a small cove where our sand beach is located, but there is a finger of water that extends to the north of our house site, creating a narrow bay. There are certain conditions that make a safe landing difficult. One of those is when the lake is a virtual mirror, and it is so calm, nary a ripple can be found on the surface. When coming in for a landing, it is hard for the pilot to determine the plane's height above the water without some ripple or wave action to give him depth perception. It is difficult for the pilot to gauge how close to the water he or she really is. On our return trip to Hockley, our pilot lined up with the narrow bay, came in, and was flying just above the water. The bay is perhaps half mile long, if that, so we needed to set down in short order. The end of the lake is treed, so it was imperative to land quickly or we were going to fly into the trees.

I remember skimming above the water, flying directly towards the forest at the end of the lake. I thought to myself "Ok, time to land, come on, put it down."

We were close to the point of no return when the pilot made the decision that he couldn't judge where the mirror-like surface of the water was, so he reached over, gunned the throttle, and with a burst of speed, pulled back on the yoke, and we easily cleared the trees. A delay of one second and things might have been different. We returned to the base without another attempt at landing. A snowy lake is another condition that makes it hard for pilots to judge how close to the surface the plane is. A gray day complicates the situation even further. It's very difficult to get any depth perception under these circumstances.

I've taken a couple of unusual trips as well. There was an occasion when I was picked up by the Cessna 185 based in La Ronge. It was a bitter cold winter day, and the temperature was close to -30°F. I always dress warm and had on my heavy coat and wool mittens.

The pilot was an older, seasoned man who had made a career of flying in the bush, and I doubt there was anything that could have rattled him. We were headed back to La Ronge, and since it was a beautiful day, we were relatively high up in altitude. Perhaps a mile up. We were about 15 minutes away from the La Ronge airport when my door popped open. Doors are hinged, so as the plane flies forward, the air pressure helps hold the door closed. In other words, there is no situation where the door can be ripped off, and I, the passenger, can get sucked out of my seatbelted position, to fall to my death, a mile below.

However, let's throw logic out the window for a minute.

I'm zooming towards the town of La Ronge, trees and objects on the ground are mere specks, and my door is flapping in the breeze. This was my first experience with a door ajar in a plane, and all I could think of was myself and my gear being drawn out through the narrow opening between the door and the fuselage with a big sucking sound.

My molecular structure, so rigid and solid, reduced to a jelly-like consistency, as the last of my body oozed through the opening due to unseen forces that only aerodynamic engineers understand.

Rationally, there wasn't much to fear, but it was disconcerting to say the least. As all this is running through my head, and my pilot looks over and calmly tells me to hold the door closed.

Well...where's the drama in that?!

For the remaining 15 minutes of the flight, my mittened hand, at sub-zero temps, accompanied by a body numbing wind chill, was outside the plane, firmly holding on to the door, keeping it shut as tight as I am able.

Although we landed just fine, there were no television or newspaper crews at the airport to interview me on how I saved the flight. I was prepared to tell them exactly how, with nothing but a mittened hand, I held the plane together just long enough for us to get on the ground!

In summer, the float plane base is a hive of activity with various planes taking off and landing in a well-choreographed routine. Many times, as soon as a plane lands, dock hands and customers are loading it for the next trip. Groups of people are milling around, anxiously awaiting their turn for their trip; fishing gear, duffle bags of clothing, large ice chests full of top priority beer, and maybe even a small ice chest filled with lower priority food, litter the dock waiting to be loaded.

On one occasion, we were scheduled to take the Beaver, a trusty mid-sized plane that can take about five people plus gear. Hockley Lake was our destination, as we had recently applied for a lease, and we wanted to spend some time camping and enjoying our new found paradise. The plane taxied alongside the dock, and Johanna and I lost no time in throwing our gear into the plane. Shortly thereafter, we were airborne, heading north. We weren't in the air very long, perhaps 10 minutes at most, when I sensed we were making a big circle.

It was subtle at first, but the guy in the copilot's seat, me, has the orienting awareness of a homing pigeon, and I wondered, was the pilot testing me?

By then, we had reversed course 180 degrees and I could make out the float plane base. Neither Johanna nor I knew why we had made a big circle back to the base. The reason became evident as soon as we pulled up to the dock; the dockhand unwound the big coil of fueling hose and turned on the fuel pump...fill 'er up! Planes fly their best when the engine runs, and we had taken off without being fully refueled.

Finally, I'll tell you about the time I purposely opened the door to the Single Otter when we were flying home. On the way between La Ronge and our home, a couple of men were in the bush struggling to move an exploration drill through the deep snow. They were using a skidder to drag the drill and had not been heard from in a few days. This drill move was supposed to only take a couple of days, but was taking much longer than anticipated, and concern was mounting for their safety.

Several boxes of supplies were prepared for them, including a radio, food, and toilet paper. Carefully packaged with loose tails of orange flagging that would flutter in the air, the boxes of survival supplies were to be dropped from the passing plane once the guys were located. It was hoped the flagging tape would make the boxes easier to see as they fell through the air and also when they were on the ground ready to be retrieved.

As it so happened, our return flight home coincided with this attempt to find the men and drop the supplies. It was my responsibility to make the drop. We took off and headed north to the general direction and area of the men. I've never been in the military and can only imagine what it's like to be part of a humanitarian mission to drop supplies to refugees, but that's the way I sort of felt. I also felt pressure not to mess up this airdrop. Once the package goes out the door, there's no getting it back. It either hits the mark or it's useless. At the speed the airplane is traveling, timing is critical.

What good are rescue supplies if they land two miles away from the intended drop zone?

From the air, the pilot was able to locate tracks in the snow. We were flying relatively low, following the tracks to see if we could find the men and their machine. It didn't take more than a minute or two to find them and we circled overhead.

Target acquired!

Now that the men were aware we were in the area, we headed away to make a large circle so that we could get lined up to make the package drops. I couldn't see where we were in relation to the guys, so I needed to rely on the pilot's cue on when to push out the boxes. I cracked the door wide enough to allow three packages to scoot by. They were on the floor of the plane, right next to the door, ready to shove out as soon as I got the signal.

Slowly, we lined up and came in low. I nervously watched for the hand signal and when it came... it was "bombs away."

I launched the three packages out the door as fast as I could, with the hope the guys could retrieve them. I later heard that, because of the depth of the snow, they only found two packages. A few days later, the men were able to get out to the road and were safe and sound. But that was certainly an interesting flying experience.

Ready to head north in the Beaver (with canoe)

Twin Otter offloading supplies at Hockley Lake

Chapter 11—

Cook Stove Delights

I would be remiss if I didn't mention the wood cook stove that has been our constant cooking companion since 1980. It is the focal point of our current Canadian house, sitting prominently in the kitchen, centrally located, on the second story. Bright, shiny chrome adorns the frame, and it is an eye-catcher to all who enter. Next to me, it is Johanna's most prized possession.

A bit of wishful thinking I guess. It *is* Johanna's most prized possession!

The Maine house had a genuine antique wood stove that I used for cooking, baking, and canning until Johanna came along. While on my own, I was quite capable of cooking a full turkey dinner-- turkey, stuffing, mashed potatoes, green beans, candied sweet potatoes, and even gravy, the elixir of life, which I can drink by the gallon if allowed.

Is there anybody else hungry, or is it just me?

Add in a favorite bread recipe and a dessert of choice, and I could keep myself well fed, but now I am far happier to leave Johanna in charge of the kitchen. I still contribute to the kitchen duties by taste-testing!

I am known to be chocolate-powered. Give me a piece of chocolate, and I'll move mountains. Fortunately, my mom has always been an excellent cook and I ate well as a youngster. Johanna likes to cook and bake, so she has taken the torch from my mom. Between the efforts of the two of them, I've never had a chocolate deficit. One is an expert with the traditional electric range, and the other is a pro with this wood cook stove.

I have no preference as to what type of oven is used as long as the dish comes out chocolate!

Virtually anything can be cooked on or in a wood cook stove. The typical electric range is impractical in an off-grid home due to its high energy consumption. Although we could have opted for a propane stove, we have stuck with the tried and true wood stove since we are surrounded by an abundant supply of firewood.

We have good, heavy stainless steel pots, but our favorite cookware is the antique cast iron skillets passed down from both of my grandmothers and Johanna's mother. For ease of cooking and cleaning, properly seasoned iron cookware can't be beat.

Seasoning is the process of baking on a thin coating of grease that protects the pan, and gives it a no-stick quality that rivals the best of Teflon pans. Additionally, we get a little added iron in our diet by ingesting food that has absorbed iron from the pan.

The only drawback to cast iron cookware is having Johanna greet me at the door with a frying pan in her hand. Then I know I'm in trouble! Just kidding. She's never done that, but I'll bet she's been tempted a time or two.

Friends and family have contributed to our cast iron cookware collection over the years, and the antique waffle maker is one of our treasured gifts. It still works fabulously. It's actually made for a wood stove and replaces one of the round access lids over the firebox. With the round stove plate removed, we place the waffle maker over the direct flame to heat. Once preheated, we open the device, pour in the batter, and close it again. Once that side is done, the waffle maker pivots and flips, allowing the other side to cook. Clever gizmo. There's nothing better than fresh waffles with real butter and real maple syrup. The fake sugar goo that passes for syrup isn't welcome here. That goo was banished from our house long ago, and now we use nothing but the real thing.

The kitchen cook stove does triple duty in our home. Not only does it cook our meals, but it also heats the upstairs and supplies our hot water needs all at the same time. When you stop and think about it, a few pieces of properly dried firewood burning in the firebox do a lot of beneficial things for us. We put a lot of effort into cutting and hauling the firewood, but the triple duty efficiency of our setup makes it all worthwhile.

Our stove has a warming oven above it, and off to one side is an attached water reservoir, which can be used for warm water. We rarely use the water reservoir since we have a hot/cold running water system, but having the extension to the stove top surface is nice, as it is a good place for a spoon and implement rest. The warming oven is a great place to raise bread dough or dry herbs spread out on a cookie sheet. As the name implies, it is a place to put food to keep warm while the rest of the meal finishes cooking. The brick-lined firebox has a water jacket mounted on one side, which allows us to set up a thermo-siphon loop for our hot water. The only caveat with the water jacket is that it needs to be filled with water before making a fire. We found out the hard way that if we don't have water in it, the heat from the fire will warp and crack the jacket.

While waiting for two replacement jackets to be flown in, we endured a month of no running hot water, and resorted to heating water in kettles and pots set on top of the wood stove, like we used to do so long ago in Maine. Replacing the broken jacket was an easy fix once the new one arrived. We are keeping the other new jacket as a spare, part of the large inventory of parts we keep on hand to deal with unforeseen problems.

We have a standard home water heater set up next to our stove. It's roughly a 50-gallon tank. And that's all it's being used for, purely a storage tank. No electricity goes to this heater. We set up plumbing from the tank to the stove's water jacket to take advantage of the flow of heated water. Just as hot air rises, the same principal applies to hot water. As water is heated in the jacket, it starts to flow upward and into the top of the water tank and is then replaced by colder water coming out of the bottom of the tank.

This is a simple and efficient method of taking some of the heat from the wood stove and using it to raise the temperature of water for household use. It works great, and it's free. There is no need for any in-line pump since the water circulates on its own. The size of the tank is balanced with the size of the stove so we don't end up with a tank of boiling water, which would happen if we had a much smaller tank. But the water does get hot. Since this is a standard insulated water tank, the water stays hot for days even if we have no fire in the stove. A pressure relief valve, standard in all homes, is a must for our system as well.

There are times when Johanna will have the stove going most of the day and then we'll run the hot water tap preemptively to release some hot water. If Johanna knows she has a day of canning or baking, she'll draw down the hot water in the system by doing a few loads of wash before the day's canning begins. This uses the available hot water and fills the system with cold water, ready to be heated while she's using the stove for the day's cooking activities. We used to have galvanized iron piping going from the jacket to the tank, but found that it clogged too easily from the minerals in the water. Copper piping is now plumbed in, and has been trouble-free for years. It's important there are no line restrictions so that the water can flow freely through the system.

Canning garden produce is an easy task with this stove. Able to handle multiple kettles, the whole cook top is one big heating element with temperatures varying across the surface, so it's a simple matter of rearranging pots on the stove top for proper temperature regulation. Whether Johanna is canning by boiling water bath or pressure canner, the key to success is getting a hot fire going. She can slide a pot anywhere on the surface so that it boils, simmers, or stays warm. This is one of the beauties of the cook stove, easy temperature control.

The stove came with a large oven, which does a marvelous job of baking. It has a set of racks in the interior like any modern oven, allowing the cook to select the appropriate area to place a cake, pan of cookies, loaves of bread, or that yummy beef roast. Depending on what's for dinner, Johanna may choose to employ a couple different sized cast iron Dutch ovens to bake the meal. Our Thanksgiving turkey, roasted in our largest Dutch oven with lid, is something we look forward to every November.

What a treat it is to be out in the middle of nowhere, the smell of the roasting turkey permeating the whole house, the golden brown bird served with great fanfare, while the dessert pies are waiting in the wings in the warming oven.

That big cast iron Dutch oven does double duty when it comes time to render the accumulated fat for soap making. Saponification is the process of taking lye and rendered fats to make soap. It's hard to believe this combination of ingredients produces the product all of us use daily to get ourselves clean. Johanna makes large batches of soap, enough to last us years. Not only is the soap good for handwashing and showering but the hard bars can also be finely grated for use in the clothes washer.

As with any wood stove, we'll need to occasionally clean it. Johanna has established a cleaning routine, whereby each week she empties the ash pan and each month scrapes out any accumulated soot from the exterior of the oven, making for improved oven efficiency. We spread the ash on the gardens or use it in our compost style toilet. The soil here is naturally acidic, and the ash helps bring up the pH to a more neutral range, helping the garden to grow.

I thought I'd include a simple recipe for oven roasted pota... one of our favorites. I'd give you my boiled water recipe that uses powdered water, but it's a family secret. Enjoy!

- 1 tbsp lemon juice
- 1½ tsp olive oil
- ¼ tsp dried savory or thyme
- pinch of salt
- pinch of garlic powder
- pinch of pepper
- 2 potatoes or ½ # equivalent (cut in chunks)

Mix and toss the above ingredients in bowl, add to preheated cast iron skillet, and bake in a hot oven (400-450 degrees) for 40 minutes. Stir halfway through and cook until tender, brown, and crispy. This makes 2 servings.

Hot water tank plumbed into stove

Johanna's kitchen

Johanna's most prized possession

Super energy-efficient frig/freezer (note the wall thickness)

Chapter 12–

Forest Fires Burn Me Up

I had been relaxing in our porch swing one evening in early June of 2010 when I casually noticed some passing black clouds and rumbling thunder in the distance. But I sure came to life when, out of the corner of my eye, I saw a bolt of lightning streak to the ground and heard a deafening crack of thunder immediately afterward.

That was close. Too close.

Scanning the skyline for smoke the following morning, revealed nothing, which suggested we were in trouble. By lunchtime, the situation had changed. After eating, I started out the downstairs door and immediately stopped in my tracks, instinctively knowing something was wrong.

Why was the lake a tan color?

My heart skipped a beat as I sprinted the short distance to a bank overlooking our bay, knowing full well what I was going to see. A nearby curtain of gray-black smoke rose skyward, with enough smoke to alter the skies overhead and cast a tannish color onto the lake surface.

"Fire!" I shouted.

"How far?" my wife yelled back from the kitchen window.

"Close!" I shouted as I ran down to our dock area.

Fear was palpable as we each carried out our prearranged assignments. My job was to start our water pump, which I had set up weeks before. One pull was all it took to get the pump engine running and water flowing from the lake, through water lines, to the installed sprinkler heads. Johanna was frantically running through the house closing windows, throwing pictures in suitcases, gathering important documents, and getting our survival suits ready.

Once we had the sprinklers running, I reported the fire to the fire base using our satellite phone, and a crew working a nearby fire was dispatched. From its inception one mile away from us, the fire increased exponentially that first day and was accompanied by an enormous mushroom cloud of smoke high overhead. Despite running six miles, the fire headed away from our homestead, allowing the firefighters time to set up another pump and five more sprinklers to increase the odds of saving our property.

We didn't feel safe at home, so that night we bailed out and pitched a tent a short distance away in a safer area. At dawn, we returned home, but conditions were so dry that by mid-morning we witnessed new columns of smoke in our vicinity. We vigilantly watched from the safety of our boat, and returned to shore only to keep the pumps fueled and sprinklers running. We continued this ritual for a couple days, with the fire moving away from us the entire time. But on the third day, just before nightfall, we watched as flames became visible on a nearby hill and we knew it was just a matter of time before the fire reached us.

The next morning we were up by 4:00 am, and with chainsaw in hand, I cut down everything that resembled a tree along our back perimeter.

I thought that if I could slow the forward momentum of the fire, the sprinklers would have a greater chance of protecting our property. I cut until I was exhausted and could see smoke rising nearby. Retreating to the safety of the boat, we watched in dread as the fire ramped up and came towards our bay. Hillsides started to burn, and flames gained a foothold at the northern end of the bay. Much to our horror, we watched yet another column of smoke start in the distance. The fire had thrown embers a quarter of a mile ahead of itself to start this new blaze.

At that moment, our morale was lifted when we heard the drone of a float plane. A fire crew was arriving to check on our safety. Temporarily docking the boat, we all met on the beach and walked to the house, where we stood on a nearby overlook and watched the flames race down the opposite side of the lake, 150 yards away from us.

It was like being in a movie theater, the big screen showing a large-as-life fire burning right in front of us, with black smoke billowing upward and a dense veil of white-gray smoke hugging the ground so thickly that the bright orange flames were visible only when they leapt skyward above the fracas. A slight diminution in the smoke allowed just enough visibility to see an orange-red glow, much like opening the door to a furnace allows a view of the orange-red coals. And, like the furnace hungrily consuming its fuel, the intensity of the forest fire's heat incinerated everything in its path.

The fire boss said there was nothing more to be done and we would have to trust the sprinklers and pumps. He considered doing a back burn, but the winds were unfavorable for this technique. We checked pumps one last time, donned smoke masks and goggles, and retreated to the boat while the fire crew took off.

Before the pilot had the float plane turned around for takeoff, we saw a towering wall of flames, well above treetop level, working its way towards the house.

There was nothing we could do, and the feeling of the situation being lost was overwhelming. Utter hopelessness!

We could hear the roar of the fire, along with the steady hum of the water pumps. The Wajax pump used by professional fire fighters has an unmistakably loud, high-pitched whine, and as we bobbed nearby in the boat, the pump hiccupped, a stutter that caused my heart to skip a beat.

Please pump, don't stop now.

And just that quick, it caught itself, smoothed out, and was fine for the rest of the ordeal. We sadly resigned ourselves to the fact everything we owned was now in the path of the approaching firestorm.

How could our house withstand the oncoming onslaught?

Flames and smoke engulfed everything in its path. We lost sight of the house and even our beach as the smoke obliterated everything within our view.

Previously, we had set up all of our sprinklers defensively around the house, arranged in accordance with the direction we expected the fire to come, the north, which was behind the house. Before long, we noticed smoke rising from a completely different location; now it was in front of the house too. The fire had thrown another coal ahead of itself and was burning in an unprotected area, working its way towards the house from the front. We watched the new ground fire crawl along the shore area, an occasional tree going up like a Roman candle, the flames working their way to the only thing defending our property, the fire pumps and their accompanying fire hoses.

Once the majority of the fuel had been consumed, the fire tapered down to hard smoking with scattered smaller fires. At this point, we boated back to our beach to determine if it made sense to fight the remaining fire with hose and nozzle. This would mean disconnecting some of our sprinklers, which would be a high-risk move. I ran up to the house and looked around. I did not feel good about the situation and promptly retreated.

Johanna had stayed with the boat, but noticed some smoking in a long pile of brush. She grabbed a bucket from the boat and threw multiple buckets of lake water on the area. If we hadn't made the run back to the house, she would never have seen that pile smoking. Since the brush pile went towards the house, she no doubt saved us from another heartache. After my quick inspection of the house site, I deemed it was too dangerous to hang around, so we beat a hasty retreat in the boat.

All we could do was bob in the boat, watch the show, and wait. Eventually, two planes circled overhead. Two fire crews had come to our rescue and were ready to tackle the fire, but they had to wait for smoke and flames to dissipate before attempting to land. They were able to land in the late afternoon, and all of us teamed up to hose down the many hot spots. The crews arrived just in time because the blaze had worked its way to within 20 feet of the water pumps. By the time things settled down and were under control, only 90 feet of unburned ground separated the homestead from the fire.

What a close call!

On June 14th, the fire crew from Southend came in to take down their sprinklers. Although there were still plenty of hotspots in the area, our little oasis was deemed safe. Over the course of the next six weeks, we still lived in fear as an occasional smoldering area would come to life and burn more forest. Some badly needed rain came on July 31, which finally put an end to the fires. The Hockley Lake fire, as this was named by the provincial authorities, burned about 173,000 acres.

Quite a bit of ground to go up in smoke, but if you'll stick with me, I'll tell you about the "big" fire.

In hindsight, it was a sign of things to come, when shortly after we moved to La Ronge, Saskatchewan, back in 1999, a fast-moving forest fire broke out that burned a number of homes and nearly destroyed part of the town. We were using La Ronge as a temporary base and had trucked all of our worldly possessions to the local storage facility. Nobody could have foreseen that everything we owned would be in the path of this fire, and the only thing saving our belongings would be the determined effort of water bombers that attacked the fire with water drops. This event was an introduction to our future in the northern wilderness.

The majority of fires in the north are set by lightning. In

summer, when an unorganized thunderstorm passes through, we sometimes have dry lightning with little to no associated rain. Jagged lightning bolts shoot down from the heavens, strike the Earth, and ignite fires if conditions are dry enough. With the vast swaths of mature forests in the northern part of the prairies, in a dry season, we are always one lightning strike away from a conflagration.

Every cloud with lightning that drifts by puts us on edge. Although, in honesty, "edge" is an understatement; it's fear we feel.

The predominant tree species in this area are jack pine and black spruce, two evergreens that will burn with a vengeance when fire gets into their crowns. In summertime, it's not uncommon for us to be able to see smoke from distant fires.

Because of this, during fire season, I go outside several times each day to look for any visible smoke in the surrounding sky. Some big fires burn for months, which leads to us living in constant fear and being on high alert. I expend large amounts of nervous energy frequently inspecting the perimeter, walking to the overlook, going down to the beach, climbing the ladder up to the roof for a look from a high vantage point, and then resting a bit before rechecking.

Smoke is a fascinating thing to watch from a distance. It tells you a lot about a fire. White smoke means the fire is mostly smoldering or perhaps burning in a bog. Gray smoke indicates the fire is burning strongly, with black smoke signaling the fire is burning with great intensity. At that point, it is likely rolling through the crowns of the trees and moving rapidly.

This is what Johanna and I witnessed in the 2010 Hockley fire when we watched the fire race up one shore of the lake. Evergreens have a volatile oil, which makes them extremely flammable. These forests are so densely packed with trees that once the fire gets up into the tree top, it spreads rapidly from tree to tree; it appears to literally roll through.

Seeing a wall of black smoke with its billowing mushroom cloud high in the sky is an amazing sight. The smoke associated with a large fire can easily rise miles into the atmosphere. Set against a sunny, blue sky, that cloud of smoke is bright white, reminding me of a giant head of cauliflower, complete with puffy lobes. More lobes appear as the cloud constantly, but slowly, changes shape. It's an awesome and stunning sight, but knowing the damage being done on the ground, which is truly frightening, detracts from its beauty.

Fires generally take a break at night--the vicious updraft of hot gases and smoke diminish, and the tall column of smoke dissipates and settles to the ground. Overnight smoldering of the fireline produces copious quantities of smoke, which lays low over a vast territory. Usually with the arrival of daylight and the rising sun, the air is heated and, before long, the fire takes off again. The heated air rises, which draws more air in and, in effect, fans the fire back to life. This is a general rule, hence the need for constant vigilance. We never take a fire for granted. Just as easily, fires *can* burn hard, well into the night.

And they did!

I can only describe seeing the distant orange glow in the sky from our dock at night as an abject sense of fear.

Since the start of our bush life 16 years ago, we've had four scares of nearby clouds of swirling smoke, surging skyward. Each time, these columns of smoke were within a mile of us.

I have mentioned the ferocious power of fires. I distinctly remember once watching a smoldering area until late in the evening. By 9:30 at night, all it was doing was throwing billowing curtains of smoke. I decided I had had enough watching for the day. I figured nothing was going to happen at that late hour, as normally fires taper off when the sun sets, air temperature diminishes, and the nighttime humidity rises.

However, at that moment, I heard a loud explosion. It was as if a bomb had gone off. Apparently, the entire area that was smoldering had caught just the right draft of air and it all went up in one big bang. The volume of air immediately sucked into the firestorm was immense, causing the wind to pick up and the trees to sway violently, as if we were in a hurricane. As we grabbed what we could and ran for our lives down to the boat, we experienced some of the most terrifying minutes we've ever encountered. That fire never got to us, but the ordeal sure was intense.

You assume risks when you are in the wilderness, and the threat of forest fires is one of those risks. We knew we would ultimately have to deal with a fire, but the scale, the frightening size, and the ferocity were a surprise to us. We used fire-resistant metal for the siding and the roofing when we built the house. This material comes in baked enamel paint of various colors. We chose two earth tones, tan and green, finishing the exterior of our home to blend in with the surroundings. The metal was lightweight and was easy to fly in and install on the house.

We had introduced ourselves to the local fire command center when we first moved out here, and we made sure they knew our exact location. To this day, to a degree, I am their eyes on the ground, and many times I will call in a fire to confirm they know about it. Between summer float plane traffic, higher altitude commercial flights, and routine fire patrols, there are a lot of watchful eyes from above, so it isn't often they aren't aware of all fires. Still, a fire can be smoldering and, until it flares up, planes going by may not notice anything unusual.

Saskatchewan Environmental Resources Management (SERM) does a marvelous job of protecting property, but there are times when conditions simply aren't safe for them to land, or manpower and equipment may be stretched thin from battling numerous, simultaneous fires. We planned for an eventual fire by buying a Honda gas-powered water pump, multiple lengths of fire hose, and sprinklers so that we would be prepared in the event the fire crews couldn't get here in time.

Our home is our responsibility to protect, and keeping combustible debris, such as leaves, away from the house and having metal roofing and exterior siding are things we can do to increase the odds in our favor.

What has saved our home twice?

Sprinklers! Both our own system and those of the provincial fire crews. Part of my spring ritual is to head to the house roof and install two sprinklers, one at each end. I also have full-length trees cut, approximately 20- to 25-feet long, and have a sprinkler head attached to the top of each of those trees. We pick locations around our house site where we can stand these trees back up, like big flag poles, and either wire each one to another smaller tree or attach a set of tripod legs to the pole, so that it can be free-standing. The higher these "flag poles," the more coverage and the better the protection. The Honda water pump with a 1½ " firehose delivers pressurized water from our lake to the input side of a manifold, and all the sprinkler feed hoses come off the output of the manifold.

When our property is being defended from a fire, the ground is crisscrossed with various hoses and water lines. The steady drone of the water pump, and the rhythmic "tick, tick, tick" of the sprinkler heads as they sweep through their circular pattern, offer reassurance, a feeling that maybe, just maybe, this will all end well. Water running off the roof, much like it does during a rain storm, reinforces the notion.

Once a fire gets into the crown of the trees, it's hard to stop. So how do sprinklers prevent property from being incinerated?

The basic premise of sprinklers is to bring up the humidity in the protected area as high as possible, before a fire arrives. The dome of humidity has a tendency to bounce the fire around it, allowing the fire to bypass the protected areas. They most certainly will not extinguish a wildfire!

For anyone living in fire-prone areas, this concept will work for you as long as you have a reliable water source. A swimming pool, pond, stream, or even household tap gives you a chance at saving your home. At a minimum, a couple of sprinklers, proper water lines, and a water pump are all that are needed for some cheap insurance.

These days the weather is becoming more extreme, and a little preparation can go a long way. Furthermore, fire isn't limited to certain countries. When conditions are right, any countryside can burn. World news frequently has a story of a major brush or forest fire somewhere in the world.

Our big fire occurred in 2002, the year right after we built and finished the house. That year, we had a late spring with ice never leaving the lake until May 27th. In mid-June, we were aware of rumbles of thunder from small thunderstorms passing through the area, but other than a few drops of rain, we remained parched.

We didn't think anything of it when several water bombers passed by headed north. I went out and waved as they flew by, oblivious to their real mission.

Soon after, the bombers returned southbound, and I noticed a column of smoke in the distant north. Just that quick, it was too late for them to do anything. The fire was out of control. The next day, a glance towards the south showed there was another column of rising smoke.

We were now sandwiched between two large fires, the Nagle fire and the Dobbin fire. The Nagle fire was about 25 miles away, and the Dobbin fire was 14 miles distant.

Can you imagine a fire approximately 25 miles in the distance eventually reaching you?

It can, and it did!

Day after day we watched the clouds of billowing smoke move ever closer. For weeks, we lived with the smell of smoke and a thick haze in the air.

Both fires were moving in our direction, even though one was north of us and the other was to our south. They were each so massive, they were interacting with each other to close the gap between themselves. Winds were ferocious some days, and I heard later that one of the fires traveled 20 miles in a day, driven by those air currents. If true, that is a remarkable rate of travel. Some mornings we awoke to terrible visibility. The smoke was so thick we couldn't see trees 100 yards away. Talk about an eerie feeling and a surreal panorama. The fires were out there, somewhere, coming from two directions, and we couldn't even see 300 feet. We were engulfed in a thick, impenetrable cloud of smoke, much like a dense fog bank enshrouds coastal areas.

These fires were not going to catch us off-guard. We lived in our survival suits during the day, ready to bail out to the lake at a moment's notice. The survival suits are heavy and hot, and on sunny, 80°F to 90°F degree days, they made for a lot of overheated discomfort. At night, I slept upstairs with one eye open and occasionally peered out the windows in all directions to make sure I couldn't see any approaching orange. Having to be constantly vigilant was exhausting.

We knew that the fire command was aware of our situation when they showed up to help with our defense by setting up their own pumps and sprinklers. What a sense of relief it was to be in such a dire situation and then have a plane come in and off-load a bunch of friendly fire personnel, along with their equipment, to give us a hand. I cut a swath through the forest, from one shoreline to the other, which effectively encircled our homestead. Two more pumps and additional sprinklers were set up to soak this cut fireline with an endless supply of water pumped from the lake. I would run the pumps for a few hours, let the water soak into the ground, and then run them another couple of hours. The objective was to keep everything good and wet.

While I was working the chainsaw, I also clearcut a large circle in the woods, big enough to allow a helicopter to land. We now had two ways, float plane and helicopter, for help to arrive if needed. As it turned out, this was a good strategy, because not long after, the chopper pad was utilized.

The fires were too close now, and we were urged to evacuate by chopper. Originally, Johanna was going to head out by herself, and I was going to remain behind to man the pumps. But the situation was so dangerous, and fire command strongly recommended I jump on board too. A helicopter was dispatched to pick us up. This was to be our first experience in a helicopter, and as the chopper circled overhead, I had mixed emotions about abandoning the place. Before we left, we double-checked our setup, made sure everything was fueled up and running, and then lifted off.

To this day, I remember the chopper hovering over our home and, through the smoke, seeing the spray from all the sprinklers as they robotically spun, watering down their individual assigned plots. When flying over the Dobbin fire, which was back-burning towards our home from the north, we could see a seemingly endless smoldering line snaking through the forest, with the occasional tree erupting into flames. Meanwhile, the Nagle fire to the south was burning far more aggressively. The helicopter ferried us to a fire camp, where we were picked up by a float plane, which took us to town, where we stayed with our friend.

My nature is not to accept the inevitable without giving it my best effort, and it wasn't long before I regretted leaving the homestead. I made the decision I was going home and, with some gentle persuasion, I was allowed to jump on a flight. I would have chartered my own flight if I'd had to.

My return came with the understanding I was on my own. This was a serious decision with potentially grave consequences, and the pilot wished me the best of luck.

I arrived home on a sunny but smoky afternoon and did what I came back to do, run water pumps. I had a couple of nervous but uneventful days.

On the day the fire arrived, I received a call via satellite phone warning me the fire was on the move, and there was a good possibility the Dobbin and Nagle fires would merge into one enormous conflagration, with me smack in the middle of the mess. With the northern part of the province immersed in heavy smoke, it was hard for the crews to know exactly what the fires were doing, due to such poor visibility. Later, I heard there were 170 fires burning all at once, and it was a daunting task trying to keep track of them all. While I was outside during that day, a squirrel in a nearby tree came down to about my shoulder height showing no fear of me.

If the squirrel could talk, I really think he wanted to say, "OK, so what's the game plan here? I sense some bad stuff coming."

I really didn't have a good answer for that.

That afternoon, a fire crew landed to fuel the pumps and to double-check our setup. Before leaving, the pilot told me not to worry, the fire was far away. But the native fire crew, who had far more experience than the pilot, told me they sensed it was on its way. They wished me well and then departed.

A few hours later, the situation was starting to look bleak. Although it was only late afternoon, it was getting dark and ash was falling. I went down to the beach and heard a faint rumbling in the distance and saw the southern sky glowing orange. It was showtime, and no force on Earth was going to stop the approach of the inevitable firestorm. I came back to the house, wrote a quick note, and stashed it in our cook stove for safe keeping. If the house burned and I didn't survive, someone, someday, would open the stove and hopefully find an intact piece of paper from me.

"6-27 Thurs. 5:25 pm

To Johanna, family and friends,

I am looking out front window. It's been dark for an hour. Lights needed. Smoke getting moderate. Visibility less than a mile. Orange glow in sky. Ash and small embers falling. Basically calm and quiet here except for faint roar in distance. If something happens to me, know that I loved this place and I wouldn't want to be anywhere else. My love to you all. I did my best.

Love, Ron"

Not long after writing my note, I could hear the freight train approaching in the distance. The freight train was the fire. A fire storm has that chugging sound when it becomes so fierce it vigorously sucks in the surrounding air.

I ran down to the shoreline and looked 4 miles distant towards the end of our lake. All I saw on the horizon was a solid curtain of intense, undulating orange and red flames towering above the treetops.

You talk about dry mouth. I couldn't swallow. My mouth went stone dry in an instant, and I needed some water. To this day, an orange sunset or glow in the sky brings me back to that day and makes my heart skip a beat.

So how now brown cow?

I seem to be in a bit of a dilemma. I could hang here for a while and potentially get trapped at this narrower end of the lake or get in the boat and head in the direction of the fire. Heading towards the fire would take me to a wider part of the lake and would give me a bit more open water as a buffer. I chose to head down the lake towards the fire.

Rarely do we see leeches around the dock, yet now there were dozens of leeches in the water as I hopped into the boat. Even they wanted no part of what was coming.

With the reassuring, steady drone of the three water pumps, I pushed off into the unknown. I spent that night in the lake, in the boat or on an island, depending on the situation. Initially, I got out of the boat and hunkered down in shallow water close to an island that was near the middle of the lake. I pulled the boat over me for protection, as if it were a big metal blanket, since I had no idea what to expect. A wet towel over my head helped to deal with the smoke. I didn't have a smoke mask or any goggles for my eyes, so the wet towel served as an air filter to facilitate breathing. After a time, I gained confidence, occasionally held the wet towel to my face, and just stood up to watch the show.

The sound was like the roar of a jet engine. Whole hillsides, nurtured by nature for decades, took only seconds to burn in one big whoosh. As the flames took out a hill, the roar reached a crescendo when the fire crested the top, the flames swirling in vortexes of hot rising gases. From my island sanctuary, I watched as the fire storm rolled up both shorelines of the lake, moving faster than a person could run. Most islands were not safe, and they burned.

Although I was safe in the middle of the lake, as far as I could see, I was surrounded, and the whole world was on fire. Even though it was dusk, I could see smoke boiling heavenward, illuminated by the glow of the flames. I heard small explosions in the distance, and at the time, I figured they were our home and fuel going up in flames. To this day, I don't know what made those sounds, other than possibly trees or rocks exploding from the heat.

After a time, a ghostly smoke-filled stillness descended over the smoldering landscape. I could still hear the fire in the distance as it moved away. By then, it was night and semi-dark and I thought maybe the worst was over. I made the decision to boat back to the house and take advantage of this lull in the storm; I would attempt to refuel the water pumps, since they had been running for hours and were at risk of quitting.

I slowly worked my way north towards home through an eerie, smoky calm. The closer I got to our homestead, the more nervous I became. My internal danger detector was going off full bore and I stopped and put the motor in to neutral to think about things.

At that moment, I was blindsided by a wall of dense smoke that raced across the lake. I never saw it coming. My eyes were stinging as I gunned the motor to get out of there. As I broke out of the smoke, I could see I was racing right for a glowing orange shoreline. I could feel the heat on my face as I exited stage right and got back down the lake to an area of safety.

There came a time when I felt the fire had run its course, since I couldn't see any serious areas of flame. I went to one of the unburned islands so I could lay down and try for a nap. Although I was able to get somewhat comfy, it was impossible to sleep. Just as well, since the wind began blowing, causing the sky to light back up in bright orange.

The fire came to life again. This thing wouldn't quit.

Hot embers pelted me as I jumped in the boat and headed to the safety of open water. With the wind blowing, the only thing I could do was keep the engine in reverse against the wind and try to stay centered in the middle of the lake, between the glowing orange shorelines. With every gust of wind, the landscape brightened to an intense orange, much like the pulsating coals in one colossal campfire. Our boat motor has always been ultra-reliable, and it proved so again that night. Thankfully!

As I was floating around in the middle of the lake, a lightning bolt flashed and a crack of thunder immediately followed.

Where did that come from?

Then another flash-bang, followed by another. I believe these were a product of the fires, as big fires can create their own weather. I'll never know for sure. I do know I was bobbing around in my aluminum can, in the center of the lake, with lightning bolts cracking all around me.

Surely I wouldn't survive the fire only to be zapped by lightning!

At this point, I was disoriented and had no sense of direction. It was dark, smoky, and starting to rain when I chanced upon an island that hadn't been burned over. Tying the boat to a handy tree, I walked inland and basically hunkered down as low as I could get until the storm passed. You might think my being out in the pouring rain was the final straw. I didn't mind though. The downpour was what really helped quell the fire.

It was 3:00 in the morning when I had just enough light to see to return home. I had no idea what I would find.

Would our house still be standing?

Exhausted and soaking wet from the rain, I sped up the lake towards home, the boat motor full throttle. I had resigned myself to the possibility of seeing a pile of ash where once a proud home had stood.

What a wave of immense relief to see the solar panels on the roof, a beacon barely visible through the haze, shouting to me that we had survived.

I drove the boat hard onto shore, where I jumped out into a dead silent world of calm. Visually, I could make out small fires and hotspots and I immediately gassed up the pumps, got them running, and attached a fire hose with nozzle.

To my amazement, one of the pumps was still fully fueled. It had shut itself down shortly after I had left the previous afternoon. Evidently, the water suction line to the lake had become blocked with floating debris. Automatic shutdown is a safety feature so the pump doesn't self-destruct in the event it runs dry of water. It was unbelievable to realize that the fire came through and one of the pumps with its associated line of sprinklers wasn't running. The fire ran right up to and then around that sprinkler line and kept on going. Fortunately, this pump had been running all day, before the fire showed up, so the area was pretty saturated, but still, we were lucky. Given the intensity of the fire, it's pretty miraculous it didn't fully penetrate that section of line and overrun our homestead.

The fire, however, did lob enough embers into our compound so there were scattered small fires, as well as a smoldering, burning line working its way towards the house. As fast as I could muster, I ran a firehose to this section and, for hours, poured water on all the hotspots. The forest floor steamed and sizzled from all the residual heat in the ground. Astounding!

I stopped the fire's advance in those early morning hours by spraying countless gallons of water on the area, the house only 90 feet from potential destruction. Because of all the smoke, the firefighters weren't able to get in that day to help, so I manned the fire hose by myself, and dealt with the various hotspots that easily could have flared up again.

The following day, crews flew in to help with hotspots that were further away from the house. They ran 800 feet of hose down the line where the burned forest met the still live green trees of the remaining woods. Imagine our surprise when we walked the line and found a grouse nest. Burned up to, and completely around it, the nest sat with five intact eggs, right on the line of fire. That brave mother grouse must have sat on it during the blaze, protecting her eggs, and the group of us could only marvel as we watched the chicks as they broke through their shells. I'm sure the mother was fine and was watching us from a distance.

I am convinced, had I not been here to deal with all the remaining fire and smoldering in the early morning hours, post fire, the outcome would have been far different. We are eternally grateful permission was granted to allow me back to protect the place.

The 2002 fire was like a death to me. The wilderness setting we lived in and adored was now blackened ground with toasted stems where living green trees had once stood. What remained was an ashen landscape where all life had been incinerated, and it broke my heart to see the devastation. In many places, the fire scoured the ground down to sand and cobblestones. Rocks split, and chips flaked off large boulders from the searing heat. The following is a poem I wrote after the fire that I'd like to share with you. Like many northern Saskatchewan lakes, our lake was named in a tribute to a Saskatchewan fallen service member from World War II. This poem "Dear Mr. Hockley" succinctly sums up that day on Hockley Lake.

Dear Mr. Hockley

The firestorm came on June 27.
The lake was consumed at night by 11.
Driven by winds that came from the south.
The wall of flames led to instant dry mouth.

The forest dwellers awoke with an uneasiness that day,
A sixth sense, an instinct that hell was on its way,

A dark foreboding that discounted any sort of play,
Replaced by an urgent need to try to get out of the way.

Smoke and embers in advance from the skies,
The smell of life burning before my eyes.
Twisted smoky shadows with lives of their own
Began with a stray lightning bolt, the seed had been sown.

Surrounded by shorelines glowing brightly you know
I'd look down the lake through a murky haze
To a darkened section with nothing to show
But a single lone tree that was fully ablaze.

Whole hillsides went up with a mighty whoosh.
As I looked around and faced the truth.
The sounds of a freight train and the scenes that I saw
Would be hard to forget, if ever at all.

Your carpets brushed black, your rock exposed,
Flames reached high above your head down to your toes.
The smoke towered as did the glow
Of a fiery orange sky, a heart wrenching show.

Safe on an island, the winds then shifted.
I was forced into the boat where for a time I drifted.
The creation of the fire, lightning, and thunder
Made me again seek shelter where I hunkered down to ponder.

The rhythms of nature over eons unaltered.
My faith in the fire crews never faltered.
Fire threat constant, the countrysides renew,
Thanks to the nameless faces for what they do.

Mortally wounded sentinels on your hill top perch
Once was beautiful spruce, pine and paper birch
Blackened silhouettes on craggy hill,
That some green remains is quite a thrill.

I'll never forget that night on the lake
Hoping much survived in the wake
Of a fire with a life and mind of its own
From small beginnings a monster was grown.

A flicker of orange now replaced by green
By pine cones and seeds that remain unseen
By a new generation that will show
That despite the odds mother nature will grow.

The Nagle/Dobbin fire burned 550,000 acres. Combined with the more recent 2010 Hockley fire, close to three quarters of a million acres have been toasted around here, but recovery is well underway.

Fire is an inevitable, natural occurrence. It's the cycle of life for a forest and plays an important role in its renewal. The burned areas are rife with blueberries and cranberries, which we take advantage of, and they become the perfect habitat for wildlife. The surrounding hillsides are green with 6- to 12-foot pine and spruce, plus even taller poplar and birch. Because fires have burned through the encompassing countryside, we are much safer now that the majority of the fuel has been consumed. Although most of the surrounding area has burned, immediately around our homestead remains a small green zone. A glance out any window makes it seem like nothing ever happened.

The experiences I've had with wildfires have left an indelible mark on me. Johanna teases me that I have a poor sense of smell, but if there's a fire anywhere around, I'll smell smoke. Like a hound dog on the scent, I can detect the slightest molecule of smoke in the air.

Despite the serious title and the scary events we have lived through, there is one humorous story I can share with you. Numerous times when fires have been near, we have had fire crews here helping us. To show our gratitude, Johanna baked and prepared nice meals for them when they stopped in.

Johanna has an herb garden out in front of the house. One year we were dealing with a fire, and she had freshly picked herbs hanging in large bunches by the stove to dry for storage. The guys came in and sat down to eat.

One motioned over to the hanging herbs and said "nice plants!"

I thought to myself, "Well thanks. It will certainly enhance our meals."

It wasn't until later, after they had left, that it hit me. The crew probably thought we had a rack full of pot drying by the stove. I wanted to yell after the plane, "I swear it's not weed, it's bergamot and anise!" But it was too late.

We are forever grateful to the guys and gals of the fire crews. Without their help, it is highly unlikely we would have a standing home in the bush. Words can't thank them enough, so to show our appreciation, I decided to do something concrete. Working with hand tools, it took me about a year to make a small end-table cabinet with a Birdseye maple top. By hand, I chipped-carved the drawer face and cabinet door with a decorative pattern.

I presented the cabinet to the fire managers and the crew in La

Ronge, who were taken by surprise that someone would make this effort. In turn, they donated the cabinet to the Royal University Hospital burn unit in Saskatoon, where it is now proudly on display in the waiting room. I am so pleased.

Hockley Lake fire viewed from homestead

Johanna watering the area

One of the many sprinklers set atop poles

Too close!

Working toward the homestead

Total devastation

View from our home of the opposite side of the bay

Chapter 13—

Dump Run Swim

Have you ever wondered what it would be like to go for an impromptu swim in 40°F lake water?

Speaking from personal experience, and a body that still quivers at the thought, I can say that while invigorating, stimulating, and otherwise bracing, the experience is far from pleasant. Let me tell you about the day I took an ice water bath.

Coexisting in an area with bears, we have to be careful about any food waste or smells around the homestead, which would entice them. Bears have an acute sense of smell and often skirt the shoreline of lakes foraging for food. In order to discourage any unwelcome visits, we are meticulous in how we deal with food scraps.

About a mile down the lake is a spot where we dump bones, corn cobs, and other hard-to-compost food items. We keep a plastic bucket with a lid downstairs in the utility area for the collection and storage of these food scraps. Over the course of the winter, we fill the scrap bucket and then make a dump run in the spring, as soon as the lake is icefree, to empty its contents. Animals always find the scrap pile and scatter things about, so every few years, before I dump the bucket, I'll rake and collect any good compost from this dump site to till into the garden.

My cold water exploit occurred within a couple of years of the big fire of 2002. Spring was delayed that year, and we patiently waited for the ice to melt from the lake. After a long winter, we had a scrap bucket brimming with smelly, decomposing food stuffs. As long as the lid was on, we were safe, but as soon as we took off the lid to add more scraps, P. U., it was a nose-holding affair. We were forced to savor the aroma long after the lid was thrust back on, as the smell lingered like a fog in a low-lying valley. Finally the day arrived when the ice departed from the lake, and I eagerly put the boat and motor into the water. It was time to take our scrap bucket for a ride.

I threw the bucket in the front of the boat (the bow for you sea-faring folk), fired up the motor, and zoomed down the lake.

How I love taking the boat out for a drive on a sunny day, with the warm breeze caressing my face, which was made nicer by the fact it was the season's first ride.

Because we live far from help, we always make it a habit to wear our life vests when out on the lake, whether in the boat or canoe. Additionally, although I have always been athletically inclined, my swimming abilities are comparable to those of a stone, and without a life vest, stone and I end up in the same place, the bottom of the lake. If I try to float, I invariably end up vertical trying to keep my nose above water. I took swimming lessons in my twenties and was told there are some people that just don't have the buoyancy to float. I'm one of them, and I know I make good entertainment for anybody watching me try. So donning life vests prior to either boating or canoeing is mandatory.

Barely a ripple was seen on the lake surface this beautiful spring day; the only air movement I felt came from the forward movement of my boat barreling down the lake, and then, all too quickly, the jaunt was over. I had reached the dump site. I let the boat drift onto the sand beach. Clambering up to the front of the boat, I grabbed the bucket and jumped out on to a narrow stretch of sand. Since this was to be a quick stop, I kept my life vest on and only pulled the boat slightly onto shore, without bothering to tie it up.

What could possibly happen in the minute it takes to walk the 15 feet to the dump pile, pull off the bucket lid, and dump out its contents?

Walking the short distance to the dump pile, I inhaled deeply, removed the lid, and vigorously shook out the contents on to the ground. The stench was overpowering as I went back to the water's edge, dipped the bucket in, swished it around, and went back to empty the rinse water onto the pile. My attention was suddenly diverted to a noise coming across the lake--a minor roaring sound off in the distance, increasing in pitch. Without thinking, I set the bucket down, then started walking along the shoreline to a clearer vantage point. From the stillness, I became aware of a gentle breeze as I got to an area where the coastline turned away from me at a sharp angle.

It was then, as an afterthought, that I turned back towards the boat and saw it had freed itself from shore. The wind was slowly taking it "out to sea."

This was an *uh oh* moment, since I was approximately a mile from home.

I had no time to ponder the event, and I immediately ran back to where the boat had just been, jumped into the icy cold water, and started swimming after my SS Minnow. I managed to get hold of the bow, which sits high above the water, but there was no way I was going to launch myself out of the water like Flipper and get back into the boat. Fortunately, a rope was tied to the bow, and I was able to grab hold and swim the boat back to the beach. Initially, the boat, blown by the breeze, was taking me further away from shore and safety, but I was able to halt its progress, reverse course, and gain enough momentum to take me and the boat toward land.

I'd like to say I put the rope between my teeth and swam with strong, muscular strokes, but in truth, I was holding the rope in one hand, while at the same time, doggie-paddling and inventing new swim strokes as I desperately inched my way back to the beach.

It took no time for me to get cold from this immersion, and I was relieved when I finally felt the lake bottom under my feet and was able to drag myself and the boat up to land. Once safely on shore, I climbed back into my wayward ship and got my chilled-to-the-bone self home. Since ice had only been out a couple days, water temperature was in the upper 30s to low 40s Fahrenheit, which was body-numbing. This episode was a valuable lesson, and now I always tie the boat to a nearby tree when I disembark.

In all the commotion of running back and swimming after my boat, I had totally lost focus on the noise that had initially caught my attention. That day I actually knew what was coming towards me from across the lake, when without thinking, I had wandered off to take a peek at it.

We have an interesting phenomenon that I've never seen anywhere else. Although I have no scientific proof, I believe it's associated with the fires we have had in the past as well as the local topography. With tree foliage burned off, the sun beats down on the exposed blackened Earth, heating the ground and creating rising air currents that interact with the nearby hills. Under the right circumstances, on dead calm, sunny days, we get mini-twisters out of nowhere. They are powerful enough to lift water off the lake and, on land, we can hear sticks and tree limbs snapping as the wind swirls around. It can be serene, and all of a sudden, we hear and sometimes see these mini-twisters coming.

As it so happened, this is what I was hearing that day and what I had set off to investigate, leaving the boat unattended. Thinking I would saunter over to get a better view and be a spectator to one of nature's mysteries, my cold water fortitude was tested when nature threw me a curve ball. Fortunately, the small twister either dissipated quickly or diverted away from me, as I didn't need to contend with any additional wind while I was out frolicking in the surf!

Looking back, I realize I was pretty lucky that day. If I couldn't have gotten that boat back to shore fairly quickly, I would have been faced with a decision. One that in hindsight, is easy, but at the time, the choice wasn't so clear cut. Do I stay and float with the boat, or do I let it go and try to get myself back to shore?

On this relatively warm day, as long as I made it to shore, I could have made the long trek around the shoreline to get home.

Using the canoe, we could have eventually paddled back to retrieve the drifting boat. Fortunately, things worked out, and I was able to boat home just fine, albeit quite chilled. I walked into the house where Johanna asked why I was all wet.

Do I tell her I just developed a condition where I sweat profusely, or do I tell her I did something stupid and I went for a swim after a renegade boat?

From now on, I'll leave the cold swim to the polar bears and patiently wait for the water to warm before taking the plunge. In case you're wondering, my vest is on even when taking a summer dip. We're much too far from help to take any chances.

Another amusing event happened more recently. It was an awe-inspiring, heroic, and jaw-dropping event. Towards the tail end of summer, we had a beautiful sunny, warm day, and I asked Johanna if she fancied a boat ride around the lake. Every year we try to cruise the entire lake shoreline at least a couple of times, just to get some fresh air and see the sights. Although the lake is only 4 miles long, by the time we travel the entire coast, in and out of bays and around islands, it's more like a 10- to 12-mile ride. Several times we've been lucky enough to be in the right place at the right time to see nesting loons and ducks or a moose cow with her calf using one of the islands as a nursery. We never know what interesting things will catch our attention.

On this particular occasion, we grabbed the life vests and made our way down to the dock. I put on my one-hundred-dollar, 30-year-old, aviator style sun glasses, since the sun was blazing, and, as I was captain, they make me look boss. We took it slowly and were putt-putting along the shoreline, enjoying the scenery and being attentive to any movements in the brush.

We had been out for about 15 minutes, and had worked our way a short distance down the lake, when some monstrosity of a fly, at least it seemed large at the time, made a bee line for me and hit me in the face. All in one motion, my head jerked back from the impact of the collision, or maybe I jerked my head back involuntarily.

Having a brain that's no match for my lightning-fast reflexes, I instinctively swatted at my face, my index finger catching the corner of the frame on my sunglasses. In the blink of an eye, my sunglasses were flung over my shoulder and into the lake.

You might have this mental image of sunglasses, flipping end-over-end in slow motion over my shoulder, as I mouth the word *nooooo*, but it was over in an instant as my glasses went *kerplunk*, headed to Davy Jones' locker.

Talk about awe-inspiring, heroic, and jaw dropping. What a moron!

The topography of our lake bottom is as diverse as the surrounding land with its many hills, valleys, and flats. Deposited by the last glaciers, rock and boulders are a prominent feature at the water's edge, extending both onto land as well as into the water. Unless I beach the boat on one of the few sand beaches, at any other location, I'll be scraping rocks as I approach the shore. Within a short distance of stepping into the water, we encounter contrasting terrain, as varied as sharp, boulder strewn drop-offs versus flat, shallow areas. For variety, a few sand bars jut out from prominent spits of land. It is this assortment of lake features that makes this body of water so interesting and suitable for fish habitat.

The particular area where my sunglasses lay on the bottom was perhaps one-hundred feet from shore. The coast along this area is scalloped into a series of increasingly deep indentations, creating small bays. Because of this land feature, and the fact I was relatively close to shore, I thought I had a shot at finding my glasses in short order.

As luck would have it, water depth was 15 feet, and no matter how hard I tried to peer into the depths, the bottom remained elusive. The clarity of the water is dependent on many factors and varies throughout the year. Our lake is clear and cold, but wind, water temperature, plant pollens, microorganisms, and seasons have a bearing on the turbidity of the water.

After finishing our cruise without tossing anything else overboard, I retrieved my snorkel face mask from the house and boated back to the area of my submerged sunglasses. I figured by kneeling in the back of the boat, with my face in the water, I could slowly troll over the area, and maybe catch a glint of sunlight reflecting back to me from the glasses below. I knew the general area to search, but it was still a fairly large area, visibility was poor, and I failed to locate my glasses.

Now I really thought my chances of finding them were slim to none. My only hope was that a fish would find my shades, put them on, and I'd catch the fish wearing them while I was out fishing.

The following week, I went back several times, tied the boat to shore, and took to the water, snorkeling over the area. I used the shoreline as a reference point and, with snorkel and flippers, slowly cruised in the straightest line I could muster. When I thought I had gone well beyond the range, I'd move over a couple yards and work my way back in a grid pattern. I even tried waiting until dark and then probed the depths with a strong flashlight, without success.

Ultimately, I did locate my sunglasses. The secret was waiting for a dead calm day with full sun overhead, but even then, swimming across the surface with snorkel and face mask, I was barely able to see them at the bottom. I marked their location with a weight and fishing bobber I had in tow, just in case I got lucky. Then I fashioned a wire hook, attached it to a couple sections of fiberglass chimney cleaning rod I retrieved from the boat, and by doing the dead man's float sprawled out in the water, over my glasses, I was just able to catch a corner of the frame with the wire hook. Gingerly, I made my way to shore with my sunglasses in tow. My frustration was over, and I was happy I had persevered.

It was a joyous reunion between me and my sunglasses. I'm back to looking boss!

Ship captain looking boss on his yacht

Chapter 14–

Slush Makes for Poor Sledding

Weather here has its extremes and challenges, but we have little to worry about as far as floods, tornadoes, earthquakes, and hurricanes are concerned. Summers can get quite hot, with readings of 90°F not that unusual. The season's first snowflakes usually arrive in September, but never stay for long. The earliest snow we have ever had was September 11th, which was much too soon. At that time of the year, the ground still has lots of residual heat from summer, so any snow accumulation is short-lived. The weather is likely to warm again for a brief period before freezing temperatures settle in for good. But those snowflakes are a warning shot of what is to come and provide the impetus to pick up the pace on any remaining outdoor work and activities.

Winter is long and cold. The -57°F I mentioned previously is an extreme example. When it's that cold, we stay inside. But many times we'll go for walks at -20°F to -30°F, and as long as I'm active, I have worked in -40°F temperatures, but that's really pushing it.

How do we deal with the cold? Clothes!

We never go out in the cold without clothes on. We'd end up as one big frost bite! Without clothes in summer: one big bug bite!

But, seriously, we have good winter clothes and coats, and dress in layers, beginning with long underwear. Both of us have good down-filled parkas and warm boots. Sometimes I wear a knitted wool face mask. Hand warmers, stowed in a pocket, are handy too. Regardless of temperature, when wearing the right clothes and expending a little energy, I can break into a sweat. Many times, I've had to open up my coat so I wouldn't overheat.

There is such a contrast between open water and ice-covered lakes. A frozen lake is static and seems so lifeless, while open water, with its accompanying waves, is so dynamic. We like both states, but feel more alive and vibrant in summer, when the lake is teeming with activity and wildlife. Even on a dead calm day, the lake surface mirror-like, there is always movement, although it may be hard to see.

Stand with me on the dock, and we'll see the splash of jumping fish or, over by the rocky protrusion of the nearby point, we'll see the surface become pockmarked with small concentric rings, signifying bait fish are feeding on specks of food that are floating along. When the light is just right, we see bugs of all kinds skittering across the surface, leaving more visible tracks than the eye can focus on.

Therein lies the secret of observation: don't focus, but let your eyes take it all in. Allow your peripheral vision to capture a world full of animation, even on this dead calm day. By not zeroing in on a specific image, you will see more of the subtle movements. A gaze into the water may reveal a school of bait fish passing through or a myriad of submerged insects, some crawling around on the bottom, which will soon become predators.

Dragonflies, hundreds of them, will emerge from their underwater world to patrol the air, thereby helping to control the bug population. How wonderful it is to have a large dragonfly land on my arm, a moose fly in its jaws, and hear the chomping sounds as it devours its meal. Wonderful, because that means there is one less blood-sucking, flying insect to torment man and beast. Rest in the sunshine for a minute, digesting your meal, dragonfly, and then go forth and catch another bug!

On a warm day, with the sun shining high overhead, we might see the 20-inch pike that rests in the shade of our dock. It used to speed off with a quick flick of its tail whenever we would walk on to the dock, but it has become accustomed to us and now just hangs suspended in the shallow water, close enough to touch.

In the blink of an eye, the stillness can be overtaken by a wind, waves driven on to the beach in rapid, frothing succession. We better hold on to our hats if we go down to the beach, when high winds are coming from the southwest. That direction allows the wind to come straight up the lake, roiling it, violently bobbing our boat at its berth, the vessel secured only by two small diameter ropes. Thanks to the wind, there won't be much in the way of biting insects today, and the boat will remain where it is, tethered to the dock, bouncing as every wave hits the bow. No boat ride today.

As I look across a snow-covered lake, the wind whipping the snow into sheets that drift into swirled random patterns as it blows across the surface, gives me the sense I'm in the middle of a frozen tundra that is devoid of all life other than the two of us.

And, yet, a walk on a more hospitable day onto this frozen tundra, an expanse of nothing but white, clearly shows the tracks of animal activity. The foot prints and subsequent glide imprints of an otter, the hurried prints of a hare running for cover, the jumbled hoof tracks of a moose that has foraged along the shoreline, or the large paw prints of a wolf traveling through the territory, are evidence we are not alone. There is life in the animal kingdom, albeit at a slower pace in this harsh environment.

Below the frozen lake surface, the fish have slowed down in their much darkened world, dark not only from the lack of sunlight due to shorter day length, but also from the snow that covers the ice surface. The thick layer of ice seals off the vagaries of weather, a tranquil world until the ice relinquishes its grip. A definite quiet descends on the world when the lake is frozen.

There are two facets of lake living we will miss greatly when the time comes to permanently leave our lake home. They are the winter freeze-up and the spring thaw. Both freeze-up and spring thaw are exciting times, and I'll try to describe what occurs during these transitions. These are the two times of the year when we are really on our own. The float planes are out of the water during freeze-up, and off the ice during spring thaw. During these time periods, we can't be reached by bush plane until the lake either freezes, so a plane on skis can land, or there is enough open water for a plane on floats to get in. The only transportation alternative is an expensive helicopter. The area I cleared during the fires is still maintained as an opening in the forest, one we can utilize as a chopper landing pad in an emergency.

This leads to some thoughts on safety. What happens if we have a fire in the dead of winter and the house burns down? That's not good.

We've given ourselves a fighting chance by having a stash of survival gear safely stowed in the woods, away from the house. Two containers serve as storage for flares, clothing, tent, and heavy sleeping bags. In the event the unthinkable happens, maybe we can survive it. With the two chest freezers outside, we are banking on them not being destroyed by a house fire. The intact contents would give us a large supply of food to sustain us until help arrives.

Freeze-up is never the same from one year to the next. Usually it is well under way by mid-November, but there was one cold autumn when the lake was skimmed over completely by the end of October. Depending on temperatures and wind, freeze-up can occur all at once on a frigid calm night, or sections of the lake can freeze over the course of a few days.

It's during these times that ice fog can develop from plummeting air temperatures, while the water is still warm. Drifting off the lake, the ice fog will create a coating of hoar frost on all surfaces and trees will have a thick, crystalline layer of frost. A glance outside makes it appear as though we had snow overnight, but it's just everything covered in a thick rime. The immediate shoreline, which is in contact with the fog, gets the brunt of this icy coating. Branches of Jack pine have needles that surround a central stem, much like a long bristle-bottle brush. Hoar frost coats the slender needles, adding up to an inch of delicate, white, crystalline encrustation. When the angle of the sun is just right, the sunlight refracts through the frosty coating, transforming the stark, cold landscape into a glittering winter wonderland. It's really quite beautiful.

Freezing lakes are noisy. Amazingly, freezing water produces a variety of sounds, and the volume of those sounds is astounding. Most of the noise occurs at night, as temperatures drop, with the first two to four weeks of freeze-up being the most active.

We are living inside a super insulated home, but we can hear the lake groaning loudly. Sometimes it rumbles like nearby thunder. Other times it booms, almost like an explosion, with reverberations echoing off the hill sides. The power is enormous when the lake ice or frozen ground makes a sudden expansive move. Although not very common, when that happens, our house shudders and shakes briefly as the tremor goes through.

Once the lake skims over, we generally figure another four to six weeks before there is enough ice to land a bush plane. The ice forms pretty quickly, as long as the weather cooperates. Significant snow fall right after the lake skims over can be detrimental, since the snow acts as an insulating layer. In that event, the ice will take longer to form. Compounding the situation, if there is enough snow on top of the ice, the weight of the snow forces water up in some areas, creating slush on the ice surface.

From the air, "spider holes" are easily seen, usually in bays, but they can be found anywhere on the lake. Having a central hole with irregular fingers radiating outward, they look like a wet area surrounded by snow. The irregular fingers serve as drainage channels through which water on the surface drains back into the hole. Perhaps they are created when warmer lake water is pushed upward through a crack in the ice and floods the lake surface. The initial flaw in the ice could be a small crack, an animal access point likely used by an otter, or even trapped air bubbles that weaken the ice in that spot. Regardless of how they form, spider holes are dangerous and should be avoided.

We likely will not know if slush exists until we either walk or snowmobile on the lake. The lake can look like a snow covered wonderland, but slush may be lurking underneath. Anybody who has snowmobiled on lakes is familiar with how bad slush can be. It can stop a snowmobile in its tracks, which is what happened to me once.

One year I headed down the lake on our snowmobile to check the safety of the ice. I like to make a solo run to be sure everything is safe, before Johanna hops on the back for an excursion. After several miles, I traveled down to a part of the lake that widens out and ultimately terminates in smaller bays. I made the mistake of riding into a small bay and, as I looped through, I started to bog down.

Until I drove into the area, I had no way of knowing that underneath the snow was a thick layer of water and slush. We have a heavy work snowmobile, and I didn't have the power or speed to get back up on top of the snow again. Although I had the throttle full bore, my forward progress slowed and then came to a complete standstill as the track spun and water and slush were thrown off behind me. I was stopped in my tracks. Once I got off the sled, I was standing in 8 inches of water, which was covered by knee-deep snow.

This water was coming from somewhere. Where's the hole or crack?

In situations like this, ice thickness is always a concern. Standing in water on top of the ice, I worried about whether there was enough ice to support me and the snowmobile. There was really no way to know unless I bored a hole with an ice auger or broke through the ice.

As a kid, I broke through the ice on a small local pond and was mid-thigh in cold water. By the time I got home, my pants were frozen. It was an experience I didn't care to repeat. This time my pants remained dry but, because my boots weren't waterproof, ice water was seeping in. To complicate matters, I was several miles from home.

Walking back home without snowshoes was a long slog, especially in water-logged boots. I managed to get home and then threw camping gear, snowshoes, shovel, and a jack on a tote sled and pushed that sucker 2 miles back down the lake to the snowmobile.

Our tote sled is a heavy metal-framed sleigh on runners with a hitch so that it can be towed behind the snowmobile, but this time I was the horsepower. It is great for moving firewood while snow is on the ground or hauling auger and fishing gear down the lake for a day of ice fishing. For this occasion, I was hauling camping gear, along with everything else, as I was prepared to camp overnight if I couldn't get the sled free by dark. As I pushed the tote sled down the lake to the snowmobile, I noticed some large paw prints in my previously made tracks. I had no idea a wolf had been following me home as I trudged through the snow. Unfortunately, I never looked back to see it.

Upon reaching the snowmobile, I placed the handyman jack under the rear bumper, raised the back end of the machine, shoveled snow under and in front of it, and then tamped down the snow. I knew if I threw enough snow into the slushy area, it would absorb the water and become a more solid mass. Temperatures were very cold, so it took no time for all of this to freeze. Once I was confident the packed snow and slush had had enough time to set, I carefully removed the jack and fired up the snowmobile. I only had one shot to accelerate and garner enough momentum to make it out, otherwise I would bog down again and have to repeat the process until I escaped the slushy area.

After the snowmobile warmed up, a nervous exhale, and a quick thought of "sure hope this works so I can get out of here," I gunned the throttle, and the snowmobile, in a burst of speed, with spinning track and flying snow, shot forward onto a solid layer a safe distance from the watery pitfall. I stopped at that point, walked back several hundred yards to retrieve the tote sled, hooked it up to the snowmobile and cruised on home with another adventure under my belt. So, yes, I can say with authority that slush does make for poor sledding.

If you think about it, slushy conditions are also pretty nasty for the float planes that fly about the north in the winter. They have to land on virgin, snow-covered lakes. Although I've never seen a float plane get truly stuck, I've seen one take a few minutes to free itself from the lake surface.

One time we had to do a little digging to free up the skis of a plane that had just brought us home. We had landed, off loaded, and the plane was ready to leave but wouldn't budge. Usually, we stand a safe distance from the plane to watch it take off. In winter, the thrust of the prop throws a wake of snow a long way behind the plane and we invariably get a face full of wind and snow, which diminishes as the plane progresses away from us.

That day, the Single Otter refused to move; the only thing that happened was we got faces full of wind-blown snow. A trick a pilot uses to free a stuck airplane is to throttle the engine up and rock the plane in order to break it loose from the frozen surface. Unfortunately, the trick didn't work this time and the pilot powered down. With a shovel, I dug the skis free in short order, and the plane was on its way.

There's something about watching a plane rev up and taxi down the lake, the shrill of the engine echoing off the hillsides. It gives us peace of mind when we see the plane safely on its way, and it's satisfying to watch a takeoff. If flying costs weren't so expensive, it'd be a cheap thrill. Back at the float plane base, there are a couple of small diameter poles laid out on the lake surface where the plane parks, so that the skis rest on these poles and not directly on the ice. Sitting on these poles, with the engine covered by a heater jacket, the plane is always ready for the next run.

From the air, experienced pilots will look for an area they are confident has the least potential for slush. Over the intercom, the pilot will tell me he's going to come in, touch down and travel on the surface some distance at full power, and then lift off again. Once back in the air, he'll circle around to evaluate the tracks he just left in the snow. They'll turn a grayish color if water starts seeping into the tracks. If there's no indication of poor conditions, he'll give another shot at landing. If the tracks start to fill with water, the pilot will repeat the test procedure in another location on the lake.

Once we have touched down, the pilot will keep us skimming across the snow at a fast clip until we reach the target drop-off zone. At this point, we'll start to circle the zone at a moderate rate of speed, fast enough to maintain adequate momentum in case we need to throttle up and exit the area. As we loop back and around these tracks many times, the pilot is looking at the ski imprints to make sure they don't start filling with water.

Basically, we make large circles where we want to be dropped off and confirm the area has little to no slush. As long as we have speed, the pilot can always throttle up and get out of a bad situation. Once he stops, we're committed, and it may be a problem moving again if the skis get mired in slush. By using this technique, the pilot has always been able to find a safe place to park the plane, long enough for us to get out and unload.

It's a rush to unload the plane so it can take off again. The colder it is, the more likely the plane's skis will freeze to the snow and the harder it will be to get airborne again. Additionally, the colder it is, the faster the engine will cool down and the harder it will be to restart. Sometimes, the pilot will pull out the engine blanket and throw it over the engine area to keep in the heat.

One particular year, we were being flown home after an extended time away. The lake had a couple feet of snow on top of the ice, temperatures were below zero, and we were returning to an unheated house that was well below freezing inside. We used the Single Otter to fly home, since we were returning with a large pile of gear and food. We landed, but because of slushy conditions, had to disembark about a quarter of a mile from the house. Not only is that a long way from the house, but it is also a long distance to break trail.

Johanna helped the pilot unload while I struggled to get to the house, post-holing through the deep snow the entire way, ice water filling my boots with each step. In a situation like this, it's a balance between getting the plane unloaded so it can get airborne again, and making it to the house to confirm communication equipment powers up. It is imperative, that, at a minimum, the computer and satellite fire up so we can communicate with the outside world. It would be bad news for the plane to leave and then we discover we have no way of contacting civilization.

Therefore, a top priority whenever we come home is not letting the plane leave without first verifying we have functioning communications. Tin cans and string won't cut it.

Once we are home and the plane has departed, it is a mad rush to get a fire going in the stove, and move all the perishables off the lake and into the house before they freeze. Crates of eggs, oranges, grapes, and the like don't take well to freezing and, at below zero temperatures, the race is on to lug them, one way or another, into the house.

Even though we are coming back to a cold house, the indoor temperature is always warmer than the outside temperature, and with the stove burning vigorously, it doesn't take long before the house is above freezing.

Before we left the house months ago, Johanna prepared the fire for lighting by placing kindling and firewood in the stove. It's just a matter of putting a lit match to it and we can begin heating the house. Hopefully, the snowmobile starts right up and it doesn't get stuck in the deep snow or bog down in the lake slush. There have been occasions when the sled did get stuck, and we had to walk every box up the hill to the house.

What grueling ordeals. By the end of the day, we were both spent!

Spring breakup is a wonderful experience. Not only are the days getting longer but animals are more active and we are secure in the knowledge we've survived another winter—not to mention it's fantastic to be outdoors on warm days. North of 56 degrees latitude, spring has the nasty habit of giving us hope one day, with 50°F temperatures and melting and then the next day dashing that hope with snow and a temperature of 10°F. But once we get over that hurdle, it is an interesting event.

Breakup begins with snow pack diminishing until all the snow has melted off the ice. Then the ice starts melting along the shoreline, slowly at first, but as more water is exposed and warms, the ice recedes more quickly. Every night the narrow band of open water along the shorelines refreezes, but each day we make a little more headway as the area that thaws becomes more expansive.

With the aid of the shining sun, melt water forms, which

collects on top of the ice, forming large shallow pools. We can see water running into holes that started as small cracks. The force of the draining water creates small eddies that swirl in the holes. With the setting sun and cooler night temperatures, the melting is arrested and those shallow pools drain. If the melted surface refreezes overnight, it will likely be white the next morning, and as melting occurs that day, the surface will eventually turn a grayish color. Sooner or later, a time will come when the night temperature stays above freezing, allowing the rate of ice melt to accelerate.

Lake ice doesn't melt like a big ice cube. As it melts, the ice starts to honeycomb and melt water trickles down through small, nearly invisible fractures. It is through these cracks and small air bubbles, which were frozen in time during freeze-up, that melt water flows, eroding the ice as it permeates the layer. The lake goes through stages of melt, with the color of the ice changing from white to gray, to dark gray, to finally black, as the thickness of the ice decreases.

When the ice turns dark, we know we are getting close to ice out. By the time the remaining ice is 6 inches thick, we are able to pick up chunks that shatter into dozens of smaller fragments, as though they were sheets of glass that had been dropped.

Wind plays a big role in how fast the ice melts. Think of it as a big fan blowing air across the surface of the ice. Once the ice sheet has melted along all of the shoreline, it becomes a free-floating mass, able to be pushed around by the wind. Holes further out will start to open as wind keeps working their edges. If the ice is weak enough around its edges, we will hear a tinkling sound as the wave and wind action loosens small shards of ice. Bays are the first to shed their icy shackles, the water no longer confined by a frozen layer. Soon thereafter, smaller ice sheets break away from the main body and are driven by the wind currents on to land or into each other. More and more chunks break off, and soon there are wide open expanses of water, not only along the shoreline but further out.

The direction ice sheets move is, of course, determined by the wind. It is both fascinating and scary to see a sheet of ice maybe ¾ mile long being pushed down the lake, towards our shoreline. Once the sheet has momentum, it's hard to stop and it will start piling up on shore as the ice keeps advancing, pushed by the wind.

All the while, it is fracturing and breaking up, and there is no mistaking the sound--a sound resembling high-volume static from a radio. If we are outside, we will hear the crunching and grinding of ice being thrust up onto the shore. We have several rocky points of land that jut into the lake where we go for a first-hand, closeup look at ice piling up on the rocks. Eventually, the sheet comes to a halt, melts a little, and then is driven on to the rocks again by the wind.

It's alarming when the sheet of ice is heading for our dock. The dock is no match and has lost every battle against the ice. It will push the dock up onto shore or tear it apart. We've seen it happen. When we hear lumber snapping into pieces, we know the dock is not faring too well. Once the ice is on the move, within a day, the lake can be ice-free. Between the melting power of the sun, the fanning action of the wind across the ice surface, the action of waves on the ice sheet edges, and the sheet being physically driven onshore, it is amazing how fast a mile-long expanse of ice can disappear.

Here today, gone tomorrow. That fast! We have gone from hopelessness that the ice will never go, to let's go canoeing--all in one day.

The last tenacious remnants of winter, scattered piles of ice on various shorelines, will quickly disappear and, with any luck, it will be the last of the frozen white stuff until next fall. We generally figure May 13th as the target for ice out. Anything before that date is a bonus. We've been ice-free as early as April 29th and, on the flip side, we have endured an excruciatingly slow melt that lasted until May 31st.

Spring breakup, getting close to ice-out

Tough sledding

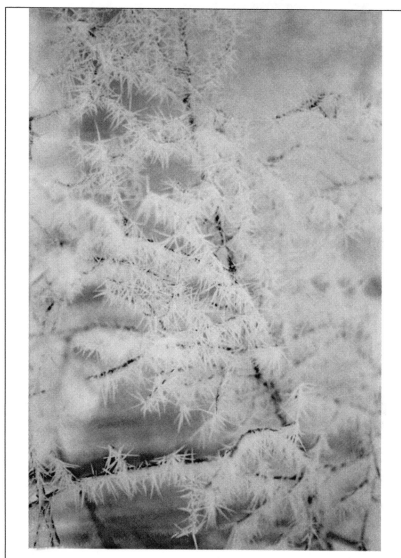

Tree branches laden with delicate crystal spikes from prolonged ice-fog

Chapter 15—

Camp Life

Living remote in the bush has many advantages. But one of the disadvantages is how unfeasible a daily commute is to a job. Neither one of us are aviators, and although I tease the pilot that flying a plane looks so easy--push that button, give it some throttle, and move that lever--we rely on the professionals who fly the charter planes whenever we need to travel in or out. Although our expenses are relatively low, having some yearly income is a necessity. Two givens in life are death and taxes, and since we're still kicking, taxes need to be paid. Insurances, satellite internet, television, and phone are some of the other monthly and yearly bills that require cash.

The quandary is, how do we get a job when we live so far away from things?

With the experience I gained building both houses, and the bandsaw mill, I had a good foundation when it came time for a job search. Carpentry, or something requiring handyman skills, might be in demand. Plus, reliable workers are a scarce commodity. In this region, having someone who is reliable and who shows up for work each day is a treasured asset.

As it so happened, I was visiting an acquaintance in La Ronge while we were out on one of our semi-annual supply runs. He caters to the mineral exploration industry building camps, delivering groceries and supplies, and generally meeting the needs of any exploration customer. Thanks to him, my first opportunity in the industry came when he asked me if I wanted to tend a camp.

Sure, I told him. What do I have to do to tend a camp?

He told me that there was a camp located well north of our home and that it was unoccupied by the exploration company's personnel. There was a caretaker on site who had been there for a while, and he was evidently anxious to go home. As his replacement, I would be responsible for protecting the company property from inquisitive people and animals while the camp was unoccupied. I would be flown in to work a five-week shift.

"Work" is a misnomer since there was very little that needed to be done. I would need to monitor the kitchen, which had fully stocked shelves of food, and fill and keep the oil stoves and generator running. Without someone around, animals would have access to a supermarket of food from the kitchen. Although this camp was a remote, fly-in location, an extensive network of ATV and bulldozer trails throughout the area could be used to access the compound. For anyone coming in by ATV, it would be a long, arduous journey, but the trip could be made, and while there, I did have several visits from people who made the trek.

Late one afternoon, in the fall of 2007, a Single Otter plane loaded with food, fuel, and supplies, stopped in to pick me up on its way north to the job site. It wasn't easy leaving Johanna out here alone for the next five weeks and, as the pilot made a last low pass over our house, I could see her waving goodbye as she stood on our dock. I worried for her safety.

The flight north lasted about an hour, and as we circled the camp in preparation for landing, I was both excited and apprehensive, wondering what the next five weeks had in store for me.

The plane touched down on a wind-blown, white-capped lake surface. A Single Otter, capable of holding up to ten passengers, is a pretty big plane, perfect for the bush, but that day we bobbed on the surface like a cork while the pilot struggled to turn us around. Planes generally land facing into the wind, and as it so happened this day, the wind was coming from a direction that required the plane to turn around on the water once we landed.

Camp was behind the aircraft and, one way or another, we had to make a U-turn. This can be a dangerous maneuver on a blustery day. All it takes is a gust of wind to catch the wing in just the right way, and in a split second, we can be flipped over, with the plane's belly facing skyward. That quick and we would be in a survival situation, a situation in which we would be forced to try to exit the plane before it fills with water. Thankfully, with skillful maneuvering, the pilot was able to time his turn to coincide with a break in the wind, and we taxied to the dock, where we were greeted by the departing caretaker.

The dock was a sturdy, wooden structure that jutted out perpendicular to shore. It was easily long enough for a plane to park parallel to it and be secured. As soon as I climbed out of the plane, I was in a rush to learn as much as I could about the camp from the outbound custodian in the short time we had together. We did a quick cursory tour, and then dealt with the cargo on the plane. We hastily off-loaded drums of fuel, cases of food, and miscellaneous supplies to the dock. These food and provisions would last at least six weeks, and all of it needed to be hauled up to camp before dark. Food consisted of the staples such as flour, eggs, bread, and sugar as well as a variety of canned goods and frozen meats. I wouldn't starve.

As he got on to the plane, my predecessor's parting advice to my continued questions was, 'You'll figure it out," and before I knew it, the plane was racing down the lake, with first one float, and then the other, lifting off the surface.

I watched as the Otter zoomed over the treetops, quickly became a speck in the distance, before it finally disappeared. I stood on the dock, overwhelmed with a sense of aloneness, as the engine sounds faded and were replaced with the only other noise, the muffled drone of the generator supplying power to the camp. I hoped I had asked all the important questions, since my answer man was now gone, and I would truly have to "figure it out."

A 4-wheeler, a conveyance I had never driven before, was hooked to a trailer, and I hauled load after load of stuff up to the camp and put everything under cover. My responsibilities became apparent once I settled into a daily routine. Fill the generator, keep a couple of heating stoves going, and fix things that were in obvious need of repair. I spent the rest of the time reading, walking, and eating, not necessarily in that order.

The camp was a small tent city with a dozen tents. Heavy canvas, insulated affairs, each tent was about 14x16 feet. There were tents set up for sleeping, core logging, office, and the kitchen/dining area. Government permits are required for setting up a camp, and although they are built as temporary shelter, if the area shows promise, a tent city can remain for years. When camp is fully occupied, there is always a flurry of activity, with the kitchen and core tents being the centers of that hustle and bustle.

Out of concern for my safety, I was requested to use a satellite telephone to make a daily call to my employer. It was a way to check in and confirm all was okay, and to discuss any needs or problems I encountered. During one of those phone calls, about a week after I arrived, I was informed that another plane load of fuel and supplies would be flying in and I could expect some company. The next day, a float plane arrived and, along with fuel and supplies, there was a small cage.

Great, I thought. They've sent me a gerbil. Upon closer inspection though, I realized it was a small puppy. Great, I thought. That should keep all the camp marauders at bay.

We've got fox, marten, wolves, bear, and barracuda, all of which could make a quick snack of the dog. Well, scratch the barracuda, I don't think they've made the transition from sea to land yet. At any rate, I appreciated the company's concern for my safety and survival, but worst-case scenario, that dog wouldn't have made much of a meal for me either.

We passed our first night together in one of the expedition tents set up as sleeping quarters. These tents were quite roomy and comfortable, with a small oil heater for warmth, a necessity since temperatures at that time of year were well below freezing. All the cot frames were constructed of 2x4 lumber, with a piece of plywood serving as the actual bed. A 5-inch-thick piece of foam, the length and width of the bed, served as the mattress, and I threw my sleeping bag on top of the foam. It was actually a very comfortable arrangement. Each corner of the tent had one of these beds. We prepared for our first night together by doing the communal bathroom visit just before going to bed.

"Come on puppy, stop exploring every tree. It's cold out. Pay attention!"

Walking up to a nearby bush, I quickly demonstrated what needed to be done, and puppy got the hint. Puppy slept on the floor, close to the stove, nestled in the blanket in which it was transported. That night, we both had a restful sleep, but I was occasionally aware of puppy moving about. The next morning, I awoke to four pleasant piles of doggie doo. At first, I was annoyed, but when I ran an imaginary line through the piles, I realized they were oriented to the four compass points.

Great, I thought, a dog with a sense of direction.

I made a quick mental note as I was enjoying the four-pile cleanup; if doggie and I get lost while on an excursion, I can just wait until my canine compass makes four deposits and then I'll be able to figure out my bearing for camp. No matter how I tried to break Puppy of her habit, she was bound and determined to carpet-bomb the camp with her personal stamp of approval. Puppy was blessed to have a highly functioning colon, and I was equally blessed to see the byproducts as I carefully maneuvered around camp.

How could such a small dog create such big piles?

Eventually, all good things come to an end and I had to leave Puppy to the next camp sitter who replaced me. As much as I wanted to leave Puppy a special pile for it to remember me by, I fought the urge and flew off into the sunset to return home.

The whole purpose of an exploration camp is to provide an environment where men and women can comfortably work in a home–away-from-home atmosphere while at the same time acquiring drill core, the ultimate goal of any exploration camp. A team of geologists and specialists make a determination on where a likely deposit might be found. Depending on the company's objective, deposits of gold, silver, copper, or any other number of minerals and gems might be sought. This particular camp was in search of uranium, as northern Saskatchewan is home to some of the richest deposits in the world.

Because drilling is so expensive, the exploration company needs to determine the areas with the highest probability of success before committing money to boring holes in the ground. Once a target area is selected, specialized teams may go in for further delineation of the ground prior to drilling. By its very nature, exploration is a gamble. One hole might prove to have positive results, but there's no certainty. Most holes come up empty. From a hole that shows a good result, samples are taken and sent to a lab. Then, most likely, more drilling will be done in the area to determine the extent of the deposit. My experience has been if a company goes to the expense of drilling one hole, multiple holes will be bored in a drill program.

Drilling in the north is frequently done in the winter when the ground is frozen, which makes access easier. On a sunny day, your eyes will be dazzled by a landscape of white ground and trees that may be laden with a heavy coat of snow frozen in place. Snow, knee-deep or more, impedes easy travel, but a bull-dozed trail through the woods makes the exploring easier.

As you walk this road, you will see the snow pushed by the dozer's blade piled high on either side, and although the imprint on the ground from the bulldozer's tracks is easily discernible, the cause of the heavy skid drag marks is more perplexing. You'll hear the steady hum of a machine in the distance, which grows louder as you approach a cleared pad in the middle of the forest. A big machine is busy at work, and the large sled runners on which it sits, make it clear what left the skid marks on the trail, alongside the dozer tracks.

A drill, a large mechanical device with a powerful motor and hydraulics, and its crew are hired to bore core. Think of core as a cross-section of rock taken from the Earth. It's a historical record of the Earth from the perspective of looking down through the crust, evidence etched in rock of all the forces that have acted on the area over eons. If you were out in the field with the drill, you would be inundated with noise as the diamond cutting head of the drill bores down through the ground. A marvel of engineering, a drill, with its big diesel engine, hydraulic cylinders, and rotating shafts all work in unison for the sole purpose of making a small diameter, deep hole in the ground.

Starting at the surface, cylindrical sections of rock, approximately 1.5 inches in diameter are retrieved, then placed in wooden boxes for evaluation by the geologist and core technician. It's important to put the core into the boxes in the proper sequence, just as it comes out of the Earth, so that if there is something of interest, the geologist has an easy way of determining at what depth this interesting feature was located.

Core technicians aid the geologist by taking basic

measurements and doing a few preliminary tests. The boxes that hold core are specially made for the purpose and, depending on the diameter of the core samples, which are determined by the size of the drill's bit, a box can hold anywhere from 10-20 feet of core. Wooden dividers in the box keep the lengths of core organized and separated. Anybody handling filled core boxes for a day will likely have tired arms and a sore back, since, in effect, they've been lugging around rock all day.

Why lift weights when you can pump rock!

One way to upset a geologist is to accidentally drop a box of core to the ground, spilling its contents, and jumbling the once organized rock sections. Thankfully, I've never done that, but others have. When this happens, the mixed up pile of core becomes a time-consuming jigsaw puzzle for the geologist, who tries to reassemble the pieces into their proper order once again.

Occasionally, I have overheard a driller say, "That was hard drilling."

Rock isn't created equal, and some rock has characteristics that make it harder to drill. Everyone in camp will know if the drilling is going well when the crew comes in from the field tired but satisfied. They generally get paid by the foot or meter, so the deeper they drill, the larger their paycheck.

Now the pressure shifts to the geologist and core technician. When the drilling does go well, core boxes can pile up outside the core tent. Long hours are spent assessing the core, and, as a core technician, I was always fascinated by the variety of material. An astounding array of rock awaits the observer--soft, hard, crumbling, fractured, speckled, layered, and every conceivable color. A neat trick is to spray the rock with water, which brings out its characteristics in vivid detail, much like finishing a piece of wood brings out the grain.

If you don't mind being in a remote setting for an extended period of time, working in exploration camps is a good way to derive some income. Residing in a camp is quite comfy; for us, really, it is just an extension of our remote living.

Since the camp life and duties were right up my alley, I became part of a team that would go to a site, build tent platforms and frames, and then set up the tents. The kitchen and the bathroom/showers would have to be plumbed, and a make-shift wiring job would be done to provide power to each tent. Most tent camps follow a basic template for the layout, which helps keep things simple and speeds up the building process.

What slows down the process is having to build at 30°F below zero and arriving to find 2 feet of snow on the ground that needs to be shoveled before any construction can begin. It's a daunting task to arrive at a site on a subzero day, trudge through the deep snow lugging work tools and supplies, and then decide where each tent should be built. Everybody grabs a shovel, and eventually the snow is flying as each scoop full is tossed off to the side.

Pretty soon, one 20-foot square has been cleared of snow. Progress! Only nine more sites to clean.

Erecting the first tent is a choreographed affair, as everybody works in unison. Oil stoves are the heat source for the tents, so a couple people install the stove, a couple more erect the chimney, while others wrestle with the 55-gallon drum of diesel fuel, which will burn in the stove. Seeing the first glow of the lit stove, and feeling the first heat radiating from it, is a welcome reward on a bitter cold day. A skilled snowmobiler from the construction crew will eventually break trail around the camp. Because it's possible to get a snowmobile stuck, having the best operator break trail in deep snow is critical, as it helps pack down the trail so it can freeze hard. Maneuvering around camp is much easier on a hard packed surface.

Ultimately, I became a camp manager, and that is how we still derive some sporadic income. Although keeping the camp functioning is my top priority, I try to help the geologist when needed. Working with the geologists has been a good learning experience for me, and I was taught to be a core technician many years ago to help assess the drill core. Johanna has been hired as the camp cook and baker in the last few camps in which I have worked. She loves cooking and baking, and the crews love having her in camp. We both get to earn some income, and she isn't left at home alone in the bush, which would be a constant source of worry for me.

Camp food is worth a mention here. You probably think food would be pretty primitive in a bush camp. Nothing could be further from the truth. I've been in numerous styles of camps, which varied from tents to multiple buildings and even trailers. It doesn't matter what the kitchen setup is, the food is terrific, and there is no sparing the expense on the quality and quantity of the food. Top-notch steaks, ribs, shrimp, salmon, the list goes on. Fresh fruits and vegetables are brought in by the case load. Well-fed crews are happy campers.

Managing the camp for a winter drill program means being able to deal with cold and problems no matter the temperature or situation. A warm day for me in winter is any temperature above 0 Fahrenheit, while a cold day is anything below that. Some days the highs are only in the -30°F range, which is hard on both personnel and equipment. If something needs fixing, I'm the guy who has to fix it. Various camp chores must be done regardless of weather conditions: Changing propane bottles when empty, keeping the generator running and serviced, fueling all the tent stoves, unloading planes or trucks full of supplies, making sure personnel returns to camp safely, and one of the more miserable jobs, keeping the camp supplied with water.

Remember, we have just set up a camp in the frozen bush. The camp is situated somewhere close to a lake for a water source, and the lake is capped with ice 24 to 36 inches thick, perhaps more in a cold winter with minimal snow cover. The trick now is to get water from the lake to large storage containers in the camp. I'll hook up a tote sled behind the snowmobile, and throw on a water pump and a gas powered ice auger.

Once out on the lake, my next challenge is pulling the auger's starter cord and getting it to run. Company equipment is often less than ideally maintained, so it is with a hope and a prayer when I yank the cord. With luck, the auger roars to life, and if I'm really lucky, the blade will be sharp enough to cut through the ice. A good running auger is a delight to use as the cutter makes short work on an 8-inch-wide hole. I can sense when I'm just about to cut through the last bit of ice, and I brace myself for the surge of water that erupts onto the lake surface.

Now, if I only had my fishing rod!

We use the same type of gas-powered water pump I use at home for fire season to pump water to camp. It's both a chore and a process to lay out hundreds of feet of stiff fire hose from the camp to the lake, as any flexibility the hose would normally have is lost at chilly temperatures. I prime the pump, hopefully it starts, and then it's a race to pump the icy lake water up to the camp and fill everything before the pump and lines freeze. It's even more of a race to drain and decouple hundreds of feet of fire hose and get the hose into a warm place before it stiffens and freezes solid. The last few camps I've worked in have had water lines in place, which made things much easier. They had installed an insulated water line with an attached heat trace. Heat trace is a wonderful electrical product, which, as long as it's powered, will produce enough heat to keep a water line from freezing.

Speaking of lakes and ice, I helped build and then manage a camp on a northern Saskatchewan lake. Because this lake was so large, in order to reach camp, over an hour of driving on an ice road was required. I was always apprehensive when I had to drive on that lake, since that's a long time to be driving on the ice.

The northern lakes are deep, and it's not unheard of for a section of ice to give way--in which case the driver would drop through and the ice would return to the same position, without anyone knowing. A more likely scenario is there would be a telltale hole of broken ice. Doesn't matter; the end result is the same. It's highly unlikely anyone would survive. Many a good man and woman has been lost from dropping through the ice into the frigid waters below. I was always glad when I got off the lake and back on to solid land.

Because of the expansion of ice, large lakes, like the one I drove on, can develop pressure ridges. A seam develops, with the ice pushing up into a small mountain ridge, sometimes extending as far as the eye can see. That winter, the pressure ridge was about 4 feet high, creating a weakened section of ice that made for a nervous minute when driving across it. In camp, we had a two-man road crew with a Snowcat, specifically for keeping the road tested and plowed while camp was in operation.

As a general rule, whenever I go on the ice, I wear my trusty orange survival suit and carry a set of ice picks. If I did drop through, the ice picks would give me a shot at clawing myself back onto the ice. Ice picks can be homemade or store-bought, but the concept is the same. They are hand-held objects with a sharp point that can dig in and give some purchase when jabbed on to the ice surface. Otherwise, the surface is too slick for my gloved or bare hands to have any chance of pulling myself out of the hole and back up and onto the ice.

If I was lucky enough to get out of the water, I would have limited time to build a fire or get help before hypothermia overtook me. My fingers would surely be numb and stiff, and it would be a difficult task to make a fire to warm up, assuming I even had access to dry matches. Hypothermia occurs when the body temperature drops to the point the body can't function properly. If it drops far enough, it's lights out.

Memo to self: don't fall through the ice!

Another general rule: I never go into an unfamiliar forest without my survival kit. Never! Whether I am at home or in a bush camp, I have enough confidence in my abilities--as long as I have my survival kit with me, I can head out on a hike or go find a drill location, without giving a second thought to any danger or risk. I'm comfortable as long as I have my survival gear, map, and GPS. My survival gear fits in a fanny pack, and includes waterproof matches and tinder, compass, whistle, snare wire, maps, GPS, spare batteries, flashlight, knife, monocular, and a multitool. I throw in a couple packaged hand warmers in the winter. Oh, and the most important thing, toilet paper in a protective plastic bag.

Medical emergencies in a camp setting are always a concern being so far removed from mainstream medical care. Most camp personnel have basic first aid training, which is an asset. As one would expect, bumps, cuts, and bruises are common among crews involved in manual labor. Minor frostbite isn't out of the question either, given the cold climes. All of these situations can be dealt with using standard first aid kits. More sophisticated equipment such as oxygen, splints, cervical collars, and basket stretchers may also be in camp.

One time, while building a camp in the bush, I had a man become ill and he had to be medevaced out. After a weather delay, the helicopter was able to fly in and pick him up with everything working out well in the end. But hearing the approach of the medevac was a reminder of how tenuous good health can be and how quickly situations can change, given the challenges of living and working so remotely.

One of the more fun and interesting things I have done in the exploration field is ride in and work with a helicopter. While I never tire of either, it's a whole different feel than taking off in a plane. Instead of horizontal lift off, we basically go straight up at first, which is a completely disparate sensation than a plane accelerating down a runway or lake surface. These helicopters are work machines, not only moving people, but also gear and equipment. Items that don't fit within the helicopter are moved by a process called long-lining, and somebody needs to be directly under the helicopter to connect the line to the load.

I'm one of the guys who does this, and it's a dangerous job with a big helicopter spinning away 100 feet above my head. There's an element of trust between me and the pilot and, with the use of hand signals, I can hook up the load, get out of the way, and watch as the load lifts up and heads away into the distance. The rotor wash, or downdraft of air from the turning blades, is a force to be reckoned with. Not only is it a powerful mass of air, but it's blowing around whatever is on the ground, creating whiteouts of snow or dust. A helmet with ear and eye protection is a must.

I've seen 4 55-gallon drums of fuel sent off as a load, 4-wheel ATVs and snowmobiles take to the skies, and cargo nets full of "stuff" delivered to the drill.

Imagine being in camp, outside, and hearing the "thump, thump, thump" of the helicopter blades in the distance. You peer in the direction of the noise and see a helicopter approaching camp with a large net full of boxes suspended below the belly, dangling by one thin umbilical cord. The next thing you see is the chopper hovering 100 feet above the kitchen delivering a cargo net full of food and groceries right to the back door, gently setting down the load so not even one egg is broken. Some of these pilots are amazing.

I was managing a camp in northern Manitoba and had a classic encounter I won't forget. A group of trailers were arranged so that there were two main access corridors, with bedrooms off of each side of these passageways. Visualize one of these long corridors, with spaced bedroom doorways and a bathroom entrance in the middle of this hallway. The bathroom is a large room consisting of multiple showers, toilets, and urinals.

One particular night, the drill ran into trouble. Generally, the drill runs around the clock, stopping only when there is a problem or when it needs to move to another location. Two crews of two men each work grueling 12-hour shifts filled with hard, dirty labor. This night, the drill foreman was in bed when he got a call about a drilling problem. It was about 4:00 in the morning when he returned, after working for hours trying to correct the problem. I know, because that was the time I got up to go to the bathroom. I came stumbling out of my bedroom, with eyes half open, and walked down the hallway. As I approached the bathroom doorway, the drill foreman came stumbling out of his bedroom, having just returned from the job site. We were both tired, but polite. Now, from the recesses of your memory, recall The Three Stooges and their classic routines.

I knew he was tired and wanted to go to bed, so I motioned to him to go into the bathroom first. He saw I had just awoke to go to the bathroom, so he motioned me through. In rapid succession, we both started and stopped multiple times, as each of us made a step for the door, but then politely motioned the other to go ahead.

Then, as precise as a military drill team, we both decided to go through the doorway together. We ended up shoulder to shoulder, wedged into that doorway, stuck, unable to move until we wriggled free. We couldn't have timed it any better. Classic three stooges routine!

Camp kitchen

Exploration camp crew erected

Slinging a load of diesel to the drill

Typical exploration camp

Chapter 16 –

Daily Life and Seasonal Patterns

We are often asked, "Don't you get bored?" or "What do you do to fill your time?"

Questions such as these are amusing to us--as if living in the wilderness offers a worry-free life with nothing to do. Or that we wake up in the morning and pray the day ends so we can get back into our suspended animation world of night. The reality is there's not a dull moment here and we are never bored. We follow the seasonal patterns, which make for an interesting and varied life.

Spring is a time of renewal and the start of outdoor work and fun. Before we put the snowmobile away for the season, we use it and the tote sled to haul firewood to the woodshed for easy stacking. This wood will replenish what we used during the past winter. It's always a good feeling to start the summer with a fully stocked woodshed. Using the summer's heat, the wood quickly relinquishes any residual moisture, allowing us to start the coming heating season with dry firewood. We also might use the snowmobile to run down the lake and do a little ice fishing on a warm spring day.

Back in Maine, when ice fishing was new and exciting to us, we'd head out and stand around all day at temperatures of -10°F, with absurd wind chills, and wait for a fish to show up and jump on our line. We no longer need to freeze to death to enjoy a day on the frozen lake. Now we can afford to be selective and choose a nice day to go fishing.

Some sunny, warm spring day, we'll throw the power auger, fishing gear, lunch, and a thermos of hot tea on the sled and take a ride down the lake to a spot we hope is teaming with fish. I'll work up a sweat as I lug the auger around to different spots, drilling numerous holes. Meanwhile, Johanna is following behind with an ice scoop to clean out the holes, and she sets the traps with a frozen bait fish. Ice fishing traps are contraptions that have a spool of line and a clever trigger mechanism that, once set, alerts the fisherman if a fish has taken the bait. An orange flag pops up and, if we are close at hand, we will hear the spool squealing as line is taken out by the running fish. We are constantly scanning the white lake surface looking for the tell-tale brilliant orange flag of a triggered trap.

Upon espying a popped-up pendant, the spotter shouts "flag!" and the race is on to get to the hole.

Carefully, one of us reaches into the hole, grabs the line and, with a gentle tug, sets the hook. Now, we bring in the fish by pulling the line hand over hand and, by timing it just right, the head is lined up with the hole in the ice so that we can pull up the fish onto the surface. Over the years, we have enjoyed many days on the lake ice fishing, getting fresh air and sun. Even when the fish don't cooperate, it's a way to take advantage of the last opportunity to be out on the ice.

A comical sequence of events has occurred with a fair degree of regularity throughout all the years we have ice fished. It is uncanny, really. We bore holes and set the traps. With high expectations, we sit on the snowmobile or pace around, waiting for a flag to pop. Nothing happens for the longest time and we end up watching each other grow a little older.

One of us will comment, "There aren't any fish in the lake."

We'll pour some tea, take the first bite of a sandwich, and then suddenly our lunch will be interrupted by a fish with a sense of humor, which decides, at that very instant, to jump on the line, sending a flag flying, breaking up our lunch. Never fails!

By March, Johanna has started our garden plants, and every window sill is overflowing with seedlings. She had the foresight to dig buckets of soil from the garden the previous fall, before the ground froze solid. She brings the buckets, which have been stored under cover in the greenhouse, into the house to thaw, and once warmed up, the medium is ready to give a germinating seed a new lease on life.

One of the benefits of ten–inch-thick walls is that they have wide window sills, making a dandy place to park potted plants and seedlings. An occasional tray rotation ensures the plants get even sunlight. Johanna starts peppers, melons, squash, Cole crops, various tomato types, and even corn indoors. Certain vegetables will be grown from hybrid seed but, as often as possible, we favor open pollinated, heirloom varieties whose seed can be saved from year to year. Not only does seed saving give us more independence, but it also allows us to save seeds from the strongest plants, plants that have adapted the best to our location and growing conditions. In other words, a tomato plant that has given us jumbo tomatoes has obviously taken to our climate and conditions, so seed saved from some of those tomatoes should give us a good chance of repeating that success in future gardens.

Despite being north of the 56th parallel, there is very little we can't grow here. We are able to grow all of our vegetables and about half of our fruit needs. Besides starting many of our seedlings indoors, we employ numerous growing tricks to help cope with our short summer season. Up here, spring has a nasty habit of returning to winter with a vengeance. So even though the calendar says May, there's no guarantee we won't have more snow and ice. Because we can have a frost in any month of the year, we are left with circumstances requiring constant vigilance regarding the weather.

We have a south-facing greenhouse that becomes home to melons, tomatoes, and peppers in late spring. But before they are planted, with snow still on the ground, we sow the seeds of salad fixings to satisfy our hankering for fresh greens after a long winter's dearth of lettuce and radishes.

Cold frames, which we set in the greenhouse, act as a sort of greenhouse within a greenhouse. A cold frame is a box with clear lid (glass or plastic), a setup that gives protection to early plantings of lettuce, kale, onions, and radishes, even when temperatures are still going down to 0°F at night.

The sun has considerable heat by this time of the year due to its higher angle in the sky so, even on cold days, the greenhouse warms up substantially. It may even need to be vented on a sunny afternoon to prevent it from getting too hot. To protect the young seedlings from the cold night, we place recycled gallon milk jugs filled with hot water in the cold frames. We ensure that the cold frame lid is closed, and then lay a heavy blanket over the box. This procedure keeps things in the box from freezing. Because of these efforts, we will enjoy our first salads while snow is still on the ground.

A few other growing tricks we employ are setting up hoop houses in the garden and using commercial garden coverings. Greenhouse plastic is supported by curved PVC pipe. From a roll of 2" PVC tubing, we cut pieces 14 inches long, which act as anchors. Driving those pieces into the ground at 3-foot intervals down both sides of a garden bed, I leave a few inches of those anchors exposed above ground level. I cut lengths of 1½" PVC tubing long enough to create arches of a desired height and insert their ends into the anchor tubes.

This is a simple way to erect and dismantle a greenhouse, as the anchors stay in the ground from year to year, while the tubes forming the arches are easily removed, stored under cover for the winter, and then reinserted the following spring. With the PVC tubing arches in place down the full length of each vegetable bed, it's an easy matter to stretch greenhouse plastic over the frames to create long tubular greenhouses. We dig a trench on one side, wrap pieces of firewood around the edge of the plastic, and set both in the trench. The pieces of firewood act as anchors for the plastic; without them, a strong wind could pull the plastic out of the ground. We learned that lesson the hard way. Once backfilled with dirt, that side of the hoop house plastic is solid and stationary. Sandbags or heavy rocks anchor the other side, making for easy access and venting of the hoop house, as the weights are movable. We can manipulate the plastic along those sides and ends as needed to vent the beds.

Late spring is a time of planting. The seedlings Johanna has carefully nurtured are set out in the greenhouse and garden. It is now my responsibility to keep them alive. Cold nights, anywhere near the freezing mark, will find me monitoring a kerosene heater in the greenhouse, since those plants are the most cold-sensitive.

After expending so much effort to start and transplant the seedlings, it would be a calamity to head to the greenhouse some morning and find everything withered from freezing. With the season so short, it would be difficult, if not impossible, to recover from that. As you recall, we can't get to a garden center to buy replacements, and there isn't enough time to restart plants from seed. Although we've planted the primary garden, at this point, little has germinated, potato sprouts and other vegetable shoots haven't pushed through the surface yet, and what seedlings are planted are somewhat cold-tolerant, such as cabbage and broccoli. Last to be planted in the garden are the temperature-sensitive plants such as corn, pumpkins, and squash.

At ground level, we use either Reemay or N-sulate, fabrics, which are commercial garden products that work well. They are made to protect plants and are laid over the planted seeds in the bed or draped over seedlings. The fabric gives an added layer of frost protection. Think of the material as a light blanket. We've had the hoop houses fully planted with seedlings, and our plants have survived temperature drops to 20°F at night. When a surprise spring snow storm hits, the plastic hoop houses do their jobs even while sagging from the weight of the snow.

Another spring chore we do is to fertilize all the fruiting plants, such as strawberries, raspberries, and saskatoons to ready them for another productive season.

Spring is one of the two times in our year when we are scheduled to fly out for appointments and resupply. It's a three- or four-day event, and our vehicle is always jam packed when we are done our shopping. By the end of our last day in town, we have had enough of a populated environment, and it's always good to get back home. Once home, we are set for the next six months.

Spring is also the time we wrestle the boat and motor into the water as soon as ice is off the lake. The boat has been stored for the winter, bottom up, near the beach, so it's a short drag to the water's edge. I used to tarp the motor and store it down near the beach, but twice bears have ravaged it, so it's now safely stored in the enclosed shed. It is heavy and cumbersome to maneuver around, and I'm glad I only have to deal with it twice a year. The aluminum boat is relatively easy for me to flip over prior to launch, but if I'm not feeling spiffy, I can always use a rope trick to generate enough leverage to roll it over.

I know spring is really here when I am able to slide the boat down the ramp, drag it into the water, and float it over to the dock, which will be its summer home. Mount the motor, throw in the oars and seats, squeeze the fuel bulb a few times, and, with a quick pull on the starter rope, the motor purrs back to life. Don life jackets and off we go. Zoom zoom!

Although we are no longer worried about a major fire, we still set up the pump at the beach and mount roof sprinklers for fire protection. But now the pump's primary function is to water the garden. It takes a delicate touch to water the gardens with the fire hose, but I sure can water them in a hurry. If I handed you the fire hose and asked you to water the gardens for us, you would have, in your hands, the power to release a mighty flood upon our vegetable kingdom. Even though I run the pump at moderate speed, a twist of the hose's nozzle changes the water flow from a gentle, wide-angle, short-distance spray, to a long range, powerful jet of water, capable of pulverizing garden plants and boring holes in the soil. So, use your power wisely.

In spring and summer, a flurry of bird and animal activity arises, including a host of different waterfowl. The forest is alive with the song of birds going about their business of securing their next generation. They will remind us of it every morning with their incessant chirping before sunrise. The occasional hum of a float plane passing by speaks of human activity, as locals and tourists re-populate the northern lakes for their vacations. We never tire of seeing a float plane fly over us, sometimes close enough that we can wave to it and see the pilot's response as he waves back, not with his hand in a window but with the whole plane, as one wing gently dips and then the other.

Summer is a time of leisure. Our screened-in porch with swing is a nice place to wile away some time reading or napping. Throughout the summer, watering and weeding all the gardens is a priority, since we count on these food sources to carry us through at least the next year. The herb plot, which sits prominently in front of the house, and the greenhouse and the vegetable garden behind the house, are pretty much Johanna's domain. I work the berry patch, which has strawberries, raspberries, and a number of other fruits. I also take care of the asparagus and apple orchard. The best the orchard has done so far is give us micro–apples, which is not exactly what we were hoping for, but the blossoms are beautiful and the small fruit makes good jelly.

On a calm night, you will find me in the boat on our beloved lake. There was a time when I felt the need to fish whenever I was out, but my fishing need has long since been satisfied and I just enjoy taking a drive or drifting in the middle of the lake with the breeze. I still throw the lure over occasionally, but not nearly as often as I used to. For exercise, I'll motor down the lake a distance and then row home.

We try to go camping once a summer. As a surprise for Johanna, many years ago, I set up a campsite down the lake on an island. I cleared out a small area, made a fire ring complete with cooking grate, and stacked up a small pile of firewood. Located on top of a knoll, the site overlooks the lake, small islands, and the surrounding hills. It's a favorite camping destination when we really want to get away from it all.

Although we have been picking continually from our gardens for fresh eating, beginning in midsummer there is a shift towards food preservation and storage. As vegetables mature, Johanna is busy in the kitchen either canning or blanching produce for the freezer. It is very satisfying seeing hundreds and hundreds of jars filled from our efforts. You might say it's a lot of work, but it saves on the food bill and makes us much more self-sufficient; we know exactly where our food has come from and how it was produced. As the garden becomes depleted, we pull the spent vines and plants, pile them in a compost bin, layer it with soil, and add them back to the garden the following summer once the material has decomposed.

After a fire, blueberries and cranberries are some of the first plants to re-populate the burned landscape. Because of the fires we've had in the area, both fruit species are abundant, with more blueberries than we could ever use. Surrounded by free food, we harvest and freeze bags of both fruits for various uses throughout the year.

Late summer will find me out in the woods with a bucket and blueberry rake. I have some favorite picking spots down the lake, the locations of which are top secret. Even Johanna doesn't know where they are.

A blueberry rake is a handy device that makes it much easier and faster to pick berries in quantity, as opposed to picking berries one at a time by hand. The rake has long tines that can get right in and snag clusters of fruit at once. The berries collect in a part of the rake that resembles a box. When the rake box is full, I empty the berries into my bucket and repeat the process. In good blueberry ground, I can pick five gallons in an hour.

Then we go through a sorting process to get rid of leaves and debris. First, we use a fan to winnow out lighter material. With the fan set on an outside table, we pour the berries in front of the fan, from one bucket to another. As the berries free-fall between buckets, the lighter leaves and debris are blown to the side by the action of the fan.

Next, we pour all the fruit through a wire mesh to sort out most of the immature green berries. The larger mature fruit stays on top of the screen, while the green berries fall through and are discarded. Finally we hand-pick through the remainder, selecting the good berries to eat fresh or freeze. The whole sorting process will take an afternoon of work. Cleaning five gallons of blueberries is a tedious activity, but one that gives us jars of jam and juice, many bags of frozen berries for pancakes and muffins, and bowls of fresh fruit.

We have some areas where the ground is a carpet of cranberries. Although they grow very close to the ground, I am able to use the rake to carefully harvest them too. We basically use the same procedure to clean them as we do the blueberries. Once cleaned, Johanna makes and cans quarts of cranberry juice, with 28 quarts being the record for a season. She also freezes bags of fruit for making cranberry sauce throughout the winter. On a cold winter day, we get a great deal of satisfaction from eating blueberry muffins or a dinner that includes cranberry sauce, both of which are made possible by the previous summer's berry-picking efforts. Wild roses also grow in some areas, and we harvest the hips for a nice tea as well as a dose of Vitamin C.

There is an air of excitement to fall as we prepare for winter's isolation. Although we are secluded year round, starting in the fall, birds are heading to warmer climates, animals are starting to hunker down, and a peaceful quiet descends over the land. Fall is the time for the second of the two scheduled trips to town for resupply. After we have returned home and off-loaded the winter's supplies from the plane, we will stand on the dock and watch the plane take off. Once it is a mere speck in the distance, well beyond hearing, we are left with nothing but a deafening silence.

It is at that moment we become acutely aware our last physical link with humanity just flew away, and we have the sense we are fully immersed in the wilderness, with no one but ourselves left on the planet. Exciting!

With the advent of cooler weather, we will have a small fire in the heater stove, when necessary, to take off the chill. Nothing signals a welcome like the curl of smoke emanating from the chimney on a calm fall day or the smell of burning firewood drifting lazily along on the air currents. Out of this smoke, memories are conjured of raw, cold fall days in Maine when the garden was spent, the wood was stacked neatly in the shed, and I eagerly awaited the arrival of the first snowflakes of the season, with the anticipation of more to follow. From a distance, the whiff of smoke was an affirmation that all was well, with the warming home fire burning.

Fall is the time to pull the boat and motor out of the lake and get all equipment maintained and winterized. I keep a maintenance log on all of our equipment so I can track what repairs and work have been done on each piece. I do any needed changes of oil, filters, or spark plugs now, so when spring shows up, we're ready to go. We inventory an assortment of repair and maintenance parts for our equipment so we can deal with most problems and breakdowns on the spot.

Autumn is also the time we put the garden to bed for the winter. We pick the remaining crops, such as potatoes and carrots, and take them down to our root cellar for storage. We harvest plants we left to mature specifically for the purpose of seed saving, their seeds now gathered and drying in various pans arranged on a counter by a window. We label each pan with the variety it contains and, when deemed dry enough, Johanna carefully packages the seeds, labels them, and stores them in the root cellar for next year's garden--a continuity of life from year to year for many of the vegetables we grow. I till the Earth as one of the last tasks, leaving the ground neatly arranged and manicured. The freshly turned soil, fluffed and ready to plant, will lie dormant under a blanket of snow waiting for the coming spring, many months away.

We adopt a slower pace of life in winter. Other than tending the home fires, there really isn't anything urgent that needs attention. It's a season of settling in and devoting more time to our hobbies. Although we engage in our hobbies year round, in winter, we have more time to dedicate to them.

Some of my hobbies include woodworking with hand tools and hand-carving. I have made everything from a small jewelry or music box to a moderate sized piece of furniture. When I had the sawmill in Maine, I sawed some logs of valuable Birdseye and Curly maple, and as a result, I have a nice inventory of sawn lumber I flew in when we moved here.

I use the computer as my source for news so I can stay abreast of world events. It is our link to the outside world, and I do our financial transactions, pay bills, and file taxes with it. Sometimes I'll dabble in stock options. I really need to change my strategy though, since the "buy high, sell low" model doesn't seem to be working for me. Listening to my music or shortwave radio, and playing chess on my electronic chess board round out my leisure activities.

Johanna's hobbies are numerous. Any sewing or needle craft such as knitting, quilting or cross stitch will entertain her. Associated skills, such as carding and spinning wool, go hand in hand with her crafts. She knitted the full face mask I wear in the winter, mentioned in an earlier chapter, from yarn she spun. I figure, if it was good enough for the sheep to wear, it's good enough for me!

She uses an old fashioned Singer non-electric treadle sewing machine for projects. She has made many shirts and pants on that machine as Christmas or birthday gifts.

She excels at cooking and baking, which makes us a good

match. I excel at eating her cooking and baking. Thankfully, I stay active and keep the extra pounds at bay. Employing our hand grinder, Johanna will periodically convert wheat berries, one of the many items we inventory, to flour. Using two hands on the grain mill's handle, she rhythmically cranks, taking her arms on a circular loop around the mill's pivot point, steadily exercising her upper body for 20 minutes or more at a time. Grinding grain for flour is hard work! Up to a point, we are both nutrition-conscious, and using whole wheat flour is one of the things we do to help meet that desire. Additionally, you will always find her in the middle of reading a book.

Winter is the time we take the snowmobile out for rides. Not only do we ride on the lake, but we also have a loop trail of 2 to 3 miles through the woods, where we snowmobile, hike, and snowshoe. When we go on a winter walk, from certain high vantage points on the loop trail we can see far in the distance to nearby lakes and hills. When I take a solitary trek, I pause on a lofty, nearby hill overlooking the homestead below and, upon seeing the smoke rise from the chimney, I feel a sense of satisfaction and pride. No matter what the Canadian wilderness has thrown at us, our little sanctuary has stood tall.

The fact that we try to get out for a walk every day makes us feel better both physically and mentally, and may be a good reason why we aren't bothered by the wintertime blahs. No cabin fever here. I think it helps to maintain our level of fitness as well. We have never caught a cold or had the flu when we've been home. The only time we get sick is when we are mingling in society.

I had mentioned earlier my first experience with the Aurora Borealis (northern lights) and how special that first sighting was. Ever since that first encounter, there have been numerous times we have thrown on hat and coat and gone outside to watch the light display. We never know when the show will materialize, but fall and winter are generally the best seasons for viewing. The nights are long and dark, and when the conditions are just right, we are in for a treat.

Every now and then, the sun rains a shower of charged particles towards Earth. Most of those particles are deflected by the Earth's magnetic shield, but some of those particles collide and interact with the various gases in our atmosphere. Those collisions with the different gases create the lights and the colorful displays we see.

Passing by a window on a winter evening, we might note the outdoors seems oddly illuminated, even though it is supposed to be dark. A quick glance through the window reveals shimmering bands of light. The bands generally emanate from a northerly direction, but this doesn't always have to be the case. Sometimes, the north sky can be dark while the sky directly overhead may be lit. The light display can take many forms. There may be bands of light, or there may be whole curtains of light dancing across the sky. At other times, there is merely a radiant glow in the sky. Rays may undulate and appear to fold in on themselves or they may ripple across the heavens.

On rare occasions, if we are lucky, pulses of colored light may shoot across the sky. Most of the time the Auroras are a whitish color, but we've seen glimpses of rose, violet, and green mixed in, a palette of color which never fails to dazzle. Sometimes the show is dominated by one special color for the night. We stand outside to watch for as long as we can, until the numbing cold drives us inside.

But that is the best time to watch, when the air is crisp and clear. There are only the two of us, necks bent skyward, eyes taking it all in, and the only sound we hear is when one of us utters, "Wow, look at that. Nice!"

During any season I'll be out cutting firewood, and Johanna will be stacking the cut pieces for later gathering. Although finding something on TV worthy of watching is getting more difficult by the day, there are a few television series with a mystery or educational bent that we enjoy watching. Occasionally, we'll wrestle with a puzzle or play a game of some sort.

Combining all our hobbies with the normal routines of daily life, the hours in the day pass quickly, and by nighttime, we're left scratching our head. Where did the day go?

Greenhouse

Johanna spinning yarn in her shop

Hand-made thank-you cabinet for Saskatchewan fire crews

One of Johanna's hand-made quilts

Our garden (note the hoops on one bed)

Ron hand-planing in his shop

Chapter 17 –

Close Encounters of the Animal Kind

As you can imagine, we experience our share of wildlife. We see the typical animals you might expect, such as hare, fox, and song birds, but seeing a small herd of caribou on the frozen lake, a lone wolf, or a marten makes for special memories.

We learned the hard way how destructive bears can be, and I've shared a few stories in this book about them. We had the occasional bear sighting when we lived in northern Maine, but sightings are far more frequent here in Canada. There's never been a year when we haven't seen at least a couple of them during spring, summer, or fall.

Unfortunately, they seem to have the innate ability to sense when we are away from home, and it is during those times when we are the most vulnerable to damage. Maybe there's a bear scout posted to our perimeter, waiting and watching for us to leave the place, and once we do, it sends word out through some kind of bear communications system to alert the rest of the clan. I don't know. Seems uncanny how they show up when we are absent.

It's disheartening to return home from a vacation or seasonal job to find tarps torn off equipment and mangled foam rubber strewn about. We can say, with some authority, that snowmobiles are a favorite snack, notably the foam rubber seats and gas tank. Our snowmobile seat has been decimated, with little remaining as a place to park my posterior, and the fuel tank has bite puncture wounds. Anything plastic, rubber, or associated with fuels seems to be an attractant. We don't know what the attraction is but, nonetheless, it is a definite problem.

We have tried two things to prevent continued bear damage to our property. The first thing was to install a solar electric fence, which has had varying degrees of success. Because our soil is sandy and well drained, it doesn't provide a good ground when it's summer dry. In that case, I doubt the bear gets more than a minor buzz. But the fence works well as long as the ground is wet, so after a rain we have the best protection. It's not as though the four thin strands of wire strung along the fence posts are going to hold back a bear, but it does provide psychological comfort to us that we are somewhat protected.

Once when I went outside, I surprised a bear that had gotten past our defenses and was on the inside of the fence line. Upon seeing me, it took off and hurdled over the highest wire, 36 inches from the ground, so not only can they run, they also have the athleticism to hurdle obstructions. I was amazed to see that. I ran track in high school and then for a track club post high school, which gave me an opportunity to run in the Penn Relays a couple of times. No matter the venue or quality of the athlete, there was no one who could run fast enough to outrun a bear. No point in even trying. An ursine sprinter will win the race hands down every time.

The second thing we do to protect our property is to place nail boards down on the ground whenever we go away. Nail boards are just as they sound. Take any scrap board or section of plywood, and pound nails in rows spaced every inch in each direction to form a grid pattern. During periods of bear activity, if we leave the homestead for any period of time, we throw nail boards down around the freezers, which are located outside under our screened porch, around the snowmobile, and at the entrances to the house and greenhouse.

Although the majority of visits occur when we are away, there is the odd time when a bear becomes a nuisance while we are home. I recall one visit right after I had painted the metal on the west side of our greenhouse with an oil based paint. We were inside the house, carrying on as usual, in fact I was watching the Stanley Cup finals, when I heard a racket emanating from outside.

What in the world is all that noise?

I ran out and around the side of the house and came face to

face with a bear which was challenging the greenhouse to a duel. He was a burly, brazen chap, unfazed by me disrupting his sparring match. The fact that he remained in place and didn't run away suggested some persuasion was needed. Retreating to the house, I fetched my shotgun, but by the time I got back outside, he had bounded away. We can only surmise the odor from the paint piqued his interest.

On a recent occasion, we had a more troubling time with a bear. Imagine this scenario for a minute.

We are occupying the downstairs bedroom, awning window cracked open a few inches, sleeping soundly, dreaming sweet dreams. Johanna thinks she hears something.

I am awakened by her whisper "I think there's something outside."

She pulls back the curtain to take a peek. "There's a bear behind the house!" she exclaims.

She quickly cranks the window shut and immediately the bear bounds around to the window and she is literally face to face with the bear as it frantically claws at the window to get in. Separated by mere feet, she is shouting and banging to scare it off. Her efforts have no effect. The bear is undeterred.

Meanwhile, I've turned the affair into a circus as I stumble out of my dead sleep.

My glance over at the window reveals the face of the bear with its paws working on the window pane. This bear wants to climb in the window in the worst way. I add my voice to the chorus of shouts.

"Where are my pants? Where are my #%*@! pants!"

I left them upstairs. I throw open the closet and get another pair of pants off the rack, and they happen to be turned inside-out. No time to mess with this. Pants go on inside-out, but now I have no way to keep them up. The button and zipper are on the inside.

"Where's my belt? Have you seen my belt?"

I run out the bedroom door, and by that time the bear has run around the house to greet me at the utility sink window. Another attempt to claw his way in fails, and the greenhouse beckons. I hear frenzied clawing and tearing as our greenhouse cover is being shredded.

Some scenario!

This was a dangerous bear that needed a serious spanking. The bear was half way into the greenhouse by the time I was able to get a shot off and scare it out of there. Once inside, it would have decimated our entire crop, so the shot came just in the nick of time. Unfortunately, it was dark, 12:30 am, and although I was 20 feet from him, I shot our greenhouse with bird shot and the bear left unscathed. He was so busy tearing into our greenhouse, he was unaware of my presence. If he had known I was out there, I do believe he would have been all over me in a heartbeat. We are convinced this is the problem bear we have dealt with through the years. He knew exactly where to tear into the greenhouse from a previous break-in years ago. Thanks to my intervention, at least our year's worth of greenhouse food remained intact.

That bear was in pure predator mode, and it was a terrifying ten-minute ordeal. Neither of us slept the rest of the night. So much for the electric fence!

Another animal strikes fear in our hearts and terrorizes the neighborhood. Hares! Furry little lawn mowers.

We weren't prepared for how destructive those little hip-pity hop-pity creatures could be to a garden and orchard. We were so excited the first year we were able to plant the gardens and strawberries. The house was finished, we turned our attention to the great outdoors, and we began establishing beds of vegetables and fruits. But as soon as the first green leaves appeared on the strawberries, they were gone the next day. It didn't take us long to figure out what was responsible for the great leaf caper. The culprits were hares, boldly running around, at least six by our count, gnawing off young shoots to ground level.

Those things breed like rabbits!

We ended up using chicken wire to fence in all of our gardens. The young apple trees were fair game too and required protection, especially when they were whips and saplings. In the early years, when the trees were getting established, it was hard to totally protect them. It was like two steps ahead, one back as the trees did their best to outpace the amount being chewed. There were years when some of our nice trees were reduced to a main stem and the side branches were reduced to stubs. Placing chicken wire fences around the trees helped.

Fortunately, the trees are pretty well-established now, so hare damage isn't much of a problem anymore. The only damage from hares these days occurs when the snow is 2 feet deep and they can walk right up to the tree branches. They can stretch and elongate their bodies, like a kid reaching for the cookie jar, to access higher branches.

The marten, a natural predator of hares, make occasional appearances, especially in the fall and through the winter. We've seen a marten chase a snowshoe hare many times from the vantage point of our upstairs windows, and it is fascinating to watch--truly a situation of the tortoise and the hare. The hare is running full bore until it thinks it's in the clear. It stops to rest. On the other side of the house, the marten is slowly scouting back and forth over the tracks and working its way over to the hare. The chase is on again. This repeats, sometimes with the hare winning and sometimes with the hare losing.

One day a chase was underway and I went outside to watch. I stood right in the animal's last tracks to see what would happen. As if I were a statue, I stood and waited, my patience rewarded when the hare raced right by my legs, followed by the marten bounding by in hot pursuit. Both were so focused on the chase, they hadn't realized I could have reached down to touch them.

We try to encourage the marten to stick around to help control both hare and squirrels. A peek out the living room window in winter might reveal a marten dangling off the bird's suet feeder, trying its best to get at the contents. I'll go out and place a chunk of suet on the ground for it, and Marty always finds the tasty morsel. Sometimes when I go out, I can get within feet of it, while other times the marten bounds away, climbs a nearby tree, and looks back at me from a safe perch. A tree is no obstacle to a marten, as it can scale to the top in seconds.

From our second-story window, we once observed a marten at the top of the tree and saw how in one leap it fearlessly dove from the tree top to the ground below, a distance of 30 feet, the deep snow cushioning its impact. We've been awakened at night by a clatter to find a marten had climbed its way to the roof. I didn't have the heart to tell it that it was unlikely a hare would be found playing on our roof. Marty was just curious I guess.

Moose were more abundant in Maine at our old homestead, but we still have the odd sighting here in Canada. It's generally the tracks we see as proof they've been around to visit. Or a broken electric fence, since they barge right through the wire. They're big animals, and a few strands of wire they may or may not see, won't deter them.

It's always memorable when you see a large bull moose with a full rack swimming across the lake, nothing but his big head and antlers exposed. Invariably, the beast walks out of the water onto a shoreline, stops, and with a big shake of his massive head and body, sheds copious amounts of water from his hide. That's unless he has been startled, in which case he will bull his way into the woods a short distance and then stop to ascertain the threat.

There was one moose I won't forget. It was early summer, and the bugs were out in force. After dinner, I went out in the boat and was paying no attention to the world. With virtually no wind, I sat drifting in the middle of the lake with my fishing line over the side.

For some reason, I felt a presence in the area, although I heard nothing. When I turned around, the head of a moose, reminiscent of a submarine periscope, was the only thing visible as he swam towards the boat. I knew there was a large, submerged body attached to that head, and the situation was a little disconcerting because I really didn't want him trying to get into the boat with me. I had no extra rod and reel for Bullwinkle. I don't know what he was planning, but I fired up the motor and kept my distance from him. Eventually he swam away and back to shore. He probably just went for a swim to get some relief from the bugs and got curious about the boat.

Having lived in Maine for so many years, we have a good reference point in regards to black flies and mosquitoes. By comparison, the bugs in Maine were much worse. They have their moments here too, but this is wilderness after all. Bugs are a part of the woods, and one learns to deal with them. Sometimes we spray on some repellent or wear a bug net if we will be stationary for any length of time. Weeding in the garden might be one of those times when we use a bug net. Late spring to early summer is the worst period, with bugs tapering off as the summer season progresses.

Birds and I get along well for some reason. I have an affinity towards them and have had some truly unforgettable experiences. I'm honored some of these birds have trusted me so much.

Many years ago, when we lived in Maine, I was sitting in our field in front of the house, just relaxing. Out of the blue, a raven set down close to me. Maybe 30 feet away. For the next five days, that raven was attached to me. If I went to the outhouse, it would land on the roof and peer in at me. If I went for a walk up the road, it would fly close behind me, land near me and walk a little, and then fly to catch up to me again. This went on for days and then, just as quickly as it arrived, it disappeared. I never saw it again and have no explanation for the occurrence. Although I don't believe in superstition, to this day, I've always had the sense there was more to it than just a bird dropping in to say hi.

Here in Canada, I have been blessed to have hand-fed Canada jays, a chickadee and pine grosbeaks. We have a feeder in a tree in front of the house, within easy sight of our living room windows. Flocks of grosbeaks have shown up throughout the years, maybe 2 dozen at a time. They have a fondness for sunflower seeds. I sit in a chair near the feeder, put feed in my hand, and before long, one brave grosbeak comes to me, followed quickly by the rest. Soon I am surrounded by grosbeaks, both at my feet and in my hand.

The chickadee is amusing when it uses my head as a perch. There have been times he has given me a good scare by coming out of nowhere and buzzing me. How astounding that a tiny bird weighing next to nothing, trusts me enough to eat suet out of the palm of my hand, while its little claws grasp my finger.

Grouse are fairly tame here. During the winter, when snow covers the ground, they can be found in the woodshed, scratching around in the dirt. There are times when a dozen will be in the nearby trees eating the pine needles, which are a favorite food. Grouse can also give us a good scare. They cope with cold winter temperatures by burying themselves in the snow, burrowing in, and then covering themselves up. When we go for winter walks around our loop trail, the bird stays buried until the last moment, and then it explodes out of its hidey-hole right in front of us--snow and wings in a frenzied swirl. I always feel bad giving it a scare, although it's a tossup who's startled the most. As we walk along, we often see a hole in the snow where one spent some time, hunkered down safe from the cold.

In early summer, I have occasionally walked through the woods with a grouse and her babies as they foraged, and several times I've sat right by them as they all went to sleep. All the young ones pile up into a compact bundle to keep each other warm, or they work their way under the mother when she lifts a wing. All these experiences are a testament to my special affection for birds.

We are thrilled when swallows or other insect-eating birds make their home in the neighborhood. In the summer of 2014, a pair of swallows decided to use our house as a nesting area, and we were only too happy to welcome them. Over our porch screen door, on the outside, there is a small, one-inch metal lip. These swallows were bound and determined to make a nest on that thin lip, a really bad choice since every time we went out the door, the nest was a foot above our head. Seemed as though the slamming of the porch door, multiple times a day as we went in and out, would be an untenable disruption for them, but they were not dissuaded.

From the kitchen window that overlooks the porch door, we watched as each swallow flew in with a mouthful of debris, and deposited this material on the narrow metal lip, most of which fell on to the steps below. At the end of each day, I took down what material did manage to stay put and stored it. I was storing the nesting material in the hopes I could persuade them to build in a more suitable location. I'd take it down and the next day they would rebuild.

This went on for a week. They were stubborn, and I was tenacious. It was an old-fashioned contest of wills.

Our porch is held up by pressure-treated posts, and on the top of each post there is a small flat spot. I noticed they would occasionally rest under the porch on one of the flat spots. What a perfect place for them to build a nest, out of the weather and yet close enough we could watch them through the front door window. When I had saved enough of their nest-building scraps, I mounded them on the top of the post on which they liked to perch and hoped they might get the message. The message being that this was a better spot for your nest.

Sure enough, they saw it and the next thing we knew, they were building the nest under the porch, right where I had placed the material. Smart birds! We could peer through the door window at night and see them hunkered down, one in the nest and the other perched on a hanging thermometer sensor wire. They had no fear of us, and we often went outside and passed within feet of them and their nest without disturbing them. We're hoping to see them again for years to come. Their summer home, still sitting on the top of the post, awaits their return.

Numerous woodpeckers also frequent the area. Some are year-round inhabitants, and others are seasonal guests. After a fire, the influx of woodpeckers taking advantage of all the wood-boring insects in the dead trees is astonishing. As evidence of their voracious appetites, there is hardly a burned tree without a pile of wood chips and bark at its base from all the drilled holes in its stem.

Every year we have at least one pair of northern flickers that have a nest in a nearby tree. They're beautiful birds. For anybody who doesn't know the flicker's habits, they love to rapidly peck on hollow trees. Their pecking resembles the rapidity of machine gun fire. Maybe part of a mating ritual?

We have a metal chimney and cap that connects to our downstairs stove, which is adjacent to our bedroom. Every year without fail, for about a month, we can count on hearing the booming echo of the flicker pecking on our chimney cap, usually very early in the morning, while we are both sound asleep. The sound comes down the chimney and is piped right into the house. Woody makes it his business to be our personal early morning alarm clock. Sometimes he changes the tone of his morning serenade by pecking on our large, unused satellite dish.

That's enough, Woody. Go away! Don't go away mad, *just go away!*

Owls are fascinating to me. If I'd hear one calling from the woods, I'd go out to search for it but had a hard time locating it, especially if it was nighttime. Once I lucked out though and found a small boreal owl in the lower part of a tree. Because it had no fear of me, I was able to get close to it and we studied each other. Another time, a larger owl was in a tree in front of the house, and I was able to get within 10 feet of it. As it so happens, we had mouse traps placed around the garden and had trapped a mouse the previous night. I retrieved the dead mouse, showed it to the owl, and set the mouse on a branch in an adjacent tree. I had other things to do, but when I came back, both mouse and owl were gone.

Speaking of mice, the forest environment is their habitat, and it's only natural we have to deal with them. All we can do is set traps around the area and rely on their natural predators to help keep them in check. In the winter, they chew and gnaw the bark of our fruit trees which can girdle and kill a good tree. It's imperative that all fruit trees have 24" or 36" tree guards, which wrap around the trunk to protect them.

In the summer, mice do extensive damage in the garden too. One day there are plants sprouting, and the next day they're gone. Spinach and pea shoots seem to be a favorite. Seedlings Johanna has carefully nurtured and transplanted have bare stalks and are devoid of their young leaves the next day. Even when plants are mature, mice do damage. They will chew through the pea pods to get to the peas, and they'll gnaw on the heads of broccoli. We've declared war on the mice and set out numerous traps during the growing season. One year we trapped a record 146 mice in the garden. There is one positive, in all these years: we have never had a mouse in the house.

In spring, before the ice is off the lake, open water starts to appear along the shorelines, just enough water for passing ducks and loons to make a splash and take a break. The first arrival of these birds signals that the long winter is finally coming to an end. In early summer, the lake is alive with waterfowl and there's no better confirmation of this than hearing a chorus of loons. Many species of ducks call this area home for the season, and there's never been a year we haven't seen a mother duck with her newly hatched ducklings swimming along the shoreline. As with my buddy the grouse and her babies, I was able to get quite close to a blue-winged teal and her ducklings. She didn't mind me rowing alongside in the boat to observe them, and they quickly got used to me.

I know it's natural selection and part of nature to lose some baby quack quacks along the way, but there was one summer when

I interceded to save them. My friend the teal and her kids fed in the weeds growing in the shallows.

One day I was in the boat fishing and heard a commotion. Looking across the bay, I saw the mother doing the lame duck routine. She feigns injury to draw predators away from her young. It was then when I noticed a couple of heads I recognized as otters swimming in the water, working the area. The babies were trapped in a small bay. I fired up the boat and zipped over in time to scare off the otters.

Every summer, we go for boat rides to explore the many bays and islands looking for duck, loon, or goose nests. One year I was able to find three loon nests. We derive a deep satisfaction from knowing the place we love and call home is the place that so many bird species call home too.

Further down the lake is a narrow section we pass through in order to access the lower part of our lake. In this lower section is an eagle's aerie. A precariously leaning tree, old and dead from the ravages of fire, yet strong enough to support the mass of twisted sticks and debris that composed the nest, was the foundation upon which the nest was built. Since our arrival so many years ago, that nest had been home to a mating pair of mature eagles and their two eaglets every other year. One summer we took a boat ride down to check on them; they were already fledged and resting in the nest. As we pulled up in the boat, one of the eaglets jumped out, made a bee line for us, slowly glided low overhead in a circle, and then returned to a tree top perch.

He peered at us as if to say, "Look at me. I can fly."

That reminded us that it wouldn't be long before they would be gone for the winter. Have a safe flight my friend, and we'll see you when you return.

With each passing summer, we wondered how long the tree would remain standing before it succumbed to the elements. Winter of 2015 took its toll; the tree and nest toppled into the lake. I'm happy to say construction of a new aerie closer to our home has been completed on "safety island," the first island I boated to seeking refuge from the 2002 fires. We should see eagles soaring for a long time to come.

In thinking about my fishing experiences, the one fish that stands out in my mind was one I caught one late fall. Generally, that is the best time to catch monster northern pike, monster meaning in the 40-inch range. Pike have large mouths, ringed by razor sharp teeth, much like a gator. And, as with a gator, you don't want that big mouth clamping down on a hand or finger.

For this reason, big pike make me nervous. Using a lure, I threw a few casts from the dock, not knowing what, if anything, I might catch. This particular day, I latched on to a pike that took a while to reel in. I knew it was big by the way it fought. The fish was a dead weight and, as soon as I would get it close to shore it would take off and spin out line again. We played this game for some time. Eventually, I landed the mighty beast. When I opened its mouth to retrieve my spoon lure, all I could see in its gaping orifice was the orange tail of a large trout. This piggy had eaten a significant sized trout, which was still on its way to the stomach, and yet it still had gone after my lure!

On another occasion, a calm summer's day, I went down to the dock and noticed a small pike about 6 inches long. The young fry must have been from the current year's crop. It noticed me but was in no hurry to leave. Slowly it swam away from the dock, parallel to the shore in shallow water of a couple inches. When it was perhaps 6 feet away, I turned my attention elsewhere.

As soon as I did, there was an explosion of noise and water, and looking in the direction of the kerfuffle, I saw on the sand beach, out of the water, the baby pike and a big pike. Both were beached, wriggling, and squirming to get back into the water. I couldn't believe it. What timing! Obviously the large pike had been stalking the little guy, and I had inadvertently forced the smaller pike away from the safety of the dock when I showed up. It was one of those occasions of being in the right place at the right time. Who needs a fishing rod when the fish throw themselves on to shore!

Over the years, I've enjoyed sport fishing, casting not only various types of metal lures, but also flies and streamers from an antique fly rod. One of Johanna's many hobbies is to make my streamers using a fly tying kit I bought her years ago. We aren't big on eating fish, so I derive my enjoyment from catch and release, along with the simple joy of being on the water. If you like fishing, this place is your dream come true, as you really have to work hard to get skunked here.

When my brother came to help with building the house, we always took time to go out and fish. He kept track of the number of fish he caught, and the tally was well over a hundred during the three weeks he was here. I'd tell him to throw the lure over here, or throw it over there, and it was uncanny how many times he caught a fish at the spot I indicated. I enjoyed it because my brother thought I was using some kind of fish ESP.

The windows of our house serve as a nice observation point, and make for unobstructed views of wildlife. We are constantly looking out the windows as we pass by them, never knowing what a random check will reveal: a large bull moose with magnificent rack right in front of the house, a lynx slinking around on a hunting trip, a lone black wolf exploring the area behind the garden, a red fox dangling feet off the ground as it tries to free the bird suet feeder from its perch, a mother duck sneaking into her nest under a nearby tree, a pair of otter swimming by the dock.

Being in and surrounded by true wilderness gives us a perspective few others enjoy and offers us a unique opportunity to view wildlife in a purely natural setting. We have been blessed to have witnessed and shared some magical experiences with animals, and it will be another facet of our lifestyle we will miss when we are no longer living in the bush.

Come fall, as the leaves drop from the trees and a cold wind blows from the north, the year's crop of hatchlings are gone. The remaining loons are visible but silent, floating on the waves, reluctant to leave the place they've called home for the last five months. The excited cackle of their return in spring is now replaced with a quiet resignation that a long flight south is imminent. The last straggler can often be seen from the dock in our bay, even as a biting wind howls, and the season's first snow coats the ground. Who can blame them for not wanting to leave.

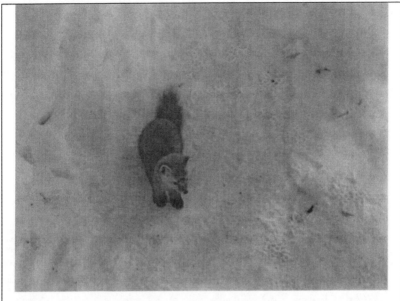

"Marty," a local marten, at the door

Eagles' home

Northern pike

Teal and ducklings

Chapter 18—

Is the Wilderness for You?

My purpose in writing this book is to share with you the culmination of an adventurous spirit, in the hope it inspires you to fulfill your dreams. The stories recorded on these pages were *our* dreams.

Your ambitions and goals will be different. Maybe they involve something extreme, such as living in the bush. Maybe it's something less earth-shattering, such as a bicycle tour. Whatever that aspiration, attaining it requires a conscious, focused effort.

However, in regards to living in the wilderness, before you pack your belongings in extra-heavy duty steamer trunks bound for the nearest float plane base, I offer the following thoughts.

What does it take to safely live in the bush?

At the very least, it takes two or more compatible yet complementary people who are knowledgeable and skilled in numerous areas: compatible in the sense that you will see your partner(s) day in and day out, seven days a week. There is no nine-to-five job to break up the day, no shopping or social events that can create a buffer of separation. In a sense, we are on an island of togetherness of our own making. If we didn't have a strong measure of harmony, we likely would not succeed. We complement each other because each of us brings a set of skills at which we excel. My weaknesses are offset by her strengths and vice versa.

You will need to be able to construct, plumb, wire, problem-solve, and be handy in mechanics. If something breaks, you'll need to know how to chew gum and work with bailing wire. If you are to be self-reliant for long periods, you will need to be a chef and baker, a master gardener, and well-versed in food preservation, including proper canning practices. You can't get to the store every week for bread, rolls, and pizza; you'll need to make foods of this nature from scratch.

You will need to be organized beyond belief. Construction of a two-story home in the bush, 100 air miles from the nearest lumber yard, illustrates the necessity for having all essential supplies on site when they are needed. Since we generally shop twice a year, as soon as we know an item is running low or needs replacing, we immediately add it to our ongoing shopping list. Nothing is left to chance or memory. The ability to plan long-range is critical for assessing what goods and supplies will be needed for half a year at a time. If we forget something while on a resupply run, we have to do without and must wait another six months until the next scheduled flight.

You'll need to have some financial resources to get started. We lived a Spartan life in Maine, homesteading off the grid for 20 years, with an outside hand pump for water and an outhouse. We scrimped and saved, paid off debts long before they were due, and worked long hours. With the money saved, combined with the money from the sale of the homestead, we were able to build a deluxe place in the bush. We still need some income and the occasional bush job supplements our finances.

Consider taking a serious first aid or Emergency Medical Technician (EMT) course. I took an EMT course for general knowledge many years ago and recently reinforced that information by taking an Emergency Medical Responder Course. Book knowledge is nice, but there is nothing like practical experience. It would be ill-advised to trot off to the bush without enough hands on experience to give you a chance at surviving an emergency.

Educate yourself on the myriad facets of homesteading and self-reliance in a setting that allows failure and learning without catastrophic consequences. Take it in small steps and develop your skills. For example, plant a small garden to familiarize yourself with the fundamentals of raising various vegetables. Learn the principles of food preservation so you have the confidence you can "put by" enough food to get through the winter. Offer to pound nails and apprentice with a friend or neighbor doing a carpentry project to learn the basics of construction. Take a chainsaw safety course and learn how to safely run the saw and fell trees.

"Jack of all trades, master at none" is a good motto. Regardless of age, suck up information like a vacuum cleaner. You never know when you will need to reach into your bag of tricks to deal with some problem. After the education, if the wilderness calls, you will have greatly increased your odds of being successful.

While nice to dream about, it's a big step going from the company of people to the silence of wilderness. Your personal demeanor will have something to do with your success or failure. You will need to be committed and determined.

Keep in mind, there is a fine line between tenacious and stubborn. If lost in the woods, tenacious is figuring out a solution to the puzzle. Stubborn is walking in circles till you drop.

If you've read this far and still desire the wilderness, you obviously have a love of the outdoors, are physically fit, are consumed with a burning desire to be independent, and are able to occupy yourself day after day without the routine of a nine-to-five job. To fill some of your waking hours, you will have the normal daily activities that are somewhat dependent on the season. Gardening in the summer, and wood-cutting and hauling in the winter are examples. Each season has its tasks to accomplish. Various hobbies can occupy your slack time.

For those of you who would feel a little anxious because the shopping center is 100 miles beyond that tree over there, or who would be bored after an hour in your porch swing overlooking your kingdom, maybe this lifestyle isn't exactly for you.

Not everyone is cut out to live this remotely, but bear in mind there are many degrees of remoteness. You can achieve more independence simply by moving from an urban setting to a less populated area so you can start raising some of your own food. Choosing to heat with wood you cut yourself could be your next step. Adding solar panels or a wind turbine further advances the cause of freedom.

We all seek out our own comfort level, and I hope my writing gives you pause to consider how far you want to push the envelope. The wilderness doesn't leave a lot of room for error. I write to give a bit of feedback and offer a dose of reality to those wanting to distance themselves from society, and wish you well if you do make the transition. I can tell you, we wouldn't want to be anywhere else. Off-grid and free in the wilderness: it doesn't get any better than that!

Eventually the day will come when, for the final time, we will watch the float plane circle overhead, drift up to our dock and, with a last look back at the homestead, we will frame indelibly in our minds the wonderful life we have had here, before stepping into the plane for our last flight.

About the Author

Living off grid since the early 1980s, Ron and his wife Johanna have spent the better part of their lives unplugged. As part of the back-to-the-land movement that originated in the 70s, they have spent their adult years living the homestead dream. They currently reside on a remote Saskatchewan lake deep in the Canadian wilderness. Access to them is via chartered float plane.

Ron is an avid outdoorsman, homesteader, and off-grid enthusiast. Some of his adventures include successfully hiking the Appalachian Trail in winter, bicycling across the United States, surviving forest fires, and being touched by Gentle Ben.

Published in *Backhome Magazine*, *Small Farmer's Journal*, and *Countryside and Small Stock Journal*, Ron and his wife also appear in *Life Off Grid*, a film and book about people living off grid throughout Canada. *Life Off Grid* is produced by Phillip Vannini and Jonathan Taggard. See http://lifeoffgrid.ca/ for more information. *Life Off Grid* aired on British Columbia's Knowledge Network in December 2015.

Ron encourages anybody with questions to contact him directly.

You can contact Ron at:
https://www.facebook.com/offgridandfree.mypathtothewilderness
http://www.inthewilderness.net/

CPSIA information can be obtained
at www.ICGtesting.com
Printed in the USA
LVOW11s1153191116
513696LV00002B/422/P